Identity, Political and Human Rights Culture as Prerequisites of Constitutional Democracy

Identity, Political and Human Rights Culture as Prerequisites of Constitutional Democracy

Miodrag Jovanović and Dragica Vujadinović (Eds.)

eleven
international publishing

Published, sold and distributed by Eleven International Publishing
P.O. Box 85576
2508 CG The Hague
The Netherlands
Tel.: +31 70 33 070 33
Fax: +31 70 33 070 30
e-mail: sales@budh.nl
www.elevenpub.com

Sold and distributed in USA and Canada
International Specialized Book Services
920 NE 58th Avenue, Suite 300
Portland, OR 97213-3786, USA
Tel: 1-800-944-6190 (toll-free)
Fax: +1-503-280-8832
orders@isbs.com
www.isbs.com

Eleven International Publishing is an imprint of Boom uitgevers Den Haag.

ISBN 978-94-6236-077-8
ISBN 978-94-6094-822-0 (E-book)

Printed in The Netherlands

Table of Contents

List of Contributors

The Editors

Miodrag Jovanović, *Professor, Faculty of Law, University of Belgrade*
Dragica Vujadinović, *Professor, Faculty of Law, University of Belgrade*

The Authors

Claus Offe, *Professor, Hertie School of Governance*
Hauke Brunkhorst, *Professor, University of Flensburg*
Milan Podunavac, *Professor, Faculty of Political Science, University of Belgrade*
Biljana Đorđević, *Lecturer, Faculty of Political Science, University of Belgrade*
David Rasmussen, *Professor, Boston College*
Axelle Reiter, *Lecturer, Verona University*
Ivana Krstić, *Assistant Professor, Faculty of Law, University of Belgrade*
Damir Banović, *Lecturer, Faculty of Law, University of Sarajevo*
Bojan Spaić, *Lecturer, Faculty of Law, University of Belgrade*

Introduction

1 Squaring the Circle: Identity, Political and Human Rights Culture in Constitutional Democracy

Miodrag Jovanović

On the eve of the full dismantlement of the Soviet-led system of real-socialism, Fukuyama famously acknowledged that we were witnessing "the end point of mankind's ideological evolution and the universalization of Western liberal democracy as the final form of human government". Even though he stressed that this victorious march of the Western liberal doctrine "has occurred primarily in the realm of ideas or consciousness and is as yet incomplete in the real or material world", he was, nonetheless, positive that the said ideal "will govern the material world *in the long run*".[1] It seemed, at that moment, that at least on European soil things were moving in the predicted direction, insofar as all the countries of the former communist block boldly entered into the process of democratic transition, and most of them clearly expressed political will to join the then European Economic Community. Just about at that time, this unique European experiment in transnational governance entered a new phase with the 1992 Maastricht Treaty. Not only did it rename the EEC as the EC, "thus dropping the word 'economic' in order to indicate that many non-economic matters had become part of its architecture",[2] but it also provided a trump card for all those arguing that some form of cosmopolitan liberal-democracy was both needed and achievable.[3]

Not much time has passed before some sobering voices occurred, noticing that a widespread triumphalism was probably premature. Hence, in an influential 1997 article, Zakaria came up with the warning argument that, contrary to the Western tacit assumption that democracy was always about *liberal, i.e.* constitutional democracy, new waves of democratization were running counter to this logic, thereby producing the rise of *illiberal* democracy. According to Zakaria, many countries around the world, including those in

1 F. Fukuyama, 'The End of History?', *The National Interest*, 1989, p. 3. This argument is fully elaborated in F. Fukuyama, *The End of History and the Last Man*, The Free Press, New York, 1992.

2 As is well known, the Maastricht Treaty also introduced the 'three pillars' structure of the EU building. W. van Gerven, *The European Union – A Polity of States and Peoples*, Hart Publishing, Oxford and Portland, 2005, pp. 7 *et seq*.

3 One of them was Held, who, despite warning that there was no such thing as a single liberal tradition, nonetheless argued already in the beginning of the 1990s in favor of some liberal form of cosmopolitan democracy. D. Held, 'Democracy: From City-States to a Cosmopolitan Order?', *Political Studies*, Vol. 40, 1992, pp. 10-39.

Central and Eastern Europe, "are settling into a form of government that mixes a substantial degree of democracy with a substantial degree of illiberalism".[4] Scholars in transitology have subsequently analyzed this trend in more detail, providing some more operative categorizations of deviations from a standard form of constitutional democracy. One of the most influential classifications belongs to Merkel, who distinguished between the four types of *defective* democracies: a) *exclusive* democracies, in which one or more segments of all adult citizens are excluded from the civil right or universal suffrage; b) *domain* democracies, in which certain political domains are out of the hands of democratically elected representatives; c) *illiberal* democracies, in which, broadly speaking, the principle of rule of law is damaged and d) *delegative* democracies, in which the legislature and the judiciary have only limited control over the executive branch, usually led by charismatic presidents. According to Merkel, one of the world regions in which various forms of defective democracy took hold was exactly Eastern Europe.[5]

Fairly unexpectedly, the European project of transnational political integration was from the 1992 inception charged for suffering of a different sort of defectiveness, which soon became known as 'democratic deficit.' Pogge speaks of the two forms of this charge. Whereas the first one boils down to the claim that "ordinary citizens of the EU have very little meaningful influence on the political decisions made in their name by the centralized organs and agencies", the second one amounts to the argument that "[o]rdinary citizens of the EU have had very little meaningful influence on the designing of the emerging European institutions, which have been shaped and modified by a small politico-bureaucratic elite".[6] Even more dramatic admonition came from the German Federal Constitutional Court, which in its famous 1993 Brunner case decision pointed out that, since democracy presupposes the existence of *demos*, no polity could be considered democratic unless its population displays some expressive features of the common belonging to the given polity. This, consequently, implies not only that the EU could transform into a democratic polity solely by moving towards some traditional nation-state model, but also that its institutions and decisions should be assessed primarily by standards of the traditional concept of liberal democratic legitimacy.[7] Essentially, what the Court conveys as the key message is that the aforementioned forms of 'democratic deficit' are unfixable as long as the EU suffers from an inherent construction failure – the lack of a prerequisite common identity that might generate an adequate political culture conducive to constitutional democracy.

This decision was harshly criticized for reducing the complex issue of devising structures of the European transnational democracy to narrowly construed concepts of *Volk* and *Staat*.

---

4 F. Zakaria, 'The Rise of Illiberal Democracy', *Foreign Affairs*, Vol. 76, No. 6, 1997, p. 24.

5 W. Merkel, 'Embedded and Defective Democracies', *Democratization*, Vol. 11, No. 5, 2004, pp. 49 *et seq*.

6 T.W. Pogge, 'How to Create Supra-National Institutions Democratically (Some Reflections on the European Union's 'Democratic Deficit')', *in* A. Føllesdal & P. Koslowski (Eds.), *Democracy and the European Union*, Springer, Berlin, 1997, pp. 160-161.

7 BVerfG 12 October 1993, BvR 2134, 2159/92.

Weiler is one of the most prominent critics in the debate.[8] He argues that, at the European level, it is both possible and necessary to go beyond the traditional analytical framework and to acknowledge the existence of multiple *demoi*, whereby individuals simultaneously express the organic-cultural identification with their nations *and* membership to European supranational values. Accordingly, whereas national citizenship encompasses the realm of ethnocultural identification and belonging,[9] the European, supranational citizenship covers the realm of law and Enlightenment, that is, civic ideals.[10] It follows, then, that regardless of how really close the Union is becoming with each successive treaty reform, "it is to remain a union among distinct peoples, distinct political identities, and distinct political communities". However, this is, somewhat paradoxically, the most potent element of European integration. Instead of trying to eliminate differences and become an indivisible one, the EU is taking the hard way, because

> it is more difficult to attain an ever closer union if the components of that union preserve their distinct identities, retain their otherness vis-à-vis each other, and do not become one flesh, politically speaking.

Herein, in Weiler's words, resides the principle of 'constitutional tolerance', which is the basis of 'constitutional discipline' in the daily functioning of the EU legal and political order. Constitutional actors in Member States do not follow this discipline because "they are subordinate to a higher sovereignty", but rather because they exercise a "continually renewed, autonomous, and voluntary act of subordination".[11] Weiler considers this acceptance and subordination as "an act of true liberty and emancipation from collective self-arrogance and constitutional fetishism, a high expression of constitutional tolerance". Its significance is particularly visible in the daily habits and practices of public administration, but it is about to become routine in policy-setting forums as well.[12] Consequently, it is this 'constitutional tolerance', rather than the Schmittian exceptionalism, which represents the "defining spiritual *Grundnorm*" of the EU constitutional architecture, and

8 See particularly, J.H.H. Weiler, 'Der Staat "über alles" – Demos, Telos und die Maastricht – Entscheidung des Bundesverfassungsgerichts', 1995, available at <http://centers.law.nyu.edu/jeanmonnet/archive/papers/95/9507ind.html>.

9 "I would argue that in the modern notion of the European organic-national nation-state, the state is to be seen principally as an instrument, the organizational framework within which the nation is to realize its potentialities". J.H.H. Weiler, 'To Be a European Citizen – Eros and Civilization', 1998 Working Paper Series in European Studies, p. 23, available at <http://aei.pitt.edu/8990/1/weiler.pdf>.

10 Weiler argues that "the Community ideal of Supranationalism is evocative of, and resonates with, Enlightenment ideas, with the privileging of the individual, with a different aspect of liberalism that has its progeny today in liberal notions of human rights. In this respect the Community ideal is heir to Enlightenment liberalism". *Ibid.*, p. 31.

11 J.H.H. Weiler, 'On the Power of the Word: Europe's Constitutional Iconography', *International Journal of Constitutional Law*, Vol. 3, No. 2-3: 2005, p. 188.

12 *Ibid.*, p. 189.

Weiler fears that the discourse of formal constitution might easily "rob Europe of this ethos of tolerance".[13]

Weiler's sustained criticism of the *no demos-no democracy* thesis of the German Federal Constitutional Court seemed to have been vindicated by more or less smooth functioning of the EU,[14] which even managed to successfully incorporate newcomers from the former communist block. However, everything changed with the 2008 global financial crisis. Abruptly, it turned out that one of the most potent forces of the post-Maastricht political integration of EU, the creation of the European System of Central Banks, as well as the European Central Bank, both in charge of conducting EC monetary policy, was in fact "the 'construction flaw' [. . .] that lacks the requisite political steering capacities". In Habermas's words, all of a sudden, everyone seemed to become aware of the fact "that the ordoliberal dream of voluntary stability criteria to which the budgets of the member states were supposed to conform has failed".[15]

This retrospectively sheds some new light on other institutional attempts of the EU aimed at overcoming the aforementioned forms of 'democratic deficit' and creating a more politically integrated supranational community. It transpires, for instance, that gradually assumed powers of the European Parliament have not triggered greater participation of the citizens in the EU-wide elections. On the contrary, the turnout in the 2009 elections was the lowest ever since direct elections for the house started in 1979 (only 43%), with one of the East European member states getting the lowest score for the second time in a row (Slovakia, with 17% turnout).[16] Similarly, once citizens of certain original member states (France and Netherlands) finally got the chance to have a say in the process of designing EU institutions, by casting votes on 2005 referendums for the Constitution of Europe, they manifestly opposed the step towards a state-like structure of the EU. Despite different

13 *Ibid.*, p. 190.

14 As already noticed, within Weiler's specific vision of the EU constitutional tolerance, the failure of the project of EU constitution was not considered to be essentially detrimental to this supranational polity, on the contrary.

15 J. Habermas, *The Crisis of the European Union – A Response* (trans. by Ciaran Cronin), Polity Press, Cambridge, 2012, p. vii.

16 To be sure, political scientists use remarkably different methodological approaches for explaining this phenomenon. The classical approach proceeds from the hypothesis that the European Parliament elections are merely 'second-order' national elections (*see, e.g.*, K. Reif & H. Schmitt, 'Nine Second Order National Elections: A Conceptual Framework for the Analysis of European Election Results', *European Journal of Political Research*, Vol. 8, 1980, pp. 3-44). A modified version of this argument states that what additionally matters are political parties' positions towards the EU. This variable explains a somewhat paradoxical trend that radical, anti-European right-wing and left-wing parties are more represented at the EU than at the national level (*see, e.g.*, S. Hix & M. Marsh, 'Punishment or Protest? Understanding European Parliament Elections', *The Journal of Politics*, Vol. 69, No. 2, 2007, pp. 495-510). Finally, some more recently conducted researches argue that concerns over both national and EU-level preferences influence voting behaviour in EP elections. *See, e.g.*, N. Clark & R. Rohrschneider, 'Second-Order Elections versus First-Order Thinking: How Voters Perceive the Representation Process in a Multi-Layered System of Governance', *Journal of European Integration*, Vol. 31, No. 5, 2009, pp. 645-664.

internal political dynamics, in both countries voters essentially perceived the emergence of the formalized constitutional EU identity as a threat to the prevailing national model of social state (France) or to national sovereignty and culture (Netherlands). Moreover, the no-vote campaigns in both constituencies largely exploited the threat of Turkish membership in the Union.[17] Finally, regardless of each successive European treaty solemnly proclaiming "an ever closer union among the peoples of Europe", being European, according to recent Eurobarometers, "matters a lot" only to 18% of EU citizens.[18]

All this seems to confirm an intricate relation between collective identity, political culture and constitutional democracy, which was correctly indicated, but probably somewhat simplistically elaborated by the German Federal Constitutional Court. As the current economic crisis unfolded on European soil, the EU was faced with having to decide between two profoundly different exit strategies. According to Habermas, one of them, actually taken by the Mercozy duo and followed by 'stability pact' measures, is deadly dangerous, because it "would invert the European project into its opposite". The unique experiment in transnational democracy "would be transformed into an arrangement for exercising a kind of post-democratic, bureaucratic rule", thus leading into a form of "post-democratic executive federalism".[19] The alternative strategy, and in Habermas's opinion the right one, would be to "continue the democratic legal domestication of the European Union in a consistent way". This route, however, decisively depends upon the possibility of developing "a Europe-wide civic solidarity".[20] This requires nothing less than the transformation of national civic solidarity and its extension so as to include the members of each of the other European peoples – from the German perspective, *e.g.*, the Greeks when they are subjected to internationally imposed and socially unbalanced austerity programmes.

Only then "would the EU citizens who elect and control the Parliament in Strasbourg be able to participate in a joint process of democratic will-formation reaching across national borders".[21] Since this is hardly a case for the moment,[22] one might say that the European experiment in transnational constitutional democracy has, ironically, found itself in the situation in which

17 S. Binzer Hobolt & S. Brouard, 'Contesting the European Union? Why the Dutch and the French Rejected the European Constitution', *Political Research Quarterly*, Vol. 64, No. 2, 2011, pp. 309-322.

18 According to the Eurobarometer 73.3, conducted in 2010, being European does not mean much or anything at all to at least 40% EU citizens, while an additional 40% of the respondents say that being European matters somewhat to them. Special Eurobarometer 73.3, New Europeans, available at <http://ec.europa.eu/public_opinion/archives/ebs/ebs_346_en.pdf>.

19 Habermas 2012, p. 52.

20 *Ibid.*, p. 53.

21 *Ibid.*, p. 46.

22 Habermas is fully aware of this fact, and, hence, he argues that the national public spheres need to gradually open themselves up to each other – "A dangerous asymmetry has developed because until now the European Union has been sustained and monopolized by political elites – an asymmetry between the democratic participation of the peoples in what their governments 'obtain' for them on the, as they see it, far-off Brussels stage and the indifference, even apathy, of the EU citizens regarding the decisions of their parliament in Strasbourg". *Ibid.*, p. 48.

a number of East European states were in the opening phase of their democratic transition. This situation is labelled by Linz and Stepan as the 'stateness problem,' which exists when "there are profound differences about the territorial boundaries of the political community's state and profound differences as to who has the right of citizenship in that state".[23] In the case of EU, the 'stateness problem'[24] is specifically reflected: in different perceptions as to whether the enlargement process should be continued, and if so, at what pace; in the dilemma whether the membership of Turkey would be irreconcilable with the political (constitutional) identity of the EU; in the question whether the institutional response to the financial crisis necessarily leads to a two-tier EU, with the insiders' 'core' consisting of 17 Eurozone countries, and the ten Euro 'outs,' which would be substantially marginalized in the decision-making processes; in the increasingly apparent lack of *federal political culture*,[25] *loyalty* (*Bundestreue*)[26] and *comity*[27] on the side of both member states and EU citizens, which are in theory considered to be necessary prerequisites for the smooth functioning of compound, ethnoculturally diverse political communities, etc.

Even though one may say that the hardest aspects of the 'stateness problem', those pertaining to the territorial delimitation of a polity, are behind the most post-communist countries,[28] those political communities are, nonetheless, still struggling with a wide spectre of issues that, broadly speaking, concern legal and political membership in the political

23 J.J. Linz & A. Stepan, *Problems of Democratic Transition and Consolidation (Southern Europe, South America, and Post-Communist Europe)*, The Johns Hopkins University Press, Baltimore, 1996, p. 16. Similarly, Rustow notices that "the vast majority of citizens in a democracy-to-be must have no doubt or mental reservations as to which political community they belong to". D.A. Rustow, 'Transitions to Democracy – Toward a Dynamic Model', *in* G. Pridham (Ed.), *Transitions to Democracy (Comparative Perspectives from Southern Europe, Latin America and Eastern Europe)*, Aldershot, Dartmouth, 1995, p. 72.

24 This problem has not been left unnoticed by scholars of European integration. In investigating what lessons the EU can learn from ethnoculturally diverse federal polities, which were often faced with the 'stateness problem', McKay noticed, as early as 2001, that "as EU responsibilities expand it is increasingly likely that the EU will experience the sort of tensions that have affected other maturing federations. This is especially so given the fact that, following the European Monetary Union (EMU), the participating countries are now locked into the sort of centralized policy imperatives more typical of nation states than of supranational organizations. These new responsibilities highlight anew the problem of the 'democratic deficit' in the EU". D. McKay, *Designing Europe – Comparative Lessons from the Federal Experience*, Oxford University Press, Oxford, 2001, p. 2.

25 This concept is in federal scholarship defined as "orientations toward the political processes based on a simultaneous loyalty to, respect for, and participation in more than one territorial community". I.D. Duchacek, 'Comparative Federalism: Agenda for Additional Research', *in* D.J. Elazar (Ed.), *Constitutional Design and Power-Sharing in the Post-Modern Epoch*, University Press of America, Lanham, 1991, p. 29.

26 On the concept of Bundestreue in the German federal practice, *see, e.g.*, H.-W. Bayer, *Die Bundestreue*, J.C.B. Mohr [Paul Siebeck], Tübingen, 1961.

27 According to Friedrich, federal comity "is manifest in the practice of fair play by both federal and local officials. It presupposes a willingness to give the other side a 'break', to be ready for compromise wherever serious strains develop, to be, in other words, pragmatic in the approach to problems on which the federal and local authorities are divided or on which their intrinsic interests clash". C.J. Friedrich, *Trends of Federalism in Theory and Practice*, Pall Mall Press, London, 1968, pp. 175-176.

28 This problem is still present in certain regions of East Europe, such as the former Yugoslavia and former Soviet states.

community. Some noticeable illiberal practices across East European countries testify to enduring defects of transitional democracies in the areas of the rule of law and constitutionalism, political and human rights culture and minority protection.[29] A number of countries from this block have experienced – and some continue to do so – a peculiar form of defunct democracy, which Smooha named 'ethnic democracy'. This is "a system that falls in between consociational democracy and non-democracy", insofar as it "grants individual and collective rights to the minority but also guarantees preferred status to the majority".[30]

Elements of this model survived in spite of the fact that some post-communist countries have in the meantime become or are just about to become members of the EU. This is, for instance, evident in the new Hungarian constitution which, although stating in its Preamble that "the nationalities living with us form part of the political community and are constituent parts of the State", has to be interpreted in conjunction with the opening phrase "we the members of the Hungarian nation". According to the Venice Commission's Opinion, the systemic reading of the Preamble suggests "that members of the 'nationalities living with us' are not part of the people behind the enactment of the Constitution". This is problematic insofar as "[t]he Constitution should be seen as the result of the democratic will-formation of the country's citizens as a whole, and not only of the dominant ethnic group".[31] A comparable Preamble was adopted in the 1992 Constitution of Estonia,[32] which along with two other Baltic states was widely criticized in the period after regaining independence for adopting discriminatory citizenship laws against the ethnic Russian population.[33] Similarly, Slovenia for twenty years defended by all available means its post-independence decision to simply erase from the official record all non-ethnic Slovenians,

29 This is certainly not the place for a more thorough elaboration whether multicultural politics of minority protection, which was introduced as the EU accession criterion for former communist states, is reconcilable with the traditional liberal model of democracy. Elsewhere I argued that the multicultural politics of recognition, even in the form of constitutionally recognized collective minority rights, is conceptually compatible with constitutionalism, understood primarily as the fettered power, and that this model of 'multicultural constitutionalism' is not incompatible with liberal democracy. M. Jovanović, 'Constitutionalism and Collective Rights: The Question of Conceptual Compatibility', *in* V. Beširević (Ed.), *Public Law in Serbia – Twenty Years After*, Esperia Publications Ltd, London, 2012, pp. 167-183.

30 S. Smooha, 'Types of Democracy and Modes of Conflict Management in Ethnically Divided Societies', *Nations and Nationalism*, Vol. 8, No. 4, 2002, pp. 426-427.

31 European Commission for Democracy Through Law, Opinion on the New Constitution of Hungary, CDL-AD(2011)016, para. 40.

32 The Preamble states: "With unwavering faith and a steadfast will to strengthen and develop the state, which is established on the inextinguishable right of the people of Estonia (in Estonian: Eesti rahvas) to national self-determination [...] which shall guarantee the preservation of the Estonian nation (Eesti rahvus), language and culture through the ages, the people of Estonia (Eesti rahvas) [...] adopted the following Constitution". As noted by one author, "the logic of the Preamble, not very explicit though, is simple: the citizens (all ethnic groups together) establish a state and adopt a constitution to preserve one ethnic group – the Estonians – and its culture". P. Järve, 'Ethnic Democracy and Estonia: Application of Smooha's Model', *European Centre for Minority Issues Working Paper*, Vol. 7, 2000, p. 7.

33 See, *e.g.*, A. Lottmann, 'No Direction Home: Nationalism and Statelessness in the Baltics', *Texas International Law Journal*, Vol. 43, 2008, pp. 502-519.

mostly coming from other parts of the former Yugoslavia, who had not managed to apply for citizenship within the stipulated period of six months.[34] Eventually, the so-called 'erased people' (*izbrisani*) won the case before the European Court of Human Rights (ECHR).[35] In November 2007, the same court condemned the Czech Republic for violating the right of Romani children to education free from discrimination by placing them in 'special schools' for children with mental disabilities, which offered lower-quality education.[36] According to the 2012 Amnesty International Report, Romani children in this EU member state are still being denied the educational opportunities offered to other students.[37] The ECHR also decided in 2006 that the 2000 Bulgarian Constitutional Court's banning of the tiny nationalist Macedonian party OMO-Ilinden, on account of being a threat to the integrity of the state and the unity of the nation, was in violation of the European Convention. However, ever since, Bulgarian authorities have denied registration of this party on various formal and procedural grounds.[38] As they prepare to become the 28th member state of the EU, the Croatian authorities are faced with massive street protests against the implementation of the provision of the Constitutional Law on the Rights of National Minorities, which stipulates equality in the official use of a minority's language and script in local self-government units where the members of a national minority make at least one third of the population. The specific target of those protests is the introduction of the Cyrillic script in the areas inhabited by the Serbs, particularly in the city of Vukovar, etc.[39]

This non-exhaustive list of deviations from constitutional democracy could hardly imply that the situation is better in other East European states that are for the moment in the status of would-be EU member states. On the contrary, as some of the contributions to this volume demonstrate, they are arguably even more exposed to the alike illiberal practices of the violation of constitutionalism, the rule of law, human and minority rights.

In spite of the fact that "universalization of Western liberal democracy as the final form of human government" (Fukuyama) happened to fail as an unrealistic utopia, the concepts of constitutional democracy, constitutional identity and political and human rights culture did not lose their relevance as the ideal-typical referential points of view. On the contrary,

34 Slovenian government for a long time even refused to apply the 2003 decision of the Constitutional Court, declaring the erasure unconstitutional. See more in P. Mindus, 'The Contemporary Debate on Citizenship – Some Remarks on the Erased of Slovenia', Revus – *European Constitutional Review*, Vol. 9, 2009, pp. 29-44.

35 *Kurić and Others v. Slovenia* (No. 26828/06), 13 July 2010.

36 *D.H. and Others v. the Czech Republic* (No. 57325/00), 13 November 2007.

37 Amnesty International and European Roma Rights Centre, Five More Years of Injustice – Segregated Education for Roma in the Czech Republic, 2012, available at <www.amnesty.org/en/library/asset/EUR71/006/2012/en/9f09fcf0-8917-43ae-a7cd-9b56e48c89cb/eur710062012en.pdf>.

38 D. Smilov & E. Jileva, 'The Politics of Bulgarian Citizenship: National Identity, Democracy and Other Uses', *in* R. Bauböck & B. Perchinig & W. Sievers (Eds.), *Citizenship Policies in the New Europe* (expanded and updated edition), Amsterdam University Press, Amsterdam, 2009, pp. 231-232.

39 Croatians protest against Cyrillic signs, available at <www.aljazeera.com/news/europe/2013/04/201347172816369285.html>.

the normative relevance of these interconnected concepts has become even stronger in times of economic crisis. Previously described dynamics of deviation from constitutional democracy both at the level of the EU polity and at the level of the East-European transitional countries prompted a group of scholars to gather and address the complex role of and mutual relation between the aforementioned concepts. This volume is a follow-up to the conference, which was organized under the title 'Political and Human Rights Culture as Prerequisites of Constitutional Democracy' at the Faculty of Political Science, University of Belgrade, from 24 to 25 November 2012.[40]

The first part of the book is devoted to practical and theoretical challenges to constitutional democracy at both the transnational and the national levels. The opening chapters deal, though from somewhat different angles, with the question of how the EU can cope with the current problems, which at first glance appear to be economic but are essentially political in nature. In his thought provoking chapter 'Europe Entrapped – Can the EU Overcome Its Current Crisis?' Offe tries to address probably the key question:

> How did we get into this situation of urgently needed yet woefully deficient European and Euro zone governing capacity? What is its pre-history of the chain effects of financial market, debt, and integration crisis?

Even though he offers a number of plausible economic explanations, it seems that the solution lies elsewhere. Once we acknowledge that "[t]he scope of functional integration is much wider than the scope of social integration", we are closer to realizing that "[t]he European political economy is experienced by its citizens as a community of fate, but not as one of fate *control*". Put differently, at the crux of the current EU crisis is the following structural problem: "Markets and the currency are international, while democratic politics remains essentially national". Consequently, mending the crisis implies addressing this political problem.

The following chapter, by Brunkhorst, tries to assess the European crisis by highlighting the paradoxes of constitutionalizing democratic capitalism. In doing so, he juxtaposes two paradigms, which were conflicting throughout the history of European integration. One is the *managerial mindset* of "possessive individualism and 'peaceful competitive struggle'", while the other is the *Kantian mindset*, which is concerned "with the constitutional realization of 'autonomy' and 'self-legislation' through 'structures of political representation.'" Brunkhorst argues that, contrary to the widely shared assumption, the struggle between the opposite logics of integration existed in the very moment of the creation of the European project. Moreover, despite the fact that the Lisbon Treaty by and large completed the political

40 The conference is organized within the project 'Constitutionalism and the Rule of Law in State-Building – The Case of Serbia', supported by the Ministry of Education, Science and Technological Development of the Republic of Serbia.

constitution of Europe, the financial crisis provided the scene for the reinvigoration of the managerial mindset.

Podunavac's chapter 'Constitutional Identity and the Construct of "Other"' focalizes the importance of identity in elaboration of a workable constitutional order. What the chapter specifically suggests is that working democratic constitutional order depends on the national, religious and cultural identity of those whose constitution it is. Secondly, there is a need for a sufficiently defined commonly shared constitutional identity in order for a constitution to function within a polity. The relation between constitutional and pre- and extra-constitutional identity is crucial for stability and legitimacy of political order. According to Podunavac, the construct of 'others' bridges these two identities.

The closing chapter of this chapter belongs to Đorđević, who investigates whether the theoretical proposal of democratic agonism (agonistic pluralism) could be successful in coping with the apparent crisis of liberal-democratic politics. The crisis reflects itself in frequent manifestations of civic distrust in politicians, political parties and the institutions of liberal democracy, apathy of citizens and low voter turnout in elections as well as low overall political participation, decreasing solidarity and increasing inequality among citizens.

Relying on works of William Connolly, Bonnie Honig and Chantal Mouffe, the author argues that "the current state of affairs in agonistic thought can be understood mainly as an alternative democratic ethos, but not an alternative democratic theory", insofar as this theoretical approach does not deal with the institutional dimension.

As the argument about the defective nature of newly emerging democracies is often based on the claim of their unsatisfactory record of human rights culture, the second chapter aims at reassessing some of the most influential foundationalist doctrines on human rights.

Rasmussen's chapter 'Rawls on Human Rights and Political Justification' deals with the problem of justification of human rights in the face "of a plurality of ideas of justice and a multiciplicity of conceptions of the good". For Rawls, this pluralism is the key challenge to the universalistic claim that has traditionally been the basis for the justification of human rights. Rasmussen begins by developing the foundations for Rawls' theory of rights in the *Law of Peoples*. In the next step, he examines the case for Rawlsian justificatory minimalism. In the concluding part of the chapter, Rasmussen provides a sketch of the argument for justification of human rights which goes beyond justificatory minimalism. This move is based on certain developments in the global development of democratic and human rights culture, which occurred in the years after the publication of the *Law of Peoples*.

The subsequent chapter is focused on Dworkin's conception of human rights. Vujadinović points out that Dworkin considers human rights universal, timeless, abstract and founded in human dignity. However, he takes for granted the concept of human dignity, and this 'no-need-for-justification argument' is problematic, insofar as it "gives a static character to human rights, while undermining social struggles as a referential framework for human rights development". That is, one can say that both human rights and human dignity "are not related to emerging political practices and dynamism either in the context of the nation-state or in the global context". Therefore, after a thorough analysis of his conception of human rights, Vujadinović concludes by noticing that while Dworkin's approach of integrity of law, politics and morality "brings with itself qualities of an admirably coherent and inherently rounded off position", it, nonetheless, "bears the danger of becoming a conception that is too hermetic (self-satisfied and self-sufficient), to really resonate with the most lively contemporary discussions and current changes in the present practice".

In her chapter 'Legal Claims, Side Constraints and the Principle of Liberty: A Libertarian Perspective on Human Rights', Reiter develops an analysis of human rights that builds on the liberal and cosmopolitan vision of democracy present in the United Nations Charter. In her opinion, this conception "is the sole paradigm that allows evading altogether the likelihood of state-promoted abuses, by conferring to individuals an unassailable sphere of self-sovereignty". Moreover, it is conducive to the peaceful coexistence of radically different conceptions of society at the international level. In that respect,

> [t]he control effectuated by the international community is comparable to that of Robert Nozick's libertarian minimal state as a framework for utopias, under which totally dissimilar societies can develop side by side as long as they abide by the basic requirement of mutual respect for the freedom of others.

Reiter argues that not only are contemporary developments in public international law inspired by a fairly similar ideal, but also that many aspects of the existing system are clear signs of the emergence of a global minimal state of such a type.

The last chapter of this volume is dedicated to the problems of identity, political and human rights culture in a selected number of transitional non-EU countries of Eastern Europe. The opening chapter of this chapter is Jovanović's and Krstić's analysis of the human rights culture in Serbia, as evidenced by the case of the treatment of sexual minorities as one of the most vulnarable social groups. The authors proceed from the definition of human rights culture "as the totality of attitudes toward and practices related to human rights, at personal, societal and institutional levels". They try to demonstrate how the robust implementation of human rights at the institutional level, or lack of it, is crucial for reinforcing, or benumbing, the human rights culture at the personal and societal levels. While arguing that Serbia has a satisfactory legal framework for the protection of the LGBT population against discrimination, Jovanović and Krstić, nonetheless, conclude that it is not fully implemented. Even more alarming is the lack of readiness on the part of some institutional actors and parts of political elites to recognize and respect the rights of this minority group.

Banović's chapter 'Political Culture in Post-conflict and Divided Societies: The Case of Bosnia and Herzegovina' deals with conditions of development of democratic political culture in a divided, post-conflict and post-socialist society. Numerous researchers

managed to identify the legacy of the socialist period in political orientations of citizens in post-socialist societies. The transitional society of Bosnia and Herzegovina is heavily burdened with the conflict and post-conflict period, where reestablishing the trust among ethnic communities and transitional justice are the preconditions for a functioning democratic political system. Finally, a viable consociational model seems to be the additional prerequisite for the development of a democratic political culture in one such society.
The volume is closed by Spaić's chapter 'Political Identities and Citizenship in Montenegro'. The focus of his contribution is on the discrepancy between the constitutional concept of citizenship and particular ethnic and national identities. According to the author, the political development in Montenegro in the last two decades could be characterized as a politics of identity, a political competition predominantly determined by, on the one hand, political parties' attitude towards identity and, on the other hand, voters' choice of identity.
Hence, Spaić tries to determine some basic characteristics of the Montenegrin political system and the dominant feature of its political culture, as well as to present the official concept of citizenship in order to provide a plausible explanation of the relationship between citizenship and politically construed national identities.

Part I
Constitutional Democracy at Transnational and National Levels – Practical and Theoretical Challenges

2 Europe Entrapped: Does the European Union Have the Political Capacity to Overcome Its Current Crisis?

Claus Offe

The European Union (EU) in 2013 finds itself at the crossroads of either something considerably better or something much worse than the *status quo*; in other words, in a crisis. That much is nearly universally understood, both within Europe and widely beyond. So I am certainly not alone in believing that the current crisis, a crisis that is the cumulative outcome of a financial market, sovereign debt and EU integration/democratic deficit crises, is an extremely serious and unprecedented one, frightening due to its complexity and uncertainty. If it cannot soon be resolved (but nobody knows how soon is 'soon enough') through a major institutional overhaul of the EU, both the political project of European integration and the global economy will suffer badly – to say nothing about the massive social suffering it has caused already in the countries of the European periphery.

2.1 The Road Forward Blocked

The seriousness of the crisis is due to one core contradiction. In a nutshell, what is urgently *needed* to be done is also extremely unpopular and therefore democratically virtually *impossible* to do. What must be done, and everyone agrees on it 'in principle' (namely large-scale and long-term debt mutualization resulting in massive redistributive measures both between member states and social classes), cannot be 'sold' to the voting public of the core member states, which so far have been less affected by the crisis than those at the periphery. Analogously, a rapid and sustained boost of the competitiveness of the peripheral countries, an adjustment of *their unit cost of labour* (defined as the ratio of real wages and labour productivity) leading at some point to their approximation to a balanced trade and sustainable levels of budget deficits – all of this is deemed to be 'needed' yet is evidently impossible to implement without wrecking their democratic political systems. Moreover, the incongruence between what is needed in economic terms and what is politically feasible, or the now symptomatically frequently invoked condition of 'ungovernability,' applies to both sides of the current and deepening European divide of core and periphery. Yet if the Eurozone falls apart as a consequence of the failure to square this circle, the EU is very likely to follow suit. I believe that Chancellor Merkel is right in saying so – although she forgot to add what by now is also evident: It is the untamed and institutionally unembedded dynamics of the EMU and the Euro that threatens to disintegrate the EU.

The chasm between what is 'needed' as a set of promising policy responses to the crisis and what is 'feasible' in terms of member state politics and available as political support applies to *both* sides of that new European divide. Northern 'populists' (as well as centrist political parties fearing the success of populist competitors) reject further tax-funded transfers and credit guarantees, while their Southern friends (or, rather, enemies) reject measures being imposed upon them that can be denounced as being part of a counter-productive austerity conditionality. Both profit from the crisis in widening their political support. The neo-Nazi party Golden Dawn in Greece has now grown to be the third largest party, as has the rejectionist and anti-political Grillo party in Italy. The moment such a party, together with other rejectionist forces, comes to be part of a governing coalition, the Euro would be a matter of the past due to immediate responses of ECB, IMF and the financial markets.

2.2 No Return to Square One

On the other hand, if a cooperative way forward appears to be blocked, why not simply go back to pre-Euro conditions? I do not think that is an option, which is why I speak of a trap where one cannot move in either direction. Even if it were widely agreed by member states that the introduction of the Euro into a fundamentally flawed currency zone was a huge mistake, the same applies by now to simply *undoing* that mistake. Legally, part of the commitments the new member states made at the point of their accession was a promise to transform their economies in ways that made them viable, as prescribed by the Maastricht criteria, as members of the Euro zone. In return, they were endowed with the entitlement to financial aid from EU funds which supposedly (yet so far widely unrealistically) would help them to boost productivity and competitiveness of their national economies along a trajectory of 'cohesion' and 'convergence'. If these mutual commitments were to be suspended, an avalanche of adverse economic consequences would be triggered: The re-nationalization of monetary policy would allow peripheral countries to devalue their currency yet leave them all the more deeply in trouble with the challenge of servicing the Euro-denominated debt they have accumulated. Also, private sector financial lenders would immediately increase their pressure ('spreads') on member states that have not yet left the Euro, thus causing the incalculable costs of a domino effect that eventually would also threaten the economy of the trade surplus countries because they would lose substantial parts of their export markets. Moreover, leaving the Euro would force leavers to also leave the regulatory regime of European law, as compliance with its rules would instantaneously become unaffordable to them. The dissolution of the Euro zone and, as an inescapable medium-term consequence, the EU would be equivalent to a tsunami of economic as well as political regression.

The EU has served so far, apart from being a machinery of economic liberalization, as a monitoring and regulatory device through which major deviations from standards of human rights and liberal democracy can be kept under control, and be it, in addition to judicial devices, by the 'soft' mechanisms of naming, blaming and shaming of violators (such as the Orban government in Hungary). The EU is also the only institutional location where binding rules governing the economic and fiscal interaction between member states can be decided upon and implemented, if so far evidently to an insufficient extent. As a supranational authority, it is a common political resource that can be used, if properly designed and further developed, for bringing order and control to not just the political economy of Europe, but also for defending peace and democratic civility on the continent. It could even be argued that the distinctiveness of cultural legacies and identities of European nations can be preserved and protected against homogenizing market forces only through the help of supranational agency. In view of these precious capacities of the EU of being a catalyst of supervisory control and cooperation, it appears frivolous to even consider the dissolution of the EU through a dynamic of re-nationalization as an acceptable way out of the crisis. Such re-nationalization would benefit neither individual member states nor the EU as a whole. Instead, it would cement European divisions.

2.3 An Unsustainable *Status Quo*

At the same time, there is no denying that the Euro was a mistake from the beginning. If one puts Greece and Germany, just to mention the two extreme cases, into one and the same currency zone, one unleashes pressures and economic constraints on the poorer, less productive participant, the one with higher unit costs of labour and hence less competitiveness in international trade, and deprives them of the possibility of *external* adjustment of their national currencies. True, in that regard the Euro ties everybody's hands. Yet the inclusion of the less competitive periphery into the Euro zone was one of those vicious mistakes that, once having been made, preclude the option of undoing them by returning to the *status quo ante*.

Currency exchange rate flexibility means that less productive national economies remain free (within limits) to devalue their currency in order to make their exports cheaper and imports more expensive, thus imposing an implicit extra tax on domestic consumers of, say, German luxury cars and Scottish whisky. Once one has adopted the Euro, the devilish implication which people start now to feel is that you cannot devalue your currency any more. Instead, countries must now engage in some kind of *internal* adjustment in order to compensate for large trade deficits, with 'internal adjustment' being a euphemism for vast cuts applying to both the state sector and labour – unless, that is, they manage somehow to increase tax revenues from high incomes and wealth, which most political forces, including all social democrats, consider hardly feasible today. Why? Because, as borders are open,

wealth can escape to national regimes with lower taxes and has done so, since the financial market crisis began, by the hundreds of billions (the 'Depardieu effect'), depriving countries from which they escape of much of available capital for investment. And why is that? Because a EU-wide tax harmonization has not (yet) been accomplished.
So after the option of external monetary adjustment is taken out of the game for Euro members, the only remaining options for adjustment are labour and the public sector. The trade and budget deficits must be compensated for through pressures on wages, pensions, labour market regulations and public services such as health and education. In addition, deeply indebted states are mandated by supranational authorities (the 'Troika' of ECB, the Commission and the IMF) to privatize state-owned assets, their political 'family silver', in exchange for financial relief (that mostly serves to recapitalize troubled national as well as international banks anyway). Everything that is financed, provided and regulated by the state now needs to be 'liberalized'. Hence, the new and already ubiquitous semantics of 'reform'. It used to be the case that by the term 'reform' we meant something proactive and 'progressive', a step towards more distributional justice. Now we see that the opposite is meant by reform: budgetary emergency measures with regressive distributional implications. Virtually the entire political elite of Europe and of member states proclaims that reforms (in the new sense) are necessary, urgently called for, and unavoidable as a *quid pro quo* for financial aid. Besides, whatever the economic virtues of any reform proposal may be held to be, such proposals are most unlikely to be adopted if they are promoted not by a democratic political process of legislation but by foreign imposition and perceived blackmail. Little wonder that this causes a social uproar and huge protest movements. Unions fight with their back to the wall; at times, we saw explosions of these leftist populist mass movements almost every Sunday in the capitals and provincial towns of Greece, Portugal and Spain. Italy is a little better off (but perhaps not so any more, after the outcome of the February 2013 elections); then comes France, where Holland is trying to assume the position of a mediator. At the same time, the twin motivators of greed and fear lead financial wealth to flee to presumably safe and profitable places, be it within Europe or off its shores.
To provide some statistics, which I found quite telling concerning what measures of 'internal adjustment' are aiming at: For the Greek balance of external trade to become even, that country needs to become no less than 40% less expensive in Euro terms. On the other side, German exports would have to be 20% more expensive in order to reduce that country's export surplus to zero.[1] Incidentally, German export surplus for 2011 has been, relative to GDP, *twice* that of China. Yet a balancing of international trade seems quite inconceivable to happen, as neither Greek workers, pensioners and political parties trying to defend their interests would allow this to happen nor German employers or any

1 W. Schäfer, 'Die Eurozone leidet unter intern verzerrten Wechselkursen', *Frankfurter Allgemeine Zeitung*, 27 August 2013.

conceivable minister of finance. What makes things worse is that even *if* the Greek state budget were to be shrunk nearly as much in response to the dictates of the EU, the ECB and the IMF by some authoritarian technocrat at the top of the country's government, the net effect on the debt-to-GDP ratio would not be favourable, but strongly *negative*.[2] As the debt is made to shrink, the GDP would shrink even more rapidly, thus driving the ratio of the two *up* due to the negative multiplier effect of austerity measures. And as financial investors know that only positive growth prospects (a 'credible business plan' of a country, as in Japan) will generate the future tax base out of the taxation of which their claims can be serviced, they are likely to respond to the worsening debt/GDP situation by either punitively denying credit or increasing the spread to even less sustainable levels to the extent such growth prospects are quite plausibly deemed to be missing, an assessment that in turn triggers a self-fulfilling prophecy of economic decline.

2.4 SOLIDARITY?

So the overall question is: How might such huge and persistent trade imbalances be remedied *within* the framework of the Euro? Or can it at all be remedied? Or should Europeans give up trying? The main ideas are a European clearing union, fiscal union or debt mutualization, most practically in the form of Euro bonds, a mechanism that is currently disallowed by the Treaties and would amount to export surplus countries sharing with net importers the substantial (interest rate, tax revenues, as well as external exchange rate) benefits that they derive from their comparatively good standing with the financial and export markets. And something of the sort is being tried now, if with extreme suspicions on the part of public opinion, especially in the northern countries. The EU is, after all, not a federal state with the normal mechanisms of fiscal federalism and a central government that is constitutionally committed to take care of some permanent form of inter-state redistribution. Publics in core countries such as Germany have so far failed to appreciate – and political parties have to a disastrous extent failed to enlighten the public about – the (uncontroversial, behind closed doors) fact that measures such as debt mutualization are not a matter of 'transfers' or 'altruistic donations', but a matter of *solidarity* in the proper sense. That is to say, solidarity means to do *not* what 'is good for *you*', but what 'is good for *all of us*'. Instead, the ruling misunderstanding that mistakes acts of solidarity (in the sense just specified) for altruistic charitable donations invites the frame of asking: 'Why should *we* pay for *them*?'

This frame is something right-wing populist parties (as well as many forces in centrist parties) are taking advantage of and using for their campaign purposes, thus preventing national and European elites from pursuing a democratically broadly supported strategy

2 O. Blanchard & D. Leigh, 'Growth Forecast Errors and Fiscal Multipliers', IMF Working Paper, 2013.

mandated by 'self-interest, rightly understood' (as Tocqueville famously put it in a different context), *i.e.*, solidarity. In the EU, the notion of a 'we' that defines the scope of solidarity is, however, poorly established as a reference of a shared identity. The contours of the entity called 'all of us' for whose benefit solidarity is to be practiced are only 'objectively' clear (namely 'all EU member states', the number of which is also involved in an ongoing process of expansion and thus remains a moving target), while they are blurred and contested in the subjective perceptions of member state elites and masses alike. The horizon of the solidarity that is called for is not a state, least of all a 'family', and not an association that members are aware of having voluntarily joined and therefore obliged to practice solidarity. It is rather an extensive community that is *still under construction* and hence weak (and getting weaker under the impact of the crisis with its winners and losers) as a source of solidarity obligations.

On the other hand, what a (currently shrinking) minority of EU enthusiasts among elites and non-elites would dream of for many years in terms of deepening the integration process has suddenly, under the impact of the crisis, turned into the road map for an urgent rescue operation that makes the empowerment of fiscal and economic governing capacities at the EU level a plain imperative. Yet as this rescue operation lacks the support of political parties (and hence voters) both in the still prosperous and in the declining countries of the EU, the rescue operation is still unlikely to succeed, particularly as it is being conducted in an undemocratic, depoliticized and technocratic mode that violates standards of democratic accountability that publics in European member states have (fortunately) learned to consider non-negotiable essentials of political life. Even in case the urgent fusion of supranational powers does succeed, it can thus easily be denounced by democrats as what it actually (and at best) is likely to be: A technocratically imposed, incompletely considered, judicially vulnerable, belated emergency operation with a dubious potential for putting the financial markets to rest and under control. On the contrary, as member states undergo a metamorphosis from classical 'tax states' to debt states,[3] they become ever more vulnerable to the vagaries of the financial markets.

2.5 The Financialization of States and Their Inadequate Governing Capacity

Both proponents of the political left and the centre-right have recently called for referenda as an institutional device to bolster the democratic legitimacy of rescue operations initiated by 'Brussels', with the left reluctantly betting on a 'pro' outcome and the right on the opposite due to the prevalence of notions of 'national' interests and growing mutual resentments between supposed winners and losers of the rescue operation. But, again,

3 W. Streeck, *Gekaufte Zeit: Die vertagte Krise des demokratischen Kapitalismus*, Suhrkamp, Berlin, 2013.

before preferences of voters can be *counted*, they must first be *formed*, and formed in the light of consensual normative reasons and the 'enlightened understanding'[4] of the nature of the situation and the alternative escape routes and their consequences. In the absence of a Europe-wide party system with some hegemonic potential that could provide such enlightening orientation, and given the power of national blinders in the formation of voters' preferences, it is not easy to be confident about the 'emergency legitimation' referenda's capacity to provide support for strong interventions at the European level.

The supreme policymaking body of the EU is the non-partisan intergovernmental (as opposed to supranational) European Council (EC, not to be confused with the Council of the EU, a quasi-federal chamber that plays a major role in European law making). It consists of the heads of state or heads of government of member states. It meets four or more times per year and defines the directions and priorities of the EU and gives 'impulses' for EU policies; it is not involved in European lawmaking. (After its sessions, almost always in Brussels, a subtotal of the members, those belonging to the Euro zone, stay on for separate consultations.) The mode of decision making of this body (that meets behind closed doors) is peculiar: no votes are taken, but the president of the Council draws a 'conclusion' that is considered adopted as a consensual policy document once none of the members registers a formal disagreement. It also reflects power relations that serve to silence potential opponents to the (normally) prevailing French–German consensus. This unanimity rule represents the smallest common denominator that national top politicians of member states are able to strike a compromise on. If it were otherwise and some kind of qualified majority rule were to apply, the national constituency of presidents or prime ministers who find themselves in the minority could (and certainly would) protest that they have been made subject to some kind of 'foreign rule', the rule of the majority countries. This arrangement severely limits the potential *effectiveness* of (the non-legislative, but 'impulse-giving') governance by the EC. Its democratic *legitimacy* is limited by the fact that members, while certainly being elected into their offices of prime minister, etc., are thereby mandated to serve the good of the *country* in which they have been elected, not that of the *EU*; in contrast, members of the European Parliament are expressly elected to represent the European citizenry in EU legislation.

How did we get into this situation of urgently needed yet woefully deficient European and Euro zone governing capacity? What is the pre-history of the chain effects of financial market, debt and integration crisis? One element of the answer is the inexplicable (as it seems from today's perspective) failure of national and European authorities to regulate the financial industry in ways that might have prevented the chains of banks defaulting and governments stepping in to bail them out – a notable *attention deficit*[5] that has

4 R. Dahl, *Democracy and its Critics*, Yale University Press, New Haven, 1989.

5 R. Posner, *The Crisis of Capitalist Democracy*, Harvard University Press, Cambridge, 2010.

afflicted policy elites not just on Europe's side of the North Atlantic. Let me just allude to some of the deeper mechanisms that seem to have played a role in this extremely complex field. Part of the explanation of the story is that the states are so badly indebted and thus so vulnerable to the vagaries of financial markets because they had to bail out their banks, at least those which are proverbially 'too big to fail'. The public costs of saving private banks at the taxpayers' expense has added to the fiscal crisis, which in turn allows the banks to profit from crediting states – a manifestation of the banks' 'second strike capability' that is an obscenity in itself.

If one were to put oneself in the shoes of a financial investor, he wants one of two things (and there is a trade-off between these two things): *Security* for the financial investment (a positive assessment of the probability that the loan will be serviced and paid off) and a high *yield* in terms of interest (as a partial compensation for the remaining risk that the debtor defaults). *States* used to be preferred debtors because they have two advantages, as seen by lenders, compared with private debtors. First, they have the political authority to *impose* taxes on citizens to service their debt. Second, they can *print* money and thus devalue their debt in real terms through inflation. The latter attraction is no longer valid if the debtor state is a Euro state, thereby being prohibited from printing its own money. The former attraction has also been rendered questionable, from the point of view of financial investors, as states are rightly perceived by them to relate to each other, as EU member states with open borders, as rivals in a game of *tax competition*. Raising taxes in order to provide assurance to creditors is not an option either if that came to be seen by investors to undercut the state's international economic competitiveness, hence its future tax base, and hence the ability to service its debt. In an open economy, states must be cautious about imposing taxes on corporations and the earners of high income; if they cannot rely, instead, on imposing them upon ordinary workers and consumers, and to the extent they cannot cut their expenditures, there remains no alternative other than relying on loans from private creditors – loans that become less readily available (or more expensive) due to the two points just made.

Throughout the period of global liberalization, *i.e.*, since the early 1980s, the total debt of OECD states has thus been continuously growing. (Incidentally, the gradual transition from the taxing state to the borrowing state has some interesting distributional implications: The *taxing* state *diminishes* the disposable income of the well-to-do through (progressive) taxation, while the *borrowing* state *increases* that income by paying interest on what the well-to-do can well afford to lend the state.) Throughout the same period, the volume of the financial sector as a whole and the portion of the revenues it derives from the financing of public debt has been growing, while the portion of income that financial investors derive from borrowers in the 'real' economy has been shrinking.

It has been argued by the German sociologist Christoph Deutschmann that the shift of the financial industry from financing investments in the 'real' economy to financing sovereign debt and speculative trading in debt is due to a relative shortage of 'classical' debtors – debtors who take out loans in order to finance investment in productive activities, the returns from which allow them to service their debt.[6] This shortage of demand for credit in the 'real' economy can arguably be attributed to the combined effect of the demographic change of aging societies (wealthy pensioners acting as *rentiers* rather than entrepreneurs) plus a secular decline of economic growth rates throughout the OECD world (as Robert J. Gordon has argued in an influential paper on US long-term growth prospects).[7] To the extent it does take place, *growth depends on credit* that is granted to states, firms and households. (As Streeck has shown in his new book, the total indebtedness (or degree of 'financialization' of the economy and polity) has increased to a factor of *eight* times the annual GDP in Germany and of *nine* times that of the US, roughly doubling since the 1970s in the US and since the early 1990s in Germany, in the latter country mostly due to debt-financed unification.)[8]

Yet it is also true that *credit depends on growth* for its sustainability. Moreover, the stability of a capitalist society critically depends upon growth. The one thing that capitalist societies, even the most prosperous of them, cannot afford is to *stagnate* (contrary to the hopes and predictions of J. S. Mill, who foresaw a liberal steady state economy[9]). For if growth were not anticipated for at least the medium-term future, investors would have no reason to invest and workers no opportunity to work and earn an income from being employed. To deepen the dilemma even further, let me just point to the currently widely shared doubts whether we in the advanced societies can at all *afford* growth ('as we know it') for environmental and, in particular, climate change considerations. Taking these considerations together, we get three propositions, each of which is as plausible as they are mutually incompatible: (1) growth is indispensable, (2) growth rates are approximating zero in advanced economies and (3) growth becomes unaffordable in view of its negative externalities.

I lack both the space and the competence to do more here than just raise these questions rather than outline answers concerning what happens in a zero growth condition. Instead, let me return to the configuration of forces and strategies in the current debt and Euro crisis. Bailing out Greece (and now Cyprus), to say nothing about Spain, Portugal and Italy, through debt mutualization, Eurobonds and other mechanisms of burden-sharing among member states is likely to turn out to be an extremely expensive transfer that would have to be paid through inflation and/or increased budget deficits in the North. That is to say, it is extremely unpopular in countries that would be seen and see themselves as net

6 C. Deutschmann, 'Limits to Financialization. Sociological Analyses of the Financial Crisis', *Archives Européennes de Sociologie LII*, No. 3, 2011, pp. 347-389.

7 R. J. Gordon, 'Is US Economic Growth Over? Faltering Innovation Confronts the Six Headwinds', *CEPR Policy Insight*, No. 63, 2012.

8 Streeck 2013, p. 233.

9 J.S. Mill, John Stuart, *Principles of Political Economy*, Oxford University Press, Oxford [1848], 2008.

contributors to the rescue operation. The only argument to possibly convince 'northern' voting publics that burden sharing (of course with harsh conditionalist strings attached) is still an acceptable idea is the argument that *failing* to do so might be even *more* expensive. This is an entirely prudential argument, not one from solidarity obligations. Nobody can know for sure what is going to happen if *nothing* happens, *i.e.*, if some form of debt mutualization does *not* materialize. The most recent prognostics from a Bertelsmann study[10] suggest a disaster: a domino effect throughout the northern Mediterranean, including France and perhaps Belgium, would be hugely destructive for the global economy, and in particular the entire European economy. Germany, as well as Finland and the Netherlands, would be very badly affected, too. So, as a matter of prudence rather than solidarity, it is better to bail out Greece in order to stop the predators of the financial industry from imposing ever higher 'spreads' on one after the other of the countries in question. To be sure, the financial institutions will warmly welcome such acts of anxiety-driven supranational 'solidarity', as these acts assure them that their risk will eventually be covered, at least to an extent that allows them to stay in business. Yet more than temporary transfers is needed in order to restore the trust in the debtor countries' ability to pay and to service their debt: In order to fully assure long-term investors, what Greece would need is not just the (at any rate limited, in both time and financial volume) willingness of vicarious debtors to step in by paying for Greek debt, but a recovery of the tax base of the Greek economy so that, at some point in the fairly distant future, Greece can cover its financial obligations from its own production (plus from permanent transfers from EU funds, such as an economically backward province would be entitled to receive from the central government of an ordinary federal state). That is to say, in order to prevent the banks from anticipating (and thereby causing in a self-fulfilling loop) the risk of default of Greek and other Mediterranean states, the EU, instead of urging counter-productive austerity and 'reforms', thereby further undercutting growth prospects and stirring up disruptive social conflict, would have to become instrumental in rebuilding the ailing and largely uncompetitive economies of the Southern Euro zone. But no one, argues Streeck[11], pointing to the (presumably 'easier') intra-state examples of the post-GDR *Länder* and the Italian *Mezzogiorno*, knows how to accomplish that in an effective and robust manner. Besides, the sobering fact is that the EU in its present shape (lacking its own taxing power and with its medium-term budget just having been significantly decimated, in early 2013, by member states' governments) is neither institutionally nor economically nor politically willing and able to take the initiative towards any of those things. A minimally promising 'Marshall Plan for Greece' is not forthcoming from 'Brussels'. Besides, if it were, it would not fall on the fertile

10 Bertelsmann-Stiftung, 'Wirtschaftliche Folgen eines Euro-Austritts der südeuropäischen Mitgliedsstaaten", Policy Brief, 2012.

11 Streeck 2013.

ground of a post-war reconstruction boom, as did its predecessor. As long as nothing of the kind is likely to happen, the banks are bound to have the final say on what happens to the populations and economies of the South.

In an economic space where national borders are perforated so that people, investments, goods and services can freely move from member state to member state, a web of causalities and interdependencies emerges the scope of which vastly exceeds the scope of control, or governing capacity. What 'all of us' are passively affected by cannot be actively shaped and managed by any agency that is endowed with legitimate power. This gap between the horizon of causation and the horizon of control applies with particular force to members of the Euro zone: they are disempowered to manage their national currencies (as there is none anymore) yet unable to collectively establish the governing capacity that would allow them to manage their interdependency in ways that are tolerable for all and capable of curbing the power of the financial sector. The ECB, being the supreme fiduciary institution of the Euro zone and remote from any political accountability has neither mandate nor nearly the capacity to fill this control gap.

Sociologically speaking, the scope of functional integration is much wider than the scope of social integration, or what we are passively *affected by* is beyond our collective capacity to *act upon*. The European political economy is (at best) experienced by its citizens as a community of fate, but not as one of fate *control*. Markets and the currency are international, while democratic politics remains essentially national and framed in the code of what has been called 'methodological nationalism'. The twist, however, is that some participants of this game, such as Germany, have no urgent reason nor incentive to remedy this imbalance because they can live with it or are even favoured by its outcomes, while others are on the receiving side of massive and uncontrolled negative externalities, *i.e.* the beggar-my-neighbour effects originating from member states that have managed to combine high productivity with wage restraint, together yielding low unit costs of labour and high export surpluses. Yet with the EU having no taxing authority of its own, any permanent and appropriately large-scale international redistribution initiated by the Commission would meet with the complaint of 'taxation without representation.' But this imbalance can be taken care of in either of two ways: either by further cutting the budget of the EU or by endowing the EU with a democratically accountable taxing and spending authority of its own (which, to be sure, would require not only amending the Treaties, but also national constitutions, such as the German *Grundgesetz*).

It used to be the case that, in order for one country or a group of countries to take full control of the economy and polity of another country, the former must *occupy* the latter by military means. This is no longer needed. Today one can have perfectly peaceful relations with a particular country and still literally own it – simply by appropriating its economy through a permanent trade surplus and by destroying its sovereignty by depriving the country (in an *ad hoc* fashion of rescue conditionality, if not through European law) of its budgetary and other legislative autonomy. Just an example: 40% of the manufacturing sector of Hungary is estimated to be owned or jointly owned by German companies. And these are only German (co-) owners – if you add France, Austria and Great Britain, this must amount to the majority of all assets of that country. Given this constellation of economic and political power, it does not come as a surprise that within those countries the situation is perceived as a new version of imperialism and dependency – a view the anti-European mobilizational potential of which yields very gloomy prospects for the future of European integration.

2.6 WHOSE RESPONSIBILITY?

Coming back to the question of who can or must be 'blamed' for such international power imbalances deepening within the European political economy and the Euro zone, the only 'agent' we can point at is the institutional set-up of the EU and the 'attention deficit' of its designers. Their design of the Euro zone was a giant mistake from the beginning because of the (further deepening) heterogeneity of the economies it comprises, as was the failure of the Maastricht treaty to provide effective sanctioning mechanisms for the violation of its criteria as well as the failure of the Lisbon treaty to establish an adequately capable regime at the European level for the implementation of supranational economic, fiscal and social policies. Nor can any 'automatic' adjustment of socio-economic imbalances be expected to take place, be it through the lowering of wages and prices in the less prosperous parts of the system or through outward migration of labour to the more prosperous ones; the latter adjustment through labour mobility is largely hindered, within the EU, by its multilingual nature of the EU with its no less than 23 official languages. To top it all, there was the mistaken political decision to engage in the competitive liberalization of the financial industry, in Germany (under the Red-Green Schröder administration) and elsewhere. So it seems that 'all of us' have made great, serious and highly consequential mistakes.

Yet this insight, though widely and occasionally even ruefully shared by today's political elites in Europe, does not really help to redesign policy. What would help, in my view, is not to allocate *blame* retrospectively, but what I would call forward-looking *remedial responsibility*. The moral principle underlying this move is simple. It postulates that the *less* an agent (member state and its economy) has suffered as a consequence of the mistakes collectively made or the *more* it has even benefitted from them having been made (through interest rates that are lower than they otherwise would be, and external exchange rates of the Euro more favourable), the *greater* the share of the burdens the agent must shoulder in compensating others for adverse consequences resulting from the original mistake. This moral calculus can even be read in a deontic and a consequentialist perspective – the latter because the beneficiary will have a long-term interest in preserving an arrangement that has yielded it so many benefits at comparatively low costs and sacrifices. Yet however one is to read it, the answer to the question who that agent might be bearing the greatest remedial responsibility in today's Europe is compelling: Germany. Yet German political elites and publics are far from *appreciating* this answer as compelling and from acting accordingly – quite the contrary and certainly not at a time when incumbent parties and governments are facing national elections.

What we have here is one of the rare cases where the demands of moral duty *coincide* with those of well-considered long-term interests. Yet its practical implications are still virtually universally being rejected. Needless to say, a proposition to

- partially sacrifice national sovereignty and substantial economic resources, for the sake of
- creating an enhanced European-level governing capacity, for the sake of
- bailing out member states and subsidizing their economic recovery as well as alleviating the misery of their social conditions, for the sake of
- appeasing the financial industry and restraining its charges of interest, in order to
- consolidate the Euro zone and eventually the EU...

  such a complex chain of strategic moves is a non-starter in terms of national politics, and not just due to its complexity and the uncertainties involved. Whoever were to advocate this line of action would have to face fears, resentments and nationalistic backlash on a massive scale from the entire spectrum of political forces.

2.7 The Poverty of Party Politics

To repeat, we face the abysmal gap between policy and politics. Political parties – preferably supranational political parties addressing a Europe-wide constituency – would have to be able to bridge this gap by shaping and educating public opinion. Instead we see parties desperately clinging to national frames and short-term cost calculations as they are afraid to provoke the worst resentments of the voters and of losing votes to populist competitors as a consequence. What their leaders say and decide behind closed doors in Brussels is often risky to state openly and defend at home in the national media because of the omnipresent suspicion of betrayal of 'national' interests. Political parties as power-seeking organizations are corrupted by the positivistic opportunism of responding to voters' *given* preferences, while shying away from the challenge of *shaping* these preferences in the first place – which is arguably the supreme mission of democratic political parties.

If that mission were to be fulfilled, parties would have to accomplish a switch from the dominant code of 'nation *vs.* nation' to an at least supplementary code of 'social class *vs.* social class.' That is to say, two Germans, one of whom is threatened by long-term unemployment, have probably *less* in common, as far as their socio-economic interests are concerned, than two Europeans being threatened by unemployment (or, for that matter, deriving income from financial investments), one of whom happens to be a German.

As a rule of thumb, politicians can afford to be more consistent the further they are from a direct involvement in national policymaking. Populist leaders, both on the left and on the right, are often quite consistent precisely because they cannot hope for government office anyway. As long as governing responsibilities are out of reach, they can be denounced as 'sour grapes,' and office holders denounced as self-serving, incompetent and corrupt. Populists are obsessed with what Max Weber called 'negative politics': politics of obstruction and anti-politics. Populists such as the Italian *Cinque Stelle* movement float mobilizing demands for the benefit of their campaign that they do not expect to have to implement as the makers of public policy. Another current example is Horst Seehofer, the Bavarian prime minister. As his role in EU crisis policy is at best a very limited one, he can well afford to 'be tough on the Greeks' – a position from which he has to retract, however, when it comes to demonstrating support for Merkel's coalition government, of which his party is a junior partner. On the other hand, I am less optimistic than, for instance, Habermas[12] that political parties *are* in fact able and willing to shape public opinion through argument and persuasion in order to generate support for far-sighted and inclusive policies. What would be needed for political parties to shape preferences through persuasion and argument is the capacity to overcome widespread fears, sentiments of distrust, short-sightedness and suspicion.

One of those popular attitudes that parties are typically not capable of coming to terms with is the suspicion that if 'we' make sacrifices in favour of 'them,' 'they' will use 'our' generosity as an opportunity to take unfair advantage of 'us.' In short, 'they' are portrayed as engaging in the frivolously self-serving behaviour that economists call 'moral hazard.' The cognitive bias of mass constituencies that parties fail to overcome is the understanding that a problem is 'their' problem, not a problem of 'all of us.' This weakness could perhaps be remedied if parties were able to switch from their dominant 'nation *vs.* nation' code to the 'class *vs.* class' code.

Yet the primary problem is the widely shared *perception* of such threat of moral hazard and its anticipated turn into a negative-sum game. If 'we' are generous to 'them,' 'they' will respond by exploiting the situation by ceasing to perform 'their' obligations, thus spiralling 'all of us' into a bottomless pit. If that were so, 'we' would do better to stop making mindless sacrifices, which is a politically popular conclusion that drives the whole scenario. It stands in the way of the acceptance of socially inclusive and far-sighted policies. Yet the negative-sum scenario is not just driven by the interests of potential donors in finding an excuse for not donating, but it is often also provided plausibility by observations on how recipients actually *do* behave and are induced by their institutions and traditions to behave. In several of the Mediterranean Euro countries, there is in fact credible evidence of tax authorities and entire political elites being corrupt, tax evasion being considered a mark of cleverness, special interest being institutionally privileged and tax-exempt, organized crime playing a

12 P. Bofinger, J. Habermas & J. Nida-Rümelin, 'Einspruch gegen die Fassadendemokratie,' *Frankfurter Allgemeine Zeitung*, 3 August 2012.

big role in the making (or at least sabotaging) of public policy and agents in public administration and the judiciary deviating far from what in other parts of Europe is considered an appropriate ethos of public service. It is the evidence of these deficiencies (that are hardly to be overcome by foreign pressures, threats and moralizing accusations) that nourishes negative perceptions and resentments on the part of those in the North of Europe who have an interest in excusing themselves from duties of solidarity, if not even a plain propensity to victim blaming. If neither the Greek state nor European legislation finds means to prevent rich citizens of Greece from reportedly transferring every year an estimated 40 billion Euros out of the country into their Swiss bank accounts or elsewhere, this fact, as processed by media reporting, is quite unlikely to stimulate other Europeans' sense of obligation and responsibility. While Greece is probably the most ethno-nationalistic country in the EU, its economic culture is arguably also the least patriotic.

We know from surveys that in none of the countries that suffer from great trade and budget deficits do majorities favour the idea of leaving the Euro – quite the contrary. The economic and political reasons are obvious. First, by exiting from the Euro they would lose their 'nuisance value' – the capacity to pressure the EU to rescue their banks, budgets and economies. Second, they would still have to service their Euro-denominated debt on the basis of a heavily devalued new national currency. Also, no reasonably responsible politician in the rest of Europe would urge them to leave, as chain reactions affecting other countries would be likely (and at least highly incalculable as to their costs) as a consequence.

The EU and its member states suffer from three deficits that are by now almost proverbial: The deepening *trade* deficits of the poorer economies, the ubiquitous (except for Sweden) *budget* deficits and the glaring *democratic* deficit at the level of EU governance. To briefly illustrate, GDP per capita relates from the (admittedly: outlier of) Luxemburg at the peak to Bulgaria at the bottom as 17 relates to 1, with ten of the twelve new member states together making up the lower end of the distribution. There is not a single Euro country where public debt levels comply with the Maastricht limit of 60% of GDP. And the European institutions, in spite of the direct and deep impact they have upon the life of citizens, operate in stratospheric distance from democratic mechanisms of accountability and representation. The most supranational and most democratic of the EU institutions, the European Parliament, suffers from the anomaly that it does not meet (and will hardly ever attain) the standard of a 'people's chamber', or a normal legislature; for that, it would have to comply with the 'one man one vote' rule and the principle of equal weight of each vote. As, for instance, the populations of Germany and Luxemburg relate to each other in quantitative terms as 204:1, the constituency of Luxemburg (or Malta or one day Iceland) would hardly ever agree to be massively downgraded in its representational weight in the EP through an abolition of the rule of 'degressive proportionality' currently in force; yet that rule has already been declared 'undemocratic' in lower houses by the German Constitutional Court.[13]

13 Bundesverfassungsgericht, Judgment of the BVferG on the Treaty of Lisbon. Available from <www.bverfg.de/entscheidungen/es20090630_2bve000208.html>, 2009, paras 274-295.

These three deficits are tightly interrelated, with the last one, the democratic deficit, being the strategic leverage point for any promising attempt to deal with the other two. In order to have a steep increase in terms of integration, fiscal pact and permanent oversight of the Commission; in order to make a regime controlling banks and budgets a stable regime (rather than an *ad hoc* emergency measure adopted behind closed doors); and, most of all, in order to implement the large-scale redistribution (both inter-state and inter-class) that such a regime would entail, one certainly cannot do without the political support of the European citizenry that expresses its will, as shaped and guided by political parties, in general elections and referenda. And, as democratic procedures go, the outcome can be yes, or it can be no; democratic processes are open-ended choices. Their outcomes depend upon the capacity of political parties to persuade and enlighten citizens. If we were to leave choices concerning policy, but also those concerning institutions, to the technocrats to decide upon, then chances are that everything they decide will be worthless the day after tomorrow, *i.e.*, after the day national constitutional courts or the ECJ have passed their judgements. In order to create solidity, permanence, calculability and continuity of the terms of integration, we need democratic legitimation. This is a functional argument: if we want to be effective, we cannot do without democratic legitimacy in the first place in order to endow policies and institutions with the authority and validity that the (alleged) expertise of technocrats cannot possibly substitute for through 'output legitimacy'.

At any rate, the way forward cannot be charted by Thatcher's (and Merkel's) TINA maxim that 'there is no alternative' to what incumbent elites declare the only way out. Invoking TINA is just tantamount to admitting that previous policies have failed their mandate to *keep* choices open, thereby trapping all of us in an allegedly alternative-less situation.

No doubt, there is a problem here. Liberal democracy has been suspected to be both procedurally slow in recognizing and addressing societal problems and myopic (inadequately 'future-regarding') in setting agendas as elites are fixated on what can be achieved by the date of the next election. (Either of these defects can be easily illustrated using current climate change politics and policies as an example.) On the one hand, it is in the very nature of democratic processes, including appropriate information gathering, will formation through public debate and deliberation, coalition building, campaigning etc., that it is highly time-consuming, compared with decision making in depoliticized technocratic committees. This applies *a fortiori* to democratic institution building: the time needed to accomplish a major overhaul of the Treaties governing the EU can safely be estimated as ranging between five and ten years. Yet in order to produce a viable response to emergency situations in financial markets, one often has a day or two. Sometimes it is even a matter of hours: Brussels' decisions on how to appease financial markets must be out at 2 am Sunday night, *i.e.*, before the Tokyo stock exchange opens. Yet still, those making such decisions must be capable of being held democratically accountable or at least be able to claim legitimacy on the basis of a fiduciary mission democratically granted to them.

The solution to this problem might be that policies become more proactive, anticipating and paying attention to seemingly remote possibilities (remote both in time and in probability) in order to be prepared – the opposite of the case in the financial market crisis of September 2008.

Besides, the absence of choice is often a false claim of politicians and their ideological preoccupations and ways of framing political and economic realities. Take the familiar case of a gaping budget deficit. The technocratic answer is the call for austerity. Yet instead of cutting expenditures, the gap can also be closed by raising taxes. Yet that would antagonize investors, whose resistance would have to be neutralized by, among other things, harmonizing the system of direct taxes throughout the EU. But trying to do so would provoke objections in the new member states that feel compelled to compete for investment through low (and often flat rate) corporate income tax rates, and so on. Claiming 'no alternatives' is often just a cover for surrendering to perceived (and no doubt accurately perceived) power relations, the powers that defend the *status quo* of the free movement of financial capital.

Europe consists of nation states, citizens and social classes; there are plenty of alternatives concerning how we want to engage all these various forces and actors into the democratic process. Generally speaking, *input* legitimation is indispensable, particularly at present when *output* legitimacy – the legitimacy claimed for the making of effective decisions – is in such a miserable state. If one thinks of the so-called permissive consensus in favour of Europe that prevailed until a decade ago, virtually nothing is left of it. Mass constituencies are up in arms against 'Brussels', 'Berlin', and 'Europe' – thus we need to rebuild Europe on the basis of democratic mechanisms of representation and accountability.

There is no shortage of policy proposals that serve as proof that there *are* 'alternatives.' A EU-wide tax harmonization applying to direct taxes would help to disincentivize 'regime shopping' practices and transnational capital mobility – a mobility with which labour cannot cope, partly because labour speaks in 23 languages, while capital is 'speechless.' Budget deficits can be addressed not just by austerity measures and 'internal' devaluation; they can also be solved by increasing taxes on high income and wealth, and be it by forcing the wealthy to buy government bonds. Indirect taxes have the great advantage that their tax base cannot flee the country and the well-known downside that their incidence is regressive: the relatively poor spend greater parts of their income and thus shoulder a greater proportion of the burden of indirect taxes. Why not apply a progressive schedule on Y - S = C per tax year, *i.e.*, annual income per person minus documented savings/investment as the basis of progressive taxation instead of a flat sales tax, thus combining the advantages, in terms of distributional fairness, of direct and indirect taxation? Furthermore, proposals have been made to Europeanize the systems of unemployment insurance[14] and

14 S. Dullien, 'Eine Arbeitslosenversicherung für die Euro-Zone', SWP-Studie, 2008.

social assistance/poverty relief,[15] the realization of which may well boost, as a side effect, the mass identification with Europe as a political entity. Moreover, without violating the 'subsidiarity' principle enshrined in the Treaties, a European legislation could be launched that specifies maximum permissible Gini coefficients for member-state societies, with the level inversely tied to their current GDP per capita values. Also, commercial banks can be prohibited from accepting deposits from financial investors who can be identified as fleeing from debt-troubled countries. All of this *can* be done, but it has not been done. These and other policy proposals can largely be implemented through European legislation. The problem is that before that can happen, a basic 'mental reframing' of the situation is called for in that the prevailing 'methodological nationalism' code of 'nation vs. nation' must be partly substituted and supplemented by a code of 'losers versus winners' of the crisis, if not socioeconomic 'class versus class.'

Institutionally, and in order for any of those proposals to win favourable prospects, the European Parliament needs to be strengthened and the Commission needs to be transformed into something like a parliamentary government. It is precisely those EU institutions that have the *greatest* impact on daily life of people that are so far the *farthest* from democratic accountability: the European Central Bank, the European Court of Justice and the European Commission. They are completely depoliticized and thus can act in majestic independence of whatever citizens, parties and parliaments prefer or reject. Again, we face a deep divorce between politics and policy: On the one hand, there is often populist mass politics (including identity-related 'culture wars') that has no perceptible implication for policymaking on citizens' core interests and bread-and-butter issues. On the other hand, there is elitist policymaking that has no roots in, no links to, nor legitimation through politics. This is the deepening bifurcation of those two spheres within the European polity. Political elites are increasingly unable to achieve outcomes that voters desire and to convince voters that their interests are in their, the elites', trustworthy and competent hands. What voters need and want is beyond the capacity of the political system to deliver, without the latter being able to explain to the former what the hindrances are and how they might be removed. It is as if one has mail-ordered a shirt and is supplied a pair of socks. The promises and appeals by which political power is *acquired* (*i.e., politics*) are disjointed, under the dictate of financial markets, from the purposes to the achievement of which power resources mandated to governments are *effectively employed* and used for the making of *policies.*

To this situation elites (as well as commentators and academic observers) respond by diagnosing and complaining about an emerging condition of 'ungovernability.' Non-elites feel cheated and follow the appeals of ever shriller and ever more anti-political forms of fundamental opposition campaigns, such as that of Grillo in Italy who, right after winning

15 P. Van Parijs, 'No Eurozone Without Euro-Dividend' (unpublished manuscript, 2012).

a spectacular quarter of the popular vote in the February 2013 national elections, gleefully predicted the Italian Republic's disintegration and exit from the Euro zone within a matter of six months due to its manifest fiscal starvation.

What if the Euro fails and the losers of the Euro game are forced to leave the common currency area? I suppose there are lots of drawers in lots of government offices that are filled with emergency plans for the hour when all the rescue plans have turned out futile. I have not seen these plans, nor has anyone I know. If the EU disintegrates, in 'controlled' ways or otherwise, we'll stand at the beginning of a giant negative-sum game in which everyone is going to lose. That much is well understood, and widely. As I have pointed out, one core problem for the saving of the Euro is that the banking crisis has spilled over into a debt crisis, and the debt crisis in an EU integration crisis. The latter crisis consists in the re-nationalization of horizons of solidarity and rich countries of Europe dictating to the poorer ones the austerity cure in order for them to regain the trust of the financial industry. They do so in spite of all the evidence that austerity is a highly poisonous medicine, an overdose of which will kill the patient (rather than stimulate growth and expand the tax base), in which case the weakest Euro zone members (and eventually all of them) become ever more dependent on lenders and allow them to charge ever higher and ever more unsustainable rates. It is becoming ever more difficult to envisage the bootstrapping act by which European political elites might escape from this vicious circle. I think it will eventually need the protest and resistance of those suffering most from the crisis to push those elites on a more promising path. But nobody, as of today, can claim the possession of valid knowledge on what that path may be, nor who may assume a leadership role in guiding us there.

3 Beheading of the Legislator: The European Crisis – Paradoxes of Constitutionalizing Democratic Capitalism

Hauke Brunkhorst

In the beginning was not the affirmation of *peace*, the protection of which now is the reason why the EU got the Nobel Prize last year (although, at the same time, the Union or its Member States are at war in several parts of the world).

In the beginning was not peace but the *negation of fascism*: that is, the *emancipation* of Europe from the dictatorship of the Third Reich.

In the beginning was not the *managerial mindset* of possessive individualism and 'peaceful competitive struggle'.[1] In the beginning was political autonomy.

In the beginning was not rational choice and strategic action enabled by rule of law, but the emancipation from any law that was not the law to which we have given our agreement.[2] Martti Koskenniemi calls the latter the *Kantian mindset*, in contrast to the managerial mindset.[3] For Kant in his time, the scandal of so-called absolutism was not a lack of *Rechtsstaat* or rule of law. Kant had no doubt that the contemporary monarchy was a state of law. For Kant the scandal of that monarchy was its lack of political 'autonomy' and 'self-legislation,' and the absence of 'structures of political representation.'[4] Historically, the Kantian constitutional mindset is the mindset of the French Revolution as it was once expressed strikingly by the young Karl Marx in one short sentence: "Die gesetzgebende Gewalt hat die Französische Revolution gemacht". [The legislative power has made the French Revolution.][5]

Today the memory that it was the same constituent legislative power of the peoples of Europe that has made the EU between Fall 1944 (the last year of World War II in Europe)

---

1 K. Marx, *Der 18. Brumaire des Louis Bonaparte*, p. 98, English translation from <www.marxists.org/archive/marx/works/1852/18th-brumaire/ch02.htm> (last accessed 19 March 2012).

2 A. Somek, 'Europe: From Emancipation to Empowerment' (unpublished e-man., University of Iowa, Utah, 2012.)

3 M. Koskenniemi, 'Constitutionalism as Mindset: Reflections on Kantian Themes About International Law and Globalization', *Theoretical Inquiries in Law*, Vol. 8, 2006, pp. 9-36.

4 *Ibid.*, p. 26.

5 K. Marx, 'Kritik des Hegelschen Staatsrechts (pp. 261-313)', *MEW*, Vol. 1, Dietz, Berlin, 1972, p. 260. Because of the indeterminacy of law application, also the application and concretization of legal norms is not simply a politically neutralized business of managerial experts but, as Kelsen, Merkel and Heller have rightly argued already in the 1920s, any "determining the content of the legal norm [is] a political question". (Koskenniemi 2006, p. 29).

and 1957 has been repressed and displaced by the managerial mindset that had already become hegemonic during the 1950s. However, the European unification did not begin with the Treaties of Paris and Rome in 1951 and 1957, but with the *new constitutions* that all founding members (France, Belgium, Italy, Luxemburg, Netherlands, West Germany) had given themselves between 1944 and 1948. Moreover, the foundation of the first Communities in 1951 and 1957 was an effect of a *global revolutionary transformation of national and international law* that was as deep as that of the French Revolution.[6] All constitutions of the founding members were made by *new representatives* of the respective peoples.

1. All founding members had *changed their political leaders* and had *replaced great parts of the former ruling classes* with former resistance fighters or emigrants who had defected. They gained a power that did not exist before or during the time of the Nazi occupation. Rebels, guerrillas and exiled politicians became heads and members of government. They risked their lives, not solely as patriots, but as democrats or socialists who had struggled for certain rights and universal constitutional principles.[7]
2. All constitutions of the founding members were *new* or in important aspects *revised* and *more democratic than ever before*. Only now did *all* of them stipulate *universal adult suffrage*.
3. All had *eliminated* the remains (or after 1918 newly invented structures) of *corporatist political representation* of society. For the first time the system of political democracy was completely autonomous and could *cover and control the whole society through parliamentary or popular legislation alone* (as was the case with Kelsen's Austrian constitution of 1918 that was then a lone exception).[8] The German *Grundgesetz* even constituted a completely *new state*.[9]
4. All constitutions of the founding members expressed a strong emphasis on *human rights* and had *opened themselves* (more or less) *to international law*. The founding members of the European Communities designed their newly constituted states as *open states* – open to the incorporation of international law and international cooperation; an important example of this is, in the German Basic Law (*Grundgesetz*), the obligatory *Völkerrechtsfreundlichkeit* [*openness to international law*] established in Article 24(1).[10]

---

6 *See* H. Brunkhorst, *Legitimationskrisen – Verfassungsprobleme der Weltgesellschaft*, Nomos, Baden-Baden, 2012.

7 J. Osterhammel & N.P. Petersson, *Geschichte der Globalisierung*, Beck, München, 2007, p. 85; E. Hobsbawm, *Das Zeitalter der Extreme. Weltgeschichte des 20. Jahrhunderts*, Hanser, München, 1994, pp. 185-187. This does not mean that there did not remain strong continuities in all countries; in particular in Germany the Nazi-continuities of the elites were still strong but silenced and displaced, strikingly described by Hermann Lübbe as "kommunikatives Beschweigen brauner Biographieanteile"); *see* H. Lübbe, 'Der Nationalsozialismus im politischen Bewußtsein der Gegenwart', *in* M. Broszat *et al.* (Eds.), *Deutschlands Weg in die Diktatur*, Berlin, 1983.

8 See already D. Jesch, *Gesetz und Verwaltung. Eine Problemstudie zum Wandel des Gesetzmäßigkeitsprinzips*, Mohr, Tübingen, 1961.

9 See H. Kelsen, 'The Legal Status of Germany According to the Declaration of Berlin', *American Journal of International Law*, Vol. 39, 1945, pp. 518-526.

10 See R. Wahl, *Verfassungsstaat, Europäisierung, Internationalisierung*, Suhrkamp, Frankfurt, 2003; U. Di Fabio, *Das Recht offener Staaten. Grundlinien einer Staats- und Rechtstheorie*, Mohr, Tübingen, 1998.

5. Finally, and crucially for the foundation of Europe, the new constitutions declared the *strong commitment of their respective peoples to the project of European unification*, which was to be realized in the near future (e.g., preamble in combination with Article 24(1) of Basic Law). All founding members of the European Communities bound themselves *by the constituent power of the people* to the project of European Unification, which then, from 1951 onwards, became constitutive for all European constitutional (or quasi-constitutional) treaties.[11] The only instance of a constitution of a founding member that made no declaration about Europe, the Constitution of Luxemburg, is in itself a revealing case. In 1952 in Luxemburg, its *Conseil d'Êtat* decided that the Constitution implicitly committed the representatives of the people to join the *European Coal and Steel Community* and to strive for further European unification.[12]

In all, the Founding Treaties of Paris and Rome were directly legitimated by the *constituent power of the peoples*.[13] Consequently, it can be concluded that, from the outset, the EU was not founded as an international association of states. On the contrary, it was founded as a *community of peoples* who legitimated the project of European unification *directly* and *democratically* through their combined, but still national, constitutional powers (represented later in the *Council of the EU* and the *EC*). At the same time and with the same founding act, these peoples, acting plurally, constituted a single *European citizenship*, embodying *new rights for the European citizen*, which were different from the rights of the citizens of the respective member states (represented later by the *European Parliament*). These remained implicit for the first decades, but the ECJ made them explicit in *van Gend en Loos* and *Costa* in 1963 and 1964. The community of European citizens as a whole thus now constitutes a second and independent 'subject of legitimization.'[14] From the beginning, the Treaties were not just intergovernmental, but *legal documents with a constitutional quality*.

1 J.E. Fossum & A.J. Menéndez, *The Constitution's Gift. A Constitutional Theory for a Democratic European Union*, Rowman, Plymouth, 2011, p. 175.

12 It is argued that, even if the constitution of Luxemburg did not contain anything vaguely resembling a proto-European clause, the Conseil d'Êtat constructed its fundamental law along very similar lines. When reviewing the constitutionality of the Treaty establishing the Coal and Steel Community, the Conseil affirmed that Luxembourg, not only could, but should, renounce certain sovereign powers if the public good so required. *See* the Report on the 1952 judgment of the Conseil d'Êtat and Fossum & Menéndez 2011.

13 Fossum & Menéndez 2011.

14 On the double legitimization of the EU by the community of peoples of the member states and the people of the EU *see* J. Habermas, 'Die Krise der Europäische Union im Licht einer Konstitutionalisierung des Völkerrechts' (manuscript of a lecture given at the Humboldt University in Berlin on 16 June 2011). For a striking comparison with the development of the United States founded by a similar kind of 'double sovereignty' (which is still a technical term of constitutional law in the US), *see* C. Schönberger, *Föderale Angehörigkeit, Habilitationsschrift*, Freiburg, 2005. *See also* M. Forsythe, *Unions of States. The Theory and Practice of Confederations*, Holmes, New York, 1981. Augustine Menendez has made an important contribution to that thesis, comparing in a case study the implementation of federal taxes in the US and the EU, demonstrating the striking parallels. A.J. Menéndez, 'Taxing Europe – Two Cases for a European Power to Tax', Cidel Working Papers, Vol. 3, 2003.

However, as one can also observe in other cases of national or transnational constitutionalization, the constitutional moment was followed by an unspectacular evolutionary incrementalism and a silent but gradual and steady process of ever denser integration. The *managerial mindset* took over soon after the first big changes. However, it has not only *replaced and repressed* the *Kantian mindset* of revolutionary foundation but – in a paradoxical move – also *stabilized* and *realized it step by step legally.*[15] In European law today the Kantian mindset is expressed in the reference of the preambles of the European Treaties to 'solidarity,' 'democracy,' 'social progress' 'human rights' and 'rule of law.' Solidarity is mentioned again and again; however, the Treaty also states that solidarity should be for free (as in David Cameron's first sentence when the crisis erupted: "No money for the Greeks!"). Nevertheless, the Kantian mindset is implemented in many single articles and legal norms of primary and secondary European law, such as the famous Article 6 of the Treaty of Maastricht, or Articles 9-12 of the Lisbon Treaty. Moreover, the Kantian mindset also underlies legal precedents such as the famous cases Costa and van Gent en Loos from the early 1960s that refer to the subjective rights that we have *as* European citizens ('direct effect' plus 'European law supremacy'). Finally, the Kantian mindset found its way into numerous juristic commentaries and treatises, that is, the emergence of a European *Rechtsdogmatik* (legal doctrine),[16] and became part of the European common law.[17]

At the end of the day, and after the symbolic re-establishment of state-sovereignty through the constitutional court of the European hegemon in Karlsruhe – the counter-hegemonic Czech constitutional court in its judgement on the Lisbon Treaty stated that the *EU today*

15 An illuminating case study is M.R. Madsen, *The Protracted Institutionalization of the Strasbourg Court: From Legal Diplomacy to Integrationist Jurisprudence*, Oxford University Press, Oxford, 2011, pp. 55-59. On the general need of the 'Kantian' mindset of normative social integration for systemic and 'managerial' stabilization see J. Habermas, *Theorie des kommunikativen Handelns*, Vol. 2, Suhrkamp, Frankfurt, 1981, p. 228; *see* A. Nassehi, *Der soziologische Diskurs der Moderne*, Suhrkamp Verlag, Frankfurt aM, 2006, pp. 126-127.

16 A good explication of the Kantian democratic and even cosmopolitan mindset of the Lisbon Treaty is A. von Bogdandy, 'The European Lesson for International Democracy: The Significance of Articles 9-12 EU Treaty for International Organizations,' *The European Journal of International Law*, Vol. 23, No. 2, 2012, pp. 315-334; see already (in respect of the Maastricht-Amsterdam Treaty and in particular the Constitutional Treaty that failed in 2005 but to a large extent is identical to the Lisbon Treaty) C. Callies, 'Das Demokratieprinzip im Europäischen Staaten- und Verfassungsverbund,' *in* J. Bröhmer *et al.* (Eds.), *Internationale Gemeinschaft und Menschenrechte*, Heymanns, München, 2005, pp. 402-404.

17 What German lawyers observe as the emergence of an autonomous legal doctrine is reflected by a Scottish observer as the emergence of European common law that transcends the pacta sunt servanda validity of international law. European "institutions and organs", Neil MacCormick argues, "have had a continuous existence over several decades and through many changes of personnel. They have become central institutional facts in the thinking of Europeans. Citizens and officials throughout Europe have interpreted the norms of and under the treaties as having direct effect on private persons and corporations as well as on states. Over more than four decades this has proceeded with impressive continuity" (N. MacCormick, *Questioning Sovereignty. Law, State and Nation in the European Common Wealth*, Oxford University Press, Oxford, 1999, p. 139).

forms a complete and gapless system of democratic legitimization, and rightly so.[18] Legally Europe no longer has a crucial democratic deficit. It is already a fully fledged democracy on both levels: the national *and* the transnational.

The problem is that nobody knows it.

The problem is not just the managerial mindset but the *hegemony of the managerial mindset*, and the *reduction* of politics to technocracy that today allows the political and economic elites to bypass and manipulate public opinion and democratically legitimated public law *on both levels*: the European *as well as* the respective national level. At the same time as it is growing legally, the public power of the people and its representative organs is increasingly deprived of real power and replaced by grey networks of *informal government*[19] – called 'good governance'[20] instead of democratic government, called 'administrative accountability'[21] instead of parliamentary responsibility, called 'deliberative democracy' instead of egalitarian decision making.[22] In a world where good governance has replaced democratic government, where administrative accountability has replaced parliamentary responsibility, where deliberative democracy of educated middle classes has replaced egalitarian procedures of decision making, where the semantic of pluralized civil societies has replaced the unity of capitalist society, where competition has replaced cooperation, where the managerial mindset of individual empowerment has replaced the Kantian mindset of emancipation – public contestation over real issues, public debate and public struggle over substantial alternatives are just 'not helpful' (*nicht hilfreich*), to say it in the matchless managerial language of Angela Merkel. In Angela Merkel's world, deliberative democracy begins when the doors are closed.

Hence, and this is my *overarching thesis*, the Kantian mindset of revolutionary foundation has been concretized and stabilized throughout the gradual evolutionary process of constitutionalization. This evolutionary process developed under the lead of the managerial mindset of Europe's political elites and professional experts. However, the hegemony of the managerial

18 I. Ley, 'Brünn betreibt die Parlamentarisierung des Primärrechts. Anmerkungen zum zweiten Urteil des tschechischen Verfassungsgerichtshofs zum Vertrag von Lissabon vom 3.11.2009', *Juristen-Zeitung*, Vol. 65, No. 4, 2010, p. 170.

19 C. Möllers, 'Transnationale Behördenkooperation. Verfassungs- und völkerrechtliche Probleme transnationaler administrativer Standardsetzun', *Zeitschrift für ausländisches öffentliches Recht und Völkerrecht*, Vol. 65, 2005, pp. 351-389; C. Möllers, *Gewaltengliederung, Habilitationsschrift*, Heidelberg, 2003. *See* M. Hardt & A. Negri, *Empire. Die neue Weltordnung*, Campus, Frankfurt, 2002; T. Prien, *Fragmentierte Volkssouveränität*, Nomos, Baden-Baden, 2010; A. Fischer-Lescano & G. Teubner, *Regime-Kollisionen*, Suhrkamp Verlag, Frankfurt, 2006; on white, grey and black networks *see* W. Matiaske, 'Gullivers Fesseln: Corporate Social Responsibility als Normbildung?' (lecture, Flensburg University, Flensburg, 5 June 2012).

20 *See* M. Zürn, *Regieren jenseits des Nationalstaats*, Suhrkamp, Frankfurt am Main, 2004.

21 *See* R.W. Grant & R.O. Keohane, 'Accountability and Abuses of Power in World Politics', *American Political Science Review*, Vol. 99, No. 1, 2005, pp. 29-43.

22 For a sound criticism of these tendencies see S. Puntscher Rieckmann, 'Constitutionalism and Representation: European Parliamentarism in the Treaty of Lisbon', *in* P. Dobner & M. Loughlin (Eds.), *The Twilight of Constitutionalism?*, Oxford University Press, Oxford, 2010, pp. 120-139.

mindset had the paradoxical result that the Kantian mindset at the same time was *preserved and repressed* (or displaced), *constitutionalized and de-constitutionalized* – again and again at every stage of the twisted paths of European constitutionalization.[23]
To demonstrate that, I will combine throughout the following chapters (3-4) Koskenniemi's Kantian inspired distinction between the two constitutional mindsets with Karlo Tuori's more managerial reconstruction of the constitutionalization of Europe as an incremental evolutionary process of stages of structural coupling of law with other social systems. Through this combination, Koskenniemi's more voluntaristic distinction is transformed into a set of 'existing concepts' (Hegel) that are internal to the social evolution.[24]

3.1 Stage I: Economic Constitution

As Tuori has shown, Europe now has not only many national (and sub-national) constitutions but also many transnational constitutions that evolved gradually and in stages. The first evolutionary step was taken in 1957 with the establishment of a functional *economic constitution* that consisted in the *structural coupling* of the *legal* and the *economic system*. The establishment of the economic constitution was due to German Ordoliberalism. The Ordoliberals were a German-Austrian group of economists and jurists at the end of the Weimar Republic who were all more or less far-right-wing neo-conservatives, but with few exceptions anti-Nazis. The centre of the school was the University of Freiburg in south-western Germany. Members of the School were Franz Böhm, Walter Eucken, Alexander Rüstow, Wilhelm Röpke, Alfred Müller-Armack and Friedrich August von Hayek.[25]

---

23 On the stages see K. Tuori, 'The Many Constitutions of Europe', *in* K. Tuori & S. Sankari (Eds.), *The Many Constitutions of Europe*, Ashgate, Oxon, 2010, pp. 3-30.

24 I have tried to explain that further in H. Brunkhorst, *Critical Theory of Legal Revolutions – Evolutionary Perspectives*, Continuum, London/ New York, 2013 (forthcoming). On the 'existing concept' *see* G.W.F. Hegel, *Wissenschaft der Logik*, Vol. 2, Suhrkamp, Frankfurt, 1969, p. 481. On the (very one-sided) critique of the empty or, as Hegel says, 'abstract' ought *see* G.W.F. Hegel, *Vorlesungen über die Geschichte der Philosophie*, Vol. III, Suhrkamp, Frankfurt, 1971, pp. 369-372. Kant is not that far away from modern historical and evolutionary thinking as his critics since Hegel regularly assume, see already K. Vorländer, *Kants Leben*, Meiner, Leipzig, 1921, p. 100. Such a concept can then work in both directions dialectically: as a mechanism of stabilizing the so-called Sittlichkeit (ethical life) of the social systems of bourgeois society, capitalist or bureaucratic class-rule and authoritarian economic government, or – in dialectical retaliation – 'can strike back'. (F. Müller, *Wer ist das Volk? Eine Grundfrage der Demokratie, Elemente einer Verfassungstheorie*, Vol. VI, Duncker & Humblot, Berlin, 1997, p. 56). It can strike back because law, and in particular constitutional law, can be used by the have-nots, by peripheral states and lower classes as a legal principle, a legal claim, or even as a legal remedy to contradict its own interpretation and implementation that is in the service of the respective ruling classes.

25 Most of the school were conservative opponents to Nazi fascism. Böhm was a declared anti-Nazi, especially an early defender of the Jews, and a member of the resistance with close relations to Bonhoefer and Gördeler. Eucken was a conservative anti-Nazi who strongly opposed Heidegger as the first Nazi-Rektor of the University of Freiburg (over whose main entrance even in 2011 the 1936 dedication is still clearly visible. He was loosely associated with the conservative resistance. Rüstow was a member of the far-right shadow cabinet led by General Kurt von Schleicher. He engaged in a half-hearted attempt at an anti-Hitler

Originally the idea of an economic constitution was the invention of the German socialist left at the end of World War I, in particular Hugo Sinzheimer and his student Franz Neumann. Sinzheimer and Neumann strictly followed the Kantian presupposition that the political constitution and the parliamentary legislator should keep the absolute supremacy over the economic constitution. The economic constitution should have a mere service function: It should improve the possibilities of the democratic legislator, to place the markets, and in particular the private sphere of domination within the capitalist firm, under democratic control.[26]

At the end of the Weimar Republic, *Ordoliberals* 'rather hijacked' the idea of an economic constitution from Sinzheimer and Neumann, watered it down and reversed it severely.[27] During the 1950s they turned the idea upside down, trans-nationalized the economic constitution, decoupled it from the national political constitution and subsumed the latter to the former. Now the whole society should be 'subsumed' under the 'principle of market-compliance,' as the (at that time pious) former Nazi Alfred Müller-Armack wrote in 1960.[28] In the 1957 treaty negotiations the German Ordoliberals under the lead of Müller-Armack, and strongly supported by the American government, finally won the battle against the recalcitrant French government that, at the time, defended a constitutional project that was much closer to the original ideas of Sinzheimer and Neumann.[29]

With the establishment of the economic constitution in 1957, a Schmittian constitutional *Grundentscheidung* (basic decision) was made. It consisted in the radical 'negation of a political constitution of Europe.'[30] Instead of subsuming the economic under the political constitution, the political constitution was subsumed under the economic constitution, and therefore *Wettbewerbsrecht*, competition law, became the 'axis of the economic

coup d'état, and he had to emigrate in 1933. Röpke was attached to the conservative 'revolution' (Tat-Kreis) from the early 1920s. However, he strongly opposed German fascism as early as the late 1920s, and he emigrated (as did Eucken) to Turkey in 1933. Alfred Müller-Armack was a Nazi of the first hour. Hayek took a chair at the London School of Economics (LSE), and he left the continent by 1931. He was the most radical liberal opponent of Keynes, who already had at that time a chair at the LSE. Still the best criticism of Hayek is H. Kelsen, 'Demokratie und Sozialismus,' *in* N. Leser (Ed.), *Demokratie und Sozialismus. Ausgewählte Aufsätze*, Verlag der Wiener Volksbuchhandlung, Wien, 1954, pp. 170-210. As a legal theorist Hayek was very close to Carl Schmitt. This point is made in W. E. Scheuerman, 'The Unholy Alliance of Carl Schmitt and Friedrich A. Hayek,' *Constellations*, Vol. 4, 2004, pp. 172-188; *see* M. Vatter, 'Foucault y la ley: la juridificación de la política en el neoliberalismo' *in* V. Lemm (Ed.), *Michel Foucault: biopolítica y neoliberalismo*, Ediciones Universidad Diego Portales, Santiago, 2010, pp. 199-216.

26 Cf. F. Neumann, *Wirtschaft, Staat und Demokratie*, Suhrkamp, Frankfurt, 1978, pp. 70-74 and 79-99, in particular pp. 70, 72, 74, 87-90 and 95-96.

27 *See* Tuori 2010, p. 16. The hijacking was organized by F. Böhm, *Wettbewerb und Monopolrecht*, Nomos, Baden-Baden, 2010 (1933).

28 A. Müller-Armack, *Studien zur Sozialen Marktwirtschaft*, Institut für Wirtschaftspolitik, Köln, 1960, pp. 11-12 and 15 (my translation). For a brief and powerful criticism of the imperial tendencies of ordo-liberalism see G. Teubner, *Constitutional Fragments. Societal Constitutionalization and Globalization*, Oxford University Press, Oxford, 2012, pp. 30-34.

29 M. Wegmann, 'European Competition Law: Catalyst of Integration and Convergence,' *in* Tuori & Sankari 2010.

30 Tuori & Sankari 2010, p. 15.

order.'[31] In case of doubt, the 'concrete order' of*law and economics* trumps the formal constitution of *law and democracy*.[32] Whereas formal constitutional law still adhered to the Kantian priority of democratic legislation, the concrete order of *law and economics* became Europe's informal prerogative constitution – Europe's 'hidden curriculum.'[33] The legal link between visible constitutional law and the invisible prerogative constitution was Article 2 TEEC.[34] One of the most crucial effects was the negation of any transnationalization of the political constitution. The hegemony of the hidden curriculum stimulated and reinforced the Europeanization of big enterprises and employers' federations, but at the same time strictly limited unions' activities and employee organizations to the sphere of the national state.[35]
Ordoliberals today are proud of the fine differences that distinguish them from Neoliberalism. But it was indeed Ordoliberalism that disclosed the historical path to the latest great transformation of globalization that has lasted since the 1980s. If we resume the three basic ideas of Ordoliberalism, it becomes evident, that only one idea is different. Therefore, the relation of Ordo- and Neoliberalism resembles more a cooperative historical division of business than a fierce opposition:

- The *first* basic idea of Ordoliberalism is to*get markets rid of state control*. The spectre of 'socialism' and 'communism' must be banned as long as it is haunting Europe under the mask of macroeconomic state interventionism. Here Ordo- and Neoliberalism meet from the beginning. Today's representatives of the power elite, such as the President of the German *Bundesbank*, Jens Weidmann, or the former judge of the Verfassungsgericht, Udo DiFabio, are accusing even the President of the ECB, Mario Dragi, of creeping socialization (*schleichende Sozialisierung*) and planned central states economy

31 Wegmann 2010, p. 93.

32 C. Franzius & U.K. Preuß, *Europäische Demokratie*, Ms 2011, p. 70.

33 On the 'hidden curriculum' *see* C. Offe, 'The European Model of "Social" Capitalism: Can It Survive European Integration?', *The Journal of Political Philosophy*, Vol. 11, No. 4, 2003, p. 463. On the distinction between the two constitutional orders see E. Fraenkel, 'Der Doppelstaat', *Gesammelte Schriften*, Vol. 2, Nomos Verlag, Baden-Baden, 1999, pp. 33-266 (published 1974, originally finished 1938); *see* C. Joerges, 'Europas Wirtschaftsverfassung in der Krise', *Der Staat*, Vol. 3, 2012, pp. 360-361, 366-367 and 377-381.

34 Wegmann 2010, p. 94. Art. 2 ECC: "It shall be the aim of the Community, by establishing a Common Market and progressively approximating the economic policies of Member States, to promote throughout the Community a harmonious development of economic activities, a continuous and balanced expansion, an increased stability, an accelerated raising of the standard of living and closer relations between its Member States". Today it is replaced by Art. 2 EC: "The Community shall have as its task, by establishing a common market and an economic and monetary union and by implementing common policies or activities referred to in Arts. 3 and 4, to promote throughout the Community a harmonious, balanced and sustainable development of economic activities, a high level of employment and of social protection, equality between men and women, sustainable and non-inflationary growth, a high degree of competitiveness and convergence of economic performance, a high level of protection and improvement of the quality of the environment, the raising of the standard of living and quality of life, and economic and social cohesion and solidarity among Member States". On the term 'invisible constitution' but with a slightly different meaning *see* A. Wiener, *The Invisible Constitution of Politics*, Cambridge University Press, Cambridge, 2008.

35 *See* S. Buckel, 'Welcome to Europe', *Juridische Auseinandersetzungen um das Staatsprojekt Europa*, (unpublished Habilitationsschrift, Goethe-Universität, Frankfurt, 2012), p. 20.

(*planwirtschaftliche Zentralität*) – Dragi, the creeping socialist who learned his job at the communist cadre training centre Goldman & Sachs.[36]

- However, Ordoliberalism distrusts not only the (bureaucratic) state but also big size (that is bureaucratic) capitalism and its tendency to concentration and centralization of capital that has led to monopoly capitalism since the beginning of the 20th century.[37] Therefore the *second* basic idea of Ordoliberalism is to *get rid of monopoly capitalism*. Competition law shall keep the economic chances of *all* market participants equal *any time*. This idea is called market justice, but it is a very poor idea of justice.[38] From the beginning it was mere ideology. In fact (as Kelsen has demonstrated in his scathing criticism of Hayek already in 1955), it worked in favour of the haves who disposed over the means of production, and at best regulated *their* competition.[39] However, in this respect Ordoliberalism is clearly different from Neoliberalism. Neoliberalism has bluntly abolished competition law and reduced so called market justice to shareholder value that has then been identified with the common good by Milton Friedman and others.[40] That is why we can no longer side-step the bright lights of the latest stock market news everywhere we go.
- The *third* (and in terms of constitutional law most crucial) basic idea of Ordoliberalism is *to get rid of democratic legislative control*. Here again Ordo- and Neoliberals meet in applying the categorical imperatives: give the judges what you have taken from the democratic legislator and the parliamentary controlled government! Promote the judges to the guardians of functional *Ordnungsrecht* (regulatory law)! In the words of Ernst Joachim Mestmäcker, "Die wichtigsten Aufgaben obliegen nicht der Legislative oder der Regierung, sondern der Rechtsprechung". [The most important decisions have to be taken not by the legislator or the government but by the judges].[41] The beheading of the legislator is the true end of the French Revolution and the

36 *See* J. Weidmann, 'Die Stabilitätsunion sichern', *Frankfurter Allgemeine Sonntagszeitung*, 8 July 2012, p. 33; J. Weidmann, 'Der Euro verlangt eine Stabilitätsunion', *Süddeutsche Zeitung*, 27 June 2012, p. 28 (quoting the following article – U. Di Fabio, 'Das europäische Schuldendilemma als Mentalitätskris', *Frankfurter Allgemeine Zeitung*, 22 June 2012, p. 9.

37 *See* already K. Marx, *Das Kapital*, Vol. 1, MEW, *supra* note 5, pp. 650-657.

38 *See* M. Friedman, *Capitalism and Freedom*, Chicago University Press, Chicago, 1982 (1962), pp. 15-26, especially pp. 20-21.

39 *See* H. Kelsen, 'Demokratie und Sozialismus' (1954), *in* N. Leser (Ed.), *Demokratie und Sozialismus. Ausgewählte Aufsätze*, Verlag der Wiener Volksbuchhandlung, Wien, 1967, pp. 170-210; E. Tugendhat, 'Liberalism, Liberty and the Issue of Economic Human Rights', *in* E. Tugendhat, *Philosophische Aufsätze*, Suhrkamp, Frankfurt, 1992, pp. 352-370; W. Streeck, 'Zum Verhältnis von sozialer Gerechtigkeit und Marktgerechtigkeit' (unpublished e-man. of a Lecture, Verona, 20 September 2012).

40 See C. Crouch, *The Strange Non-Death of Neoliberalism*, Polity, Oxford, 2011.

41 E.-J. Mestmäcker, 'Einführung', *in* F. Böhm, *Wettbewerb und Monopolkampf*, Nomos, Baden-Baden, 2010 (1933), p. 9; the same argument seems to fit the present crisis, *see* E.-J. Mestmäcker, 'Ordnungspolitische Grundlagen einer politischen Unio', *Frankfurter Allgemeine Sonntagszeitung*, 9 November 2012, p. 12. In the same way Milton Friedman and the Chicago School argues that the main threat to political and economic freedom "arises out of democratic politics" and must be "defeated by political action" (G.A. Amond, 'Capitalism and Democracy', *Political Science and Politics*, Vol. 24, No. 3, 1991, p. 231.

> Kantian political era.[42] If it really comes true, it will be the final triumph of the counter-revolution that in this case is the counter-revolution against 1789: never again shall a legislator be able to effect a revolution. That was Margaret Thatcher's actual message. In 2002 Alec Stone Sweet could only state that in "today's multi-tiered European polity, the sovereignty of the legislator, and the primacy of national executives, are dead. In concert or in rivalry, European legislators govern with judges".[43] One has to add that in combining, transnational and national constitutional jurisdiction have reinforced one another, and in a way the European *Verfassungsgerichtsverbund* (Udo DiFabio) has reserved for itself the most basic functions of all three classical state powers – at least in normal times of incremental and managerial evolutionary constitutionalization.[44]

For these reasons, the implementation of the Euro without political government was not just a mistake, or the worst possible compromise – that it was, at least from the perspective of the negotiating parties[45] – but actually nothing else than, as Wolfgang Streeck says, the "frivolous experiment" to realize a "market economy emancipated" from all political bonds and to establish "a political economy without parliament and government"..[46] The implementation of the Euro finalized the prerogative constitution and perfected the hidden curriculum of European governmentality by "immunizing the markets against democratic corrections"..[47] This immediately resulted in an increase in the social differences between the rich North and the poor South. When the crisis finally came, European *Ordnungsrecht* derogated national as well as transnational *constitutional law*.[48] As a result, the social gap that separates the North from the South grew dramatically in favour of the northern hegemon: that is Germany.[49]

42 For the thesis that transnational law has already realized a mutation to a law that is no longer related to the legislative power see M. Amstutz & V. Karavas, 'Rechtsmutationen', *Rechtsgeschichte*, Vol. 8, 2006, p. 20; sceptical: K.-H. Ladeur, 'Die Evolution des Rechts und die Möglichkeit eines "globalen Rechts" jenseits des Staates – zugleich eine Kritik der "Selbstkonstitutionalisierungsthese"', *Ancilla Juris*, 2012, pp. 220-254; M. Albert & R. Stichweh, *Weltstaat und Weltstaatlichkeit*, VS Verlag, Wiesbaden, 2007.

43 A. Stone Sweet, *Governing with Judges: Constitutional Politics in Europe*, Oxford University Press, Oxford, 2002, p. 193, quoted from Buckel, 2012, p. 26.

44 *See* A. Voßkuhle, 'Multilevel Cooperation of the European Constitutional Courts. Der Europäische Verfassungsgerichtsverbund', *European Constitutional Law Review*, Vol. 6, 2010, pp. 175-198.

45 *See* H. Enderlein, 'Grenzen der europäischen Integration? Herausforderungen an Recht und Politik', (DFG-Rundgespräch in Zusammenarbeit mit der Friedrich-Ebert-Stiftung Berlin, Ms. 25 November 2011.)

46 Streeck, 2012, p. 6 (my translation), p. 8.

47 *Ibid.*, p. 6 (my translation); on the unity of ordo- and neoliberalism see also F. Scharpf, 'Integration versus Legitimation: Der Euro. Thesen', e-man., presented at DFG-Rundgespräch 'Grenzen der europäischen Integration?', Berlin, 25 November 2011.

48 See F. Rödl, 'EU im Notstandsmodus', *Blätter für deutsche und internationale Politik*, Vol. 5, 2012, pp. 5-8; Joerges, 2012; E.-W. Böckenförde, 'Kennt Europas Not kein Gebot?', *in* E.-W. Böckenförde, *Wissenschaft, Politik, Verfassungsgericht*, Suhrkamp, Frankfurt, 2011, pp. 299-303; G. Grözinger, 'Alternative Solutions to the Euro-Crisis', Ms 2012. Grözinger calls 'financial markets' strikingly "a second constituency".

49 Paul Krugman rightly states: "Fifteen years ago Greece was no paradise, but it wasn't in crisis either. Unemployment was high but not catastrophic, and the nation more or less paid its way on world markets, earning enough from exports, tourism, shipping and other sources to more or less pay for its imports". P. Krugman, 'Greece as Victim', *New York Times*, 17 June 2012, <www.nytimes.com/2012/06/18/opinion/krugman-greece-as-victim.html> (last accessed 3 November 2012)>.

Hence, by beheading the legislator, Ordoliberalism opened the evolutionary path for the neoliberal globalization of capital beyond state control. Whether intentionally or not does not matter; Ordoliberalism had done its job, Ordoliberalism could go. Once Neoliberalism was over, the *great transformation* of the last thirty years could begin: the transformation*of state-embedded and state-controlled markets* into *market-embedded and market-controlled states.*[50] The new world order of market-embedded states makes it extremely hard for any political actor to get rid of the pressure to market compliance, to gain independence from the whims of a highly sensitive class of investors, and to return to macroeconomic steering, be it national or transnational.

3.2 Stage II: Juridical Constitution

For all that, economic constitutionalization is not the only evolutionary formation of European constitutional law, and even if it remains the hegemonic constitution to date, it was and is not the last stage of Europe's constitutional evolution. The latter is, as we have seen, conducted by the managerial mindset of *law and economics*. However, once the Kantian mindset has been constitutionalized and integrated into the public authority of European law, it counteracts the managerial mindset of blind evolutionary adaption *as* a *normative constraint*. However weak it may be, it operates no longer as a Kantian (allegedly) *empty ought* but as a Hegelian *existing concept* (as a moment of objective spirit).
In the European constitutional history, the Kantian mindset of autonomy came back already in the early 1960s, together with the rapidly increasing volume of European regulations. It came back in the reduced and, for professional lawyers, manageable form of individual lawsuits over issues of *private autonomy*. In two landmark decisions of the European Court from 1963 (*van Gent & Loos*) and 1964 (*Costa*) the *emancipatory* side of the legal form flared up. As public authority with binding legal force the Kantian mindset remained, it is true, *privatized*. However, to establish only private autonomy, the judges (in a bold teleological interpretation of the Treaties) had to create an autonomous European *citizenship* and European *citizens' rights* as rights of an autonomous legal community.[51] The two decisions from 1963 and 1964 were therefore emphatically described (by European law jurists) as "the declaration of independence of Community law".[52]
However, the Kantian moment of the two landmark decisions would have disappeared immediately from the trajectory of constitutional evolution, if the two decisions had not been followed by thousands of cases appealing to European Law in national courts of all member states (and the backing of the national courts by the ECJ submission procedure

50 W. Streeck, 'Sectoral Specialization: Politics and the Nation State in a Global Economy', paper presented at the 37th World Congress of the International Institute of Sociology, Stockholm, 2005.

51 *See* D. Chalmers *et al.*, *European Union Law*, Cambridge University Press, Cambridge, 2006; P.P. Craig & C. De Búrca, *EU Law. Text, Cases and Materials* (4th edn.), Oxford University Press, Oxford, 2007.

52 Tuori, 2010, p. 17.

under Art. 267 TFEU).[53] In this case the old evolutionary insight became true that not the elites but the *masses* make the evolution, and here I mean the masses of negative legal communications that filled the variety pool of the legal evolution, and finally engendered a new constitutional formation: the European *Rechtsstaatsverfassung*, the juridical constitution of Europe. The European *Rechtsstaatsverfassung* consists in the (reflexive) *structural coupling of law and law* – or may be better: the structural coupling of *law and subjective rights.*[54] The European *Rechtsstaat* has finally transformed Europe into *one single*, internally differentiated legal order, negatively described as fragmented, positively as pluralized[55] – and it is an order that is not toothless, as just recently Hungary came to experience.[56]

However, all these legal advances remained limited to legal experts and individual plaintiffs. On the rule-of-law-stage-II of the constitutional evolution of Europe the Kantian mindset was *constitutionalized under private law* (in a kind of Teubnerian *Zivilverfassung*[57]). However, at the same time it was repressed and displaced again in public.[58] On the second stage of constitutional evolution we can become aware of a paradox: *Constitutionalization at once advances and is de-constitutionalized by its own advances.*

This paradoxical structure is due to the emergence and continuation of *formal constitutional law* together with its opposite: that is *informal prerogative law*. Both constitutional formations constitute a European *double-state*.[59] Whereas, for example, the Kantian mindset of

53 *See* K.J. Alter, 'The European Court's Political Power', *West European Politics*, Vol. 19, No. 3, 1996, pp. 458-487; K.J. Alter, 'Who Are the "Masters of the Treaty"?', *International Organization*, Vol. 52, 1998, pp. 121-147; T. Hitzel-Cassagnes, *Entgrenzung des Verfassungsbegriffs. Eine institutionentheoretische Rekonstruktion*, Nomos, Baden-Baden, 2012. (TFEU is the Lisbon Treaty on the Functioning of the European Union).

54 Tuori, 2010, p. 18.

55 On the ambivalence of the fragmentation diagnosis (that is true also for all larger national states) see C. Möllers, 'Fragmentierung als Demokratieproblem', *in* C. Franzius & F.C. Meyer & J. Neyer (Eds.), *Strukturfragen der Europäischen Union*, Nomos, Baden-Baden, 2010, pp. 150-170.

56 ECJ 6 November 2012, *EU-Commission v. Hungary*,<http://curia.europa.eu/juris/document/document.jsf;jsessionid=9ea7d2dc30db11f305cc49ce45dbba9d83a1834337eb.e34KaxiLc3qMb40Rch0SaxuKbNb0?text=&docid=129324&pageIndex=0&doclang=DE&mode=req&dir=&occ=first&part=1&cid=9743> (last accessed 7 November 2012).

57 G. Teubner, 'Globale Zivilverfassungen: Alternativen zur Staatszentrierten Verfassungstheorie', *Zeitschrift für ausländisches öffentliches Recht und Völkerecht*, Vol. 63, No. 1, 2003, pp. 1-28.

58 J. Weiler, 'To Be a European Citizen – Eros and Civilisation', *Journal of European Public Policy*, Vol. 4, 1997, pp. 495-519. Weiler writes: "[Y]ou could create rights and afford judicial remedies to slaves. The ability to go to court to enjoy a right bestowed on you by the pleasure of others does not emancipate you, does not make you a citizen. Long before women and Jews were made citizens they enjoyed direct effect". (*Ibid.*, p. 503). In cases such as *Walrave*, *Bosman*, *Viking* and *Laval* at the European Court, the basic freedoms prevail over basic rights. In an anti-democratic way basic rights are now constrained by the four basic freedoms, and in particular by the freedoms of big money, capital etc., and not – as it should be at least in an egalitarian democratic society – the other way round, *see* S. Buckel & L. Oberndorfer, 'Die lange Inkubationszeit des Wettbewerbs der Rechtsordnungen – Eine Genealogie der Rechtsfälle Viking/Laval/Rüffert/Luxemburg aus der Perspektive einer materialistischen Europarechtstheorie', *in* A. Fischer-Lescano, F. Rödl & C. Schmid (Eds.), *Europäische Gesellschaftsverfassung. Zur Konstitutionalisierung sozialer Demokratie in Europa*, Nomos, Baden Baden, 2009, p. 285.

59 Fraenkel,1999.

the formal constitution is reflected by the court's interpretation of the basic freedoms of EU Law as *anti-discrimination norms* that are constraining the *basic freedoms* through the *basic rights* of *all* European citizens, the managerial mindset of the informal constitution is reflected by the court's interpretation of the *basic freedoms* (in particular of big money and big capital) *as constraints of basic rights* (*Walrave, Bosman, Viking* and *Laval*).[60] It is this contradiction between the formal and the informal constitution of Europe that causes a latent *crisis of legitimization*. The contradiction between the two constitutional mindsets is productive as long as it becomes a driving force of further constitutionalization.

3.3 STAGE III: POLITICAL CONSTITUTION

Since the middle of the 1970s the long latent conflict between the ever closer united executive powers of Europe and the parliamentary legislative bodies became more and more manifest. At the same time the European Court of Human Rights turned into an active court. Now backed by the ECJ's doctrines of *European law supremacy* and *uniform application*, it radicalized its human rights jurisdiction.[61] This was important for the process of democratization because – different from civil and economic law – human rights have an internal relation to democracy and cannot be dissociated from public autonomy and public self-determination.[62] The pressure to reduce the growing democratic deficit of Europe finally compelled the political and professional power elites to take into account the Kantian mindset's commitment to public autonomy. Again it became evident that the *Kantian mindset* of emancipation can be repressed, "can be halted or inhibited, but it cannot be eliminated" once it is constitutionalized.[63]

Since the first direct elections of the European Parliament in 1979 the power of the Parliament increased consistently. The managerial mindset and stubborn incrementalism of everyday parliamentary work for over a quarter-century made the weak and restricted European Parliament a *controlling and law-shaping parliament* that is now one of the strongest institutions of the EU.[64] The final step to the *parliamentary legislative procedure*, taken in the Treaty of Lisbon, largely completed the political constitution of Europe.[65] The third stage of structural coupling of law and politics was achieved.

60 Buckel & Oberndorfer, 2009, p. 285.

61 Madsen, 2011, p. 55.

62 *See* I. Maus, *Zur Aufklärung der Demokratietheorie*, Suhrkamp, Frankfurt, 1992; J. Habermas, *Faktizität und Geltung*, Suhrkmap, Frankfurt, 1992; Brunkhorst, *Solidarity From Civic Friendship to a Global Legal Community*, MIT Press, Cambridge, MA, 2005; for the present legal-philosophical discussion *see* S. Besson, 'Das Menschenrecht auf Demokratie – Eine moralische Verteidigung mit einer rechtlichen Nuance', *in* G. Haller, K. Günthger & U. Neumann (Eds.), *Menschenrechte und Volkssouveränität in Europa – Gerichte als Vormund der Demokratie?*, Campus, Frankfurt, 2011, pp. 73-77.

63 With reference to the historical concept of emancipation, see Somek, 2012, p. 8.

64 See P. Dann, 'Looking Through the Federal Lens: the Semi-Parliamentary Democracy of the EU', Jean-Monnet Working Paper, Vol. 5, 2002; Fossum & Menéndez, 2011, p. 123.

65 J. Bast, 'Europäische Gesetzgebung – Fünf Stationen in der Verfassungsentwicklung der EU', *in* Franzius, Meyer & Neyer, 2010, pp. 173-180.

However, even this time the managerial mindset prevailed again. The polling stations and the market places remained empty. To the same extent that the shaping power of the parliament increased, its public legitimacy decreased dramatically from election to election.[66] The most crucial act of the Kantian mindset, the political implementation of representative government based on fierce public debate ("Freiheit der Feder"), had the paradoxical effect of generating *democratic public legislation without democratic public life*. The increase of *constitutionalization of public legislation* again came at the price of a *de-constitutionalization of public discourse*.

Here again we encounter the managerial mindset: the *bloc* of ever closer united executive bodies in concert with the politico-economic power elites, supported by the omnipresent chief economists of the big banks, by the willing legal and political experts, and by co-opted journalists (who are much better paid than ever before and trained in the same economic vocabulary, at the expense of freelance journalists, who are much worse paid than ever before) seems to prevail over the Kantian 'power of the people.'[67] Public debate is not suppressed or limited but – more effectively – bypassed by political and economic power as 'not helpful.' Again *Ordnungsrecht* derogates constitutional law and stabilizes the new collective Bonapartism of Europe.[68]

However, these days, we witness the return of the repressed. The *economic* crisis, and in particular the *banking* crisis, can no longer be displaced by the *budget* crisis. As a consequence, the long latent *crisis of political legitimization* suddenly becomes manifest. The Kantian mindset re-emerges in the streets, in Athens, in Madrid and elsewhere. What is now at stake is the *social welfare constitution* of Europe (*Stage IV*).

It appears that the structural coupling of law with the systems of social welfare and security can no longer be performed silently behind closed doors and at low costs. The crisis makes it evident: that there is *no modern mass democracy* without the *rough equality of stakeholders*, at the very least.[69]

---

66 See 'An Ever-Deeper Democratic Deficit', The Economist, <www.economist.com/node/21555927> (last accessed 18 November 2012).

67 On the strangely sustainable triumph of ordo- and neoliberal economy in global media see W. Streeck, 'Public Sociology as a Return to Political Economy, Transformations of the Public Sphere', available at <http://publicsphere.ssrc.org/streeck-public-sociology-as-a-return-to-political-economy/> (last accessed 19 November 2012); S. Schulmeister, 'Statt Sparen – New Deal für Europa', *Le Monde diplomatique*, November 2012, p. 12.

68 H. Brunkhorst, 'Bologna oder der sanfte Bonapartismus der transnational vereinigten Exekutivgewalten', *Zeitschrift für Philosophie und Sozialwissenschaft*, Vol. 1, 2006, pp. 1-6.

69 C. Crouch, *Post-Democracy*, Polity, Cambridge, 2004; see also the quintessence of the last books of the economists Paul Krugman and Joseph Stiglitz: J.S. Hacker & P. Pierson, 'What Krugman & Stiglitz Can Tell Us', *New York Review of Books*, Vol. LIX, No. 14, 2012, pp. 55-58; with instructive statistics and observations: T. Judt, *Ill Fares the Land*, Penguin, New York, 2010. On rough equality of stakeholders see T. Christiano, 'Democratic Legitimacy and International Institutions', *in* S. Besson & J. Tasaioulas (Eds.), *The Philosophy of International Law*, Oxford University Press, Oxford, 2010, pp. 130-132; on 'rough equality' as a necessary condition of modern mass-democracy see Crouch, 2004, Chapter 1.

The national state looked like the big winner after the outbreak of the global economic crisis in fall 2008 (and many political theorists and analysts proclaimed, such as once Erich Honecker, the last prime minister of the GDR: "Totgesagte leben länger". [The condemned live longer]. But in fact the state was already weak, and therefore became one of the greatest losers of the crisis. Wolfgang Streeck rightly headed an essay two years later with: "Noch so ein Sieg und wir sind verloren". [Another victory like that and we are lost]. The great crisis of 2008 has proven that the national state was already deprived of its most basic alternatives in economic and social politics.[70]

The national state's capacity to act and shape the future always relied on the existence of *two major instruments* to get modern capitalism under control, and to enforce the legislative will of democratic majorities: either the stick of the law, or the carrot of money.[71]

However, it seems that from the beginning of the present crisis, the national states were no longer able to perform *macroeconomic steering* through an effective mix of stick and carrot, of legislation and investment. The political actors had already lost most of the legislative power that is needed to regulate and control capitalist economies. They have not regained it at the global level. On the contrary, during the last 30 years of neoliberal global hegemony, the fragile balance of power between democracy and capitalism has shifted dramatically in favour of capitalism.

As long as a modern, functionally differentiated economy (with capitalist markets) is embedded in democratically controlled state power, the parties of the have-nots, either the exploited social classes or the nations who are the losers of the global economic competition between states and regions, have two means to enforce *rough compensatory justice*.[72] They can perform macroeconomic steering in times of crisis: *nationally* by legal regulation and investment, in particular by increasing taxes for high incomes and assets, and/or *internationally* by means of devaluation of their national currency.[73] In Europe today they have lost both.

Globalization has transformed tax-collecting states into debt-depending states, and hence reversed the direction of control between states and capital. The *taxing state* that is in control of capitalism has become a *borrowing state* that is controlled by capitalism.[74] The

70 W. Streeck, 'Noch so ein Sieg, und wir sind verloren. Der Nationalstaat nach der Finanzkrise', *Leviathan*, Vol. 38, 2010, pp. 159-173; W. Streeck, 'The Crisis of Democratic Capitalism', *New Left Review*, Vol. 71, 2011.

71 *See* R. Mayntz, 'Die Handlungsfähigkeit des Nationalstaats in der Regulierung der Finanzmärkte', *Leviathan*, Vol. 38, 2010, pp. 175-187.

72 On states as global economic actors see T. ten Brink, *Geopolitik: Geschichte und Gegenwart kapitalistischer Staatenkonkurrenz*, Westfälisches Dampfboot, Münster, 2008.

73 C.Offe, 'Unpublished Interview', e-man., 2012, p. 3; Streeck, 2012.

74 Offe, 2012, p. 6. On the genealogy see Streeck, 2011. What is crucial for the neoliberal triumph and sharply recognized by Reagan and Thatcher and their economic advisers: that the Unions first are losing their formerly strong political influence, and then their organizational power, either by direct oppression such as in the UK, the US and in the low intense democracies of the formerly so-called Third World, or by internal reform that makes them sometimes a powerful, quasi council-democratic participant in globally operating industrial enterprises such as Volkswagen, but at the price of the general interest of the working class. On the latter see the case study G. Herrigel, 'Roles and Rules: Ambiguity, Experimentation and New Forms of Stakeholderism in Germany', *Industrielle Beziehungen*, Vol. 15, No. 2, 2008, pp. 111-133.

implementation of the Euro has taken away all means of resistance poor countries have in their unequal competition with rich countries.

Franklin D. Roosevelt's New Deal administration in the 1930s was supported and pushed by *democratic class struggle*: a fighting working class with young and strong Unions that had nothing to lose, organized huge strikes and stay-in strikes.[75] Backed this way by a strong workers movement, the new Dealers finally regulated and controlled Wall Street, increased taxes for the rich, cut back banks and industrial corporations, created jobs administratively, printed money. In this way those politicians and other social democrats and socialists in advanced societies were able to square the circle: that is to *socialize the means of production within the capitalist mode of production*.

However, this seems no longer possible. After 2008, nowhere were taxes increased in a measure comparable to that in the US and other western countries in the 1950s and 1960s. Not one of the banks deemed 'too big to fail' was nationalized or divided. Except for Lehmann all were bailed out again and again. Moreover, in Europe the common currency excluded all possibilities of currency devaluation. Deprived of its legislative power to regulate the economy, the state no longer had an alternative, except to spend the rest of its money.[76]

Therefore, the state has become susceptible to blackmail, and Margaret Thatcher's lie, that there is no alternative, became true as a self-fulfilling prophecy.[77] Former democratic governments are now in the hands of bankers and their staff of technocrats – directly or indirectly. In states where the bankers have not yet taken the lead, their advice resembles the advice of the old Roman Senate, the *senatus consultum*. That was advice without any legally binding force: soft law. But whoever did not follow it was already a dead man, even if he left the room alive. Therefore the national state must execute the neoliberal programme with microeconomic means and "devalue labour and the public sector", "put pressure on wages, pensions, labour market regulations, public services"[78] – and then sell the whole thing as 'reform,' 'modernization,' 'new public management' and 'individual empowerment,' best served by Third Way labour parties, reformed social democrats and red–green coalitions.[79]

---

75 W. Korpi, *The Democratic Class Struggle*, Routledge, London, 1983.

76 *See* Mayntz, 2010; Streeck, 2010; see also the long time case study W. Streeck & D. Mertens, 'Fiscal Austerity and Public Investment. Is the Possible the Enemy of the Necessary?', MPIfG Discussion Paper, Vol. 11, No. 12, <www.mpifg.de/pu/mpifg_dp/dp11-12.pdf> (last accessed 19 November 2012).

77 See J. Beckert & W. Streeck, 'Die Fiskalkrise und die Einheit Europas', *Aus Politik und Zeitgeschichte*, Vol. 4, 2012, pp. 7-17.

78 Offe, 2012, p. 3; *see* F.W. Scharpf, 'Rettet Europa vor dem Euro!', *Berliner Republik*, quoted from <www.b-republik.de/aktuelle-ausgabe/rettet-europa-vor-dem-euro> (last accessed 8 May 2012).

79 See Somek, 2012. *See* H. Brunkhorst, 'Raus aus der Neuen Mitte! Umrisse einer künftigen Linken', *Die Zeit*, 25 March 1999, p. 28; H. Brunkhorst, 'Schluss mit der Kritik! Die Generation Berlin und der Affekt gegen den Egalitarismus', *Die Zeit*, 4 November 1999, p. 54; H. Brunkhorst, 'Bürgerlichkeit als Philosophie der Postdemokratie. Ein Beitrag zur Debatte um Jens Hackes Philosophie der Bürgerlichkeit', *Deutsche Zeitschrift für Philosophie*, Vol. 5, 2007, pp. 22-25.

Unfortunately, neither Keynesians nor Marxists have ever tried to develop transnational continental and global alternatives to national state power. They have socialized the means of production not only within the capitalist mode of production but also within one country. They never even envisaged a plan to establish a transnational *political power* that could measure up to global big money and the unleashed forces of the world market that are at once productive and destructive. The Ordo- and Neoliberals (and that is the historical truth of Neoliberalism) had such a plan, as we have seen, and it worked, with catastrophic results. Only that explains the strange non-death of Neoliberalism – after a crisis that (if we follow the prognosis of the Chicago doctrine of neoliberal economy) should happen only all 50,000 years.

Now national state power is over, at least as the power of the so-called sovereign state. To take up a metaphor of Eyal Benvenisti (an Israeli international lawyer), in the process of globalization the state politically, legally, economically and culturally has been transplanted completely from a detached villa into a condo in the middle of a house of 200 condos with many different and overlapping forms of real estate ownership.[80] However, the network of transnational public law and politics, and the already emerging formation of transnational statehood,[81] are far too weak to get the global markets under control again. The coordinated state powers together with international organizations can at best *make* the global market (negative integration) but are nowhere capable of *constraining* it *normatively,* that is in the general interest of all of us (positive integration).[82] In thirty years of globalization the most powerful (for good *and* for bad) states of history – Western democracies – have been turned, in the words of Streeck, "into debt-collecting agencies on behalf of a global oligarchy of investors, compared to which C. Wright Mills's 'power elite' appears a shining example of liberal pluralism".[83]

The only way out seems to be the *reinvention of democratic class struggle* on the transnational level. The chances are very small, but must not be overseen. Unions of southern Europe, for the first time in history, are beginning acting and striking transnational and beyond borders. Together with a European Parliament that now becomes publicly visible for the first time, they finally could trigger a new democratic class struggle for profane aims: a European unemployment assurance to solve the biggest social problem of Europe today that consists in the highest unemployment rate of the young people of the south

80 Quoted from A. von Bogdandy, 'Grundprinzipien von Staat, supranationalen und internationalen Organisationen', *Handbuch des Staatsrechts XI: Internationale Bezüge* (forthcoming, e-man. 2012).

81 *See* Albert & Stichweh, 2007.

82 *See* Offe, 2012, p. 457; on the concept of solidarity as the general or universal interest of all of us, *see* Brunkhorst, 2005; on normative constraints *see* Brunkhorst, 2013; on the distinction between 'positive' and 'negative integration' F.W. Scharpf, *Regieren in Europa. Effektiv und demokratisch?,* Campus, Frankfurt, 1999.

83 Streeck, 201. As a consequence, popular sovereignty has been fragmented and marginalized, beyond and within the national state, *see* Prien, 2010.

ever since the great depression of the late 1920s and 1930s.[84] The next step then could be a massive change against the deadly ailment of neo-liberalism that is called austerity. There is a simple and effective alternative to cutting expenditures, and that is raising taxes.[85] The chances seem small, but without renewed democratic class struggle that is transnational, there is no way out of crisis, and now towards a political union of Europe that is worthy of the name democracy.

84 This goes back to a suggestion of Claus Offe after a highly pessimistic lecture of Wolfgang Streek on a conference at the New School for Social Research and the Deutsche Forschungsgemeinschaft on 'Social Research in a Transforming World: Transatlantic Conversations', 28 February 2013.

85 Offe, 2012, p. 13. Offe concludes: "(The) rich countries of Europe dictate the poorer ones the austerity cure in order for them to regain the trust of the financial industries. They do so in spite of all the evidence that austerity is a highly poisonous medicine, an overdose of which will kill the patient (rather than stimulate growth and expand the tax base), in which case the weakest Euro zone members (and eventually all of them) become ever more dependent on lenders and allow them to charge ever higher and ever more unsustainable rates. It becomes ever more difficult to envisage the bootstrapping act by which European political elites might escape from this vicious circle". (*Ibid.*, p. 15).

4 Constitutional Identity and the Construct of the 'Other'

Milan Podunavac

4.1 Introduction

The problem that has arisen in connection with constitutional power-making processes for new polities in pluralistic and deeply divided societies underscores the crucial importance of identity in building up a viable and workable constitutional democracy. The apparent lack of a sufficient identity undermines the democratic legitimacy of the proposed political order. What I suggest in this study is that in many countries the main problem is a lack of a common identity to sustain stable constitutional democracies at the nation-state level. A functioning political order depends on the national, religious and cultural identity of those whose constitution is to be adopted, but for a constitution to function within the polity there is a need for a sufficiently defined and commonly shared constitutional identity. The relation between constitutional and extra-constitutional identity is crucial for the stability and legitimacy of political order. At the minimum, constitutional identity requires the recognition of three requirements: limitation of powers, adherence to the rule of law and protection of fundamental rights. Such recognition makes little sense except in the context of some particular extra-constitutional identity. Starting with the assumption that the construction of 'others' makes a bridge between these two poles, this chapter examines a deep source of democratic deficit in the post-war societies in South East Europe.

4.2 The Concept of 'Other'

In modern political societies, particularly constitutional democracies, cultural diversity poses a challenge both for government policy and political theory. Both are looking to offer political principles that answer how it might be possible for people from different cultures to live together. The challenge is posed because members of different groups demand not only recognition of their claims to equal and just shares in economic redistribution, but more importantly, recognition of their distinct identities as members of particular cultural communities within a society. That problem produces the fundamental conflict for every political community, namely a difficulty to reconcile the imperative of the individual and universal basis of fundamental rights and of group membership in a political community. As demonstrated by recent debates in contemporary political theory of citizenship, multiculturalism and the politics of recognition, there is no simple solution to that problem. That problem raises the importance of the construction of 'others', which occupies a significant place in modern political theory. Richard Bernstein is correct in arguing that the construct of the 'other' inhabits a central place in European continental political theory.[1]

Emmanuel Levinas moves the problem to the building of political and collective identity, raising the argument of the problematic (divisive) role of the construct of 'others' for political order.[2] My intention in this chapter is to contribute to the clarification and solution of this problem by reflecting on and scrutinizing a recent debate on the matter and discussing the normative role of political theory. Starting from such underlying assumptions, I would define the political culture of 'otherness' as a generic term that provides the answer to the question: what is the way in which contemporary political societies deal with the problem of 'other,' 'different,' 'alien,' 'stranger' or, in the most intensive and existential way, with the notion of the 'enemy.' For centuries since the mature Enlightenment we have conceptualized political order as legitimate only insofar as it expresses a political will that has been enforced within bounded communities. Political actors need such boundaries within which they can establish mechanisms of representation, accountability, participation and deliberation, and where some are defined as members, others as aliens. These demarcations are the basis of differentiation between 'we' and 'others,' borderlines between 'us' and 'them' which is constitutive for every political community. Citizens (members) of a state must be interconnected with each other, constituting a horizontal network of consensus and recognizing one another as equal members of the same political community. That is why the people supply the answer to two fundamental questions constitutive for every political community: 'Who are we?' and 'What is the reason that holds us together?' The modern nation state has regulated membership according to one principal category – national membership. Secularization and democratization of the modern state destroyed the old basis of legitimacy and raised the possibility of a new origin of political legitimacy and political community. If power is secular, and if everyone is equal, how can the people be expected to be loyal just to one state and not another? The only roughly clear answers to these questions have been offered by nationalism, starting from the end of the 18th century. The nationalist thesis has been that the subjects may consider the state their own, and they can be expected to make sacrifices for it willingly if the following two conditions are met. First, the subjects are bound to each other by ties of solidarity independent of their political relationships and antecedent to these. And secondly, the state is an expression of their pre-political, solidarity community. Accordingly, the fact of belonging together is a given for them, and, moreover, something that is recognized immediately. This is the basis of the distinction between 'us' and 'them.'[3] Consequently, a nation is another name for a modern political community.

Recently, much discussion has focused on the boundaries of political membership, with some theorists challenging the dominant idea that in the age of globalization, political

1 R. Berstein, *The New Constellation: Ethical-Political Horizons of Modernity*, Polity Press, Cambridge, 1991.
2 E. Levinas, *Levinas Reader*, Oxford University Press, Oxford, 1989.
3 J. Kiss, 'Beyond the Nation State', *Social Research*, Vol. 63, No 1, 1996, p. 195.

membership must still be confined within the boundaries of a nation state. The concepts of 'cosmopolitan citizenship'[4] or 'citizen pilgrims'[5] have been developed by such critics. On the other side, some theorists, particularly those committed to a civic republican tradition, are deeply suspicious of such prospects, arguing that there is something inherently contradictory in the very idea of cosmopolitan citizenship. The aim of this chapter is to continue to grapple with these contestations in political theory, but above all to delineate the distinction between two radically conflicting conceptions of modern political community. The normative stance behind this project is John Rawls's underlying assumption expressed in his introduction to the paperback edition of *Political Liberalism*, where Rawls, referring to Carl Schmitt's critique of liberalism, suggests that the cause of fall of the Weimar Republic's constitutional regime was that none of the traditional elites of Germany supported its constitution or were willing to cooperate to make it work. I share his normative warning that constitutional stability and the democratic legitimacy of liberal polity have not yet provided an undeniable request for normative authority and that these imperatives require liberal and democratic political theory.[6] That is the reason I would put these two opposing and radically conflicting political conceptions (Rawlsian vs. Schmittian) at the core of this study.

4.3 Conceptions

As previously expressed, contemporary political theory knows of at least two radically conflicting conceptions of ways to organize a political community, and there is a clash between these opposed interpretations of how to deal with the category of otherness. According to the Rawlsian conception of liberalism, I start with an implicit consensus on what we share as members of a liberal political order, and our job as political theorists is to articulate the basis of that consensus and explore its normative and political consequences. According to such a conception, political theory plays a practical role in the process of shaping the public political culture and contributes to the creation of democratic political identities. I agree with such a normative stance and try to demonstrate it in this chapter. Within the broader construct of liberal polity there are at least three different conceptions – strategies of how to deal with the category of 'otherness.'

4.4 Politics of Indifference and Passive Tolerance

The first one is built on *politics of indifference*.[7] An important strand of contemporary liberalism lends support to this reaction. That reaction is strongly grounded in the liberal

4 D. Held, *Democracy and the Global Age*, Polity Press, Cambridge, 1995.
5 R. Falk, *On Human Governance*, Polity Press, Cambridge, 1995.
6 J. Rawls, *Political Liberalism*, Columbia University Press, New York, 1996.
7 Ch. Kukathas, 'Liberalism and Multiculturalism: The Politics of Indifference', *Political Theory*, Vol. 26, No. 5, 1998, p. 691.

conception of a political nation, arguing that the ethos of liberal polity is based on two fundamental assumptions. First, there is equality before the law, and the legal and political order expresses the rule of law. In other words, every citizen enjoys equal rights regardless of ethnic and other affiliations, and no one is above the law. Secondly, at the same time, the state is not culturally neutral. Rule of law and equality before the law are not harmed by the important facts that the nature of our political community is dictated by dominant traditions and political culture. Equality before the law is upgraded by cultural hegemony of the dominant nation. Although the nation state is not culturally neutral, the legal constitution of the political nation is colour blind and has no sense for 'otherness.' When confronted with questions about how one's distinctive cultural identity as man or woman, Christian, Muslim or Jew should matter in the public forum, the typical reaction of the liberal conception of passive citizenship is misguided. It suggests, as I aim to explain, that our lack of identification with institutions that serve public purposes, *i.e.*, the impersonality of public institutions, is the price that citizens should be willing to pay for living in a society that treats them as equal, regardless of their particular ethnic, religious, racial or sexual identities. It is not only neutrality of public sphere, but also institutions of education and civil society that protect our freedom and equality as citizens. And therefore, public institutions should not strive to recognize our particular identities in treating us as equal and free citizens.

4.5 Critics of Multiculturalism: Georg Kateb and David Cameron

Can we then conclude that all demands for recognition by particular groups, often made in the name of nationalism and multiculturalism, are illiberal demands as suggested by the recent political discourse? Let me put forward two kinds of arguments. The first one is normative and belongs to Georg Kateb. In his general remarks at APSA[8] devoted to Maurizio Viroli's *The Love of Country*, he asks, "Is Patriotism a Mistake?" and then clearly argues that a defence of patriotism is an attack on the Enlightenment, as is the defence of any group phenomena related or analogous to patriotism. Defence of patriotism is simply one element of a larger particularistic stream of thought that honours membership in all groups that offer to help a person carry the burden of selfhood and individual identity. Hence multiculturalism, the new name for cultural pluralism, is all the rage. Patriotism is the strongest form of group membership, but at the same time a "deadly form of group attachment",[9] as it entails readiness to die and to kill for one's own country. Another attack is coming from politics. At the recent Munich Security Conference, the British Prime

8 American Political Science Association (APSA).

9 G. Kateb, 'Is Patriotism A Mistake?', *Social Research*, Vol. 67, No. 4, 2000, p. 906.

Minister David Cameron strongly presented a critique of 'state multiculturalism.' He pointed out that

> under the doctrine of state multiculturalism we have encouraged different cultures to live separate lives, apart from each other and apart from the mainstream. Now we must build stronger societies and stronger identity at home. Frankly, we need a lot less of the passive tolerance of recent years and much more active, muscular liberalism. A passively neutral society says to its citizens, as long as they obey the law we will just leave you alone. It stands neutral between different values. But I believe a genuinely liberal country does much more, it believes in certain values and actively promotes them freedom of speech, freedom of worship, democracy, rule of law, equal rights of race, sex, or sexuality.[10]

4.6 RESPONSE: PUBLIC RECOGNITION AND CITIZENSHIP CULTURE

I would argue that such conclusions are too hasty. Recognizing and treating members of some groups as equal seems to acknowledge rather than ignore cultural particularities, at least for those people whose self-understanding depends on the vitality of their culture. I will put aside the arguments developed by Charles Taylor, who offered an original perspective on these problems in *The Politics of Recognition*. But what seems to me of importance today, when discussing the issue of otherness in the terms of political culture, is precisely something that belongs to his argument that human identity is created dialogically, in response to our relations, including our actual dialogues with the other.[11] If human identities are dialogically created and constituted, then public recognition of our identities requires a politics that leaves room for us to deliberate publicly about those aspects of our identities that we share with other citizens. A society that recognizes individual identity will be a deliberative, democratic society because individual identity is partly constituted by collective dialogues. That moves us to something that is at the core of the political culture of democratic citizenship, which presupposes not only civil and political struggles against a political culture of incivility, a culture that articulates racist, anti-Semitic, sexist and homophobic values, but also presupposes the culture that can include both consensus and dissensus, moral agreement and moral disagreement.[12] It also presupposes a culture that tolerates and respects differences. For democratic society it is important how to

10 D. Cameron, 'My War on Multiculturalism', *The Independent*, 5 February 2011, available at <www.independent.co.uk/news/uk/politics/cameron-my-war-on-multiculturalism-2205074.html>.

11 Ch. Taylor, 'Politics of Recognition', *in* A. Gutmann (Ed.), *Multiculturalism: Examining the Politics of Recognition*, Princeton University Press, Princeton-New Jersey, 1994, pp. 25-26.

12 M. Podunavac, J. Keane & Ch. Sparks, *Politika i strah, Politička kultura*, Zagreb, 2008, p. 49.

enhance principles of (passive) tolerance with an active attitude of respect and recognition. Tolerance extends to the widest range of views, so long as they stop short of threats and other direct and indirect harms to individuals. Respect is much more demanding. Multicultural societies and communities that stand for the freedom and equality of all people rest upon mutual respect for reasonable intellectual, political and cultural differences. Mutual respect for 'otherness' requires a widespread willingness and ability to articulate our disagreement, to defend it before people with whom we disagree and to be open to changing our own minds when faced with well-reasoned criticism. The promise of a political culture of otherness depends on the exercise of this public virtue. The realm of civil society and civic education can be defined as a basic generator of the public sphere backed by a political culture of democratic citizenship. In this respect we can agree with Urlich Beck, who argues that the political project of democracy is dependent on a triangle of citizenship, civil society and political culture.[13]

4.7 What We Value About Europe: European Republican Patriotism

The kind of civic and citizenship culture described above is an important part of the European political culture, or something denoted as 'European republican patriotism.'[14] What is Europe we know and esteem. For most of us Europeans, Europe is not an external object of knowledge. As observers, we are located within the field of observation. We start by knowing Europe indirectly, through what we 'really know,' which for the majority of us is usually only a little bit more than familiarity with our own country. We are familiar with our own country because our identity has been shaped by a specific space and a specific history. This is the first step. We know our country as a European country. But, Europe is a mosaic of countries, and another step is extrapolating what we know about other countries, which may be – in terms of their institutions and habits – in some ways identical, in some ways analogous, and in other ways very different to our own. This is an important part of a political culture of 'otherness.' Another part of our common European political culture is 'Europe that we esteem.'[15] It is obvious that the Europe we esteem is a Europe of today and not of any other period. And what is it about the Europe of today that we Europeans value so much? One possible answer is that there is something that we value in fundamental dimensions of life at the present time. The question of what these dimensions are is fundamental because the answer tells us what is the telos of European political construction. We can esteem things that we assume will not destroy us. Hence, one dimension would be the absence of

13 U. Beck, 'How Neighbors Become Jews', *Constellations*, Vol. 2, No. 3, 1996, pp. 386-389.

14 J. Habermas, 'Citizenship and National Identity: Some Reflections on the Future of Europe', *Praxis International*, Vol. 12, No. 1, 1992, p. 10.

15 V. Perez-Diaz, 'The Role of Civil Nations in the Making of Europe', *Social Research*, Vol. 57, No. 4, 2000, pp. 959-960.

hatred, non-recognition, fear, etc., and the presence of tolerance between different components. In other words, this dimension is European peace. The value of public peace allows us to live side by side with each other, as distinct countries. But that public peace was built up as a tool against three negative European experiences. The first is war, another one is the totalitarian experience, and the third one is the principle of legality. The fear of despotism that Tocqueville shared with the leading liberal conservatives of his time reinforced his opinion that the principle of legality is another name for modern political order. The rule of law is a distinctive feature of the European legacy. That thesis is extremely important for the region of South Eastern Europe, which is strongly influenced by anti-legalistic ideologies. The patterns of these ideologies vary, from those glorifying spontaneous violence as a substitute for the morality of law to different forms of nihilism that see revolution as the authentic form of popular self-reflection, to various forms of anarchism and communitarism, which reject the ethic of law in the name of shared life forms. In other words, the fundamental reason for the existence of the Europe of our time and the EU is based on its order of freedom, which is an antithesis to both left-wing and right-wing totalitarianism. Lastly, I would add the figure of the European demos. For us who are looking to Europe which we love and esteem, these three normative standards are of the utmost importance.

4.8 GLOBAL CITIZENSHIP AND INTERNATIONAL JUSTICE

The third strategy, as I have noted in previous pages, is oriented mostly towards global citizenship and international justice. This strategy examines the boundaries of political community by focusing on citizenship and political membership and arguing for political principles and practices for incorporating aliens, immigrants, refugees and asylum seekers into existing politics. Discourse (republican) theory advocated soft borders, recognizing not only the administrative rights of refugees and asylum seekers, but also the regulatory rights of democracy, arguing that democracy by definition possesses transparent public spheres that are designed to translate the ethical view of citizens into positive laws of state. And it also stresses the growing 'democratic force within global civil society' that is ethically committed to the idea that legal and illegal aliens should be accorded basic human rights.[16] For the people of South Eastern Europe, that republican redeeming of political membership, citizenship and international justice is crucial. That kind of argument is strongly in opposition to the concepts of passive citizenship and passive tolerance.

According to such a conception, the voluntary assimilation of 'others' is desirable and is to be seen as a virtue. What liberal nationalists would endorse is that assimilation is voluntary

16 More: M. Nussbaum *et al.*, *For Love of Country: Debating the Limits of Patriotism*, Bacon Press, Boston, 1996; S. Benhabib, *The Rights of Others: Aliens, Residents and Citizens*, Cambridge University Press, Cambridge, 2004.

and conforms to the requirement of liberty when there are alternatives to it. The concept of a political nation grants those alternatives since it assures equality before the law to every citizen, and it does not allow the state to interfere with private relationships. The principle of neutrality of the public sphere is accompanied by the value of political tolerance.

4.9 Political Radicalism and Anti-Liberalism

Another dominant conception is grounded quite differently. According to the radical understanding which corresponds to those held by different schools of political radicalism, broad and implicit consensus shared by members of a political community does not exist. Moreover, if such consensus exists, it counts for nothing. Our responsibility is to theorize political order from the ground up. If politics must refer to anything, it must refer to the fact that an order and specific nature of this order varies according to circumstances. The 'konkretes Ordnungsdenken' doctrine of order corresponds to the situation that now exists. That doctrine is supported by two pillars. The first one is the notion of the 'enemy,' and the second one is the concept of 'substantive unity.' The former is connected to the problem of constituting political order, the latter to its political (democratic) unity.[17] Contrary to the assumption of liberalism, this theory states that the realm of the political from which all political actions and motives originate lies in a dichotomy between friend and enemy. The friend and enemy dichotomy represents the full range of intensity between union and separation, association and opposition.[18] The political enemy is essentially the 'other': compared with the aforementioned liberal concept of recognition, he is an alien in a very different, Schmittian way. Only political actors themselves in concrete situations decide whether the 'otherness of alien' will threaten to negate one's own mode of existence.[19] Thus, in extreme circumstances conflicts may occur with him. These will be conflicts that can be resolved neither by reference to commonly held norms nor by intervention of a disinterested and therefore impartial third party (*e.g.*, the liberal state). Concepts such as 'friend,' 'enemy' and 'politics' receive their true significance through the fact that they imply the real possibility of physical death. Politics is ultimately and necessarily superseded by internal and external war and thus by the possibility of "physical killing of human beings".[20] Accordingly, a political decision is an outcome between alternatives that cannot be supported by reasoning or discussion. Real politics, which is always a struggle for power, starts where communication leaves off. In politics it is important that a decision is made, not how it has been made.[21]

17 More: C. Schmitt, *The Concept of the Political* (trans. Geog Schwab), the University of Chicago Press, Chicago, 2007; W.E. Scheuerman, *Carl Schmitt: The End of* Law, Rowan & Littlefield Publisher, New York, 1999; Ch. Mouffe (Ed.), *The Challenge of Carl Schmitt*, Verso, London – New York, 1999.

18 Schmitt, 2007, p. 26.

19 *Ibid.*, p. 27.

20 *Ibid.*, p. 33.

21 U. Preuss, 'Political Order and Democracy,' in Mouffe, 1999.

4.10 The Concept of the Stranger

The idea that fearing the enemy is an integrating principle that belongs to 'negative politics' is expanded upon by Ulrich Beck, who argues that the modern nation state always legitimizes itself by way of rooting itself in two kinds of consensus.[22] The first is rooted in the voluntary consent of the people, the second – negative consensus – springs from a fear of the enemy. This form of negative consensus has always been opposed to the democratically and voluntarily achieved one, and political societies, including democracies, could never release themselves from such integration. While not new, this stimulating idea is upgraded by Beck with the notion of the 'stranger.' Strongly relying on Georg Simmel, Beck argues that the notion of 'stranger' underpins all fundamental concepts (forces) of political order. Its influence is more destructive and more repressive than the concept of 'enemy.' Generally put, the category of the stranger is central to all concepts of social order. And therein lies their irritation and provocation. Enemies themselves are, to put it sharply, in certain respects less threatening than strangers, because they obey the established order of the stereotype of the self and the other. To summarize, the peculiarity of the concept of strangers emerges because it is a concept without counter. Strangers are not just determined by the fact that they undermine and crack from inside all polar categories of social order. Strangers are neither enemies nor friends, neither natives nor foreigners, they are near and not near, far and yet here, they are neighbours, who would be closed off by neighbours, as non-neighbours, as strangers. The strangeness of strangers appears frightening and enticing.[23]

In a story from Asterix, we can read "I don't have anything against strangers. My best friends are strangers. But this stranger is from 'here'". The category of the stranger means the distancing from nearness through closeness, which in no way has to result in mutual understanding. According to Georg Simmel,

> [t]he unity of nearness and remoteness is with strangers, so understand distance means that he who loses is far and strangeness means that he who is far is near. The nearness of the stranger presupposes quiet and orderly local life-forms, only then is stranger the wanderer who comes today and stays tomorrow.[24]

Strangers are therefore neighbours, but they are not like 'us.' Strangers are, with regard to their category, a double provocation – they are local, but they do not obey the stereotypes that locals themselves develop and maintain. The relativity of strangers exists because the stranger is a concept without a counter-concept. There are natives and foreigners, friends and enemies, and there are strangers who do not fit into these categories.

---

22 Beck, 1996, pp. 380-386.

23 *Ibid.*, p. 382.

24 G. Simmel, 'Der Fremde,' *in Soziologie*, Munchen, Leipzig, 1908.

4.11 SUBSTANTIVE EQUALITY (HOMOGENEITY) AND POLITICAL (DEMOCRATIC) IDENTITY

In his critique of liberal democracy, Schmitt argued that the problem of a liberal pluralistic society could be solved only by elimination of pluralism, including its main political institution, parliamentary democracy. In the place of parliamentary democracy he proposed a 'truly' democratic leader, one who wins the acclaim of the people through his articulation of a unifying vision of the substantive homogeneity of the people. That leader will create a normal situation out of the chaos of pluralism by making a genuinely political sovereign decision. Such a decision must distinguish clearly between friend and enemy. It attempts to establish a society only by way of friends as those who fit the criteria of substantive homogeneity.

Schmitt pointed out that there is a sharp opposition between liberal individualism, with its moral discourse centred around the individual, and the democratic ideal, which is essentially political, and aims at creating an identity based on homogeneity. In his view, when we speak of equality we need to distinguish between two very different conceptions, the liberal and the democratic conception. The liberal conception of equality postulates that every person is automatically equal to every other person. The democratic conception, however, requires the possibility of distinguishing who belongs to the demos and who is exterior to it. For that reason it cannot exist without its necessary correlate of inequality. The democratic concept of equality is political; therefore it entails the possibility of distinction between 'we' and 'others.' Schmitt is quite clear: "democracy requires first homogeneity, and second, if the need arises, elimination and eradication of heterogeneity".[25] In such political construction there is no space for 'otherness.' 'Others' are the people who are excluded as foreigners or aliens. They are not part of political unity of democratic order.[26]

The political triangle we explored in previous pages – 'enemy' as the energetic principle of politics and order, 'substantive homogeneity' as the precondition of 'political unity,' and the 'ethnic concept of democracy' – provides the important basis for understanding political development in South East Europe. All of these concepts are deeply rooted in the field of belicistic political culture, which for different reasons, both historical and modern, dominates in Balkan political societies. Three negative legacies are of utmost importance: the first one being war, the second one being political memory of authoritarian regimes and the third one being nationalism. All of them are enemies of democracy, pluralism (otherness) and civil society.

---

25 C. Schmitt, *The Crisis of Parliamentary Democracy* (6th edn., trans. Ellen Kennedy), the MIT Press, Cambridge, Massachusetts, London, 2000, p. 9.

26 More: D. Dyzenhaus (Ed.), *Carl Schmitt's Critique of Liberalism*, Duke University Press, Durham and London, 1998; U. Preuss, 'Political Order and Democracy', in Mouffe 1999.

4.12 SOUTH EAST EUROPE'S PERSPECTIVE: A BELICISTIC POLITICAL CULTURE

The political culture of the South East Europe region is characterized by mis-recognition and misperception of 'otherness.' I identify that type of political culture as belicistic. It is strongly related to the idea of 'enemy' and the construct of 'substantive consensus.' If a figure of the enemy is an 'energetic principle' of political order, 'substantive homogeneity' is the core of the political unity of society. That basic feature of the South East European political culture is strongly related to a very specific form of state and nation building.

As is well known, the modern state is possible only if its subjects are recognized as equal members of state and if they recognize state authority as legitimate. But, on the other side, citizens must at the same time be connected and united by a horizontal form of consensus and loyalty, recognizing each other as members of a same political community. That pattern of state and nation building is defined as nationalistic.[27] Its result is a mono-national state. Most of the South East European countries try to imitate that pattern of state and nation building which produces structural deficit. The basic one is linked to the public good of 'identity' and strongly related to the nature of basic consensus (or lack thereof) in South East European societies. The collective identity is another name for broad social and political consensus by which people of the same political community get answers to two fundamental questions: 'who are we?' and 'why are we together?' Basic consensus has a strong symbolic effect on the unification of political community and provides to the member of the community a clue of how to delineate the borderline between 'us' and 'them.' Approaching the pattern of basic consensus and collective identity, countries in the region can be divided into two separate groups. The first one belongs to the kind of non-constituted political community without stable perceptions of common group identity. Bosnia and Herzegovina, Montenegro and Macedonia belong to this group. Another group of countries, which includes Croatia and Serbia, approximate a mono-national state and a nationalist form of state and nation building. The basic form of consensus is strongly rooted in the pre-political realm of society, stressing the crucial role of the founding myth as the deepest core of national unity. That form of collective identity is the result of very specific patterns of state and nation building, which can be defined in terms of etatization of nation. This produced specific asymmetry in the political development and has set up ethnic nationalism as the strongest and most expansive force in the region. The specific form of division of labour between nationalism and liberalism, within which nationalism is a basic form of shaping collective identity, and liberalism is a strategy of shaping individual autonomies and constitutionalism, has never come into being in South East Europe. The reception of liberalism in the region is imitative and limited. Returning to Meinecke, etatization of nation had nothing in common with the kind of long-run

27 J. Kis, 'Beyond the Nation State', *Social Research*, Vol. 63, No 1, 1996, pp. 194-209.

evolution of Western societies. The influence of expansive and uncontrolled nationalism during the process of state and nation building left open the issues of territorial scope as well as the question who belongs to whom.[28]

The absence of identity between state borders and national identity leads to the conditions that Istvan Bibo denominated as the existential and collective fear of small South East European nations.[29] He warned us that Eastern European small communities speak of nation death and annihilation, they fear genocide, oppression or assimilation, but above all, they consider the threat of overnight political elimination and the danger of their very existence. The political unity of political community is rooted in substantive homogeneity and equality. Political community requires, therefore, homogeneity and the elimination and eradication of heterogeneity and 'otherness.' According to the dominant interpretation in South East Europe, the extra constitutional entity that first brings constitutional political order into existence is understood as an ethnically homogeneous people, unbound by any normative or legal standards and characterized chiefly by its capacity to realize its 'otherness' in relation to both other people and the liberal and universalistic principles. Constituent power as a latent force re-emerges on occasion, functioning as the guardian of constituent foundation of order and preserving the original spirit of foundational politics, both understood in terms of the pre-political unity of the founding myth of nation and state. Questions of both constitutionalism and democratic legitimacy are still left open for the entire region.

The political dynamic in South East Europe is still in need of an answer to the question of how to harmonize the realm of pre-political unity of its members and consequently form a contractual and constructive agreement on moral and political principles. In the ambient where a 'common horizon of meaning' is almost destroyed under the negative legacy of war, dictatorship and nationalism, it seems that a basic consensus can be built around the thin axes of those values and principles that have unlimited meaning for all citizens and that are grounded in the constitution itself. The role of political theory in the process of moulding both public culture and democratic identity of society, civil society and education remains of utmost importance.

28 M. Ignatieff, *The Warriors Honor: Ethnic War and Modern Conscience*, Metropolitan Books, New York, 1997, pp. 34-39.

29 I. Bibo, 'The Distress of the East European Small States', *in* K. Nagy (Ed.), *Democracy, Revolution, Self-Determination: Selected Writings of Istvan Bibo*, Columbia University Press, New York, 1991, pp. 13-89.

5 Agonistic Democracy – A Controversial Attempt to Revitalize Democratic Ethos

Biljana Đorđević

5.1 Introduction

Liberal-democratic politics is in crisis. This crisis reflects itself in frequent manifestations of civic distrust in politicians, political parties and the institutions of liberal democracy, apathy of citizens and low voter turnout in elections as well as low overall political participation, decreasing solidarity and increasing inequality among citizens. The major worry of democratic theorists is of an existential nature – these developments bring into question the role and the future of democracy and democratic theory in light of rapid technological, social and economic changes.

Reactions to this crisis are twofold. Those full of resignation are cynical since the idea of democracy that has been considered victorious not so long ago, the idea that colonized our political vocabulary, has had disappointing performance. Others demand proper and deeper democratization. An unusual way to reconcile these two opposing reactions came from a relatively novel strain of democratic theory, democratic agonism (also known as agonistic pluralism) in its project of revitalizing democracy by way of returning the political to political theory and radicalizing the conflict in order to exploit its mobilizing potentials for democratic praxis.

The way of achieving this goal is by increasing citizen engagement through channelling those mobilized democratic energies towards positive directions and away from systematic marginalization, exclusion and intolerance. Is agonistic democracy a successful alternative to the current dominating democratic paradigm – deliberative democracy – as one of its proponents, Chantal Mouffe, has suggested?[1] I will argue that the current state of affairs in agonistic thought can be understood mainly as an alternative democratic ethos, but not an alternative democratic theory. The current ranges of agonistic democracy are reduced to undoubtedly innovative though controversial attempts at democratization of political ethos in order to preserve the democratic elements within the alloy of constitutional democracy. Agonistic democracy has no institutional dimension, neither does it require de-institutionalization, which is a feature of more antagonistic versions of democracy,

1 C. Mouffe, 'Deliberative Democracy or Agonistic Pluralism?', *Social Research*, Vol. 66, No. 3, 1999, pp. 745-758.

emerging as something between a sparring partner to the existing liberal-democratic order and the challenger who is not sure what it would do should he win a battle.
As I intend to show below, agonists criticize deliberation but also ask new questions, disallowing that their answers be assessed as more or less superior argumentation in comparison with that of deliberative democrats. One of the main agonistic theses has been that issues of the nature of the political and power relations have been avoided by deliberative democrats. I will rely on the work of the most prominent agonists – William Connolly, Bonnie Honig and Chantal Mouffe. These authors' appropriation of the concept of agōn – struggle – did not come directly from the Ancient Greeks, but mainly through 19th and 20th century German philosophers and political theorists such as Friedrich Nietzsche, Carl Schmitt, and Hannah Arendt with whom and sometimes against whom Connolly, Honig and Mouffe have rethought agonism. For the purposes of this chapter, I will treat their work as compatible projects of agonistic democracy. There are, of course, differences between the mentioned theorists, but I shall not focus on them in this chapter.

5.2 The Political and Politics

The central concern of agonism is genuine political action. Agonists valorize adversarial engagement by drawing attention to and affirming the centrality of conflict within democratic politics. They want to leave more up to politics, freeing citizens to contest the terms of public life and their political association. Instead of advocating for determination in advance of what is to count as legitimate political action, they emphasize the need for the radicalization of democracy by acknowledging that every aspiration for a final solution is undemocratic and metaphysical. Democracy can be rescued only when its own impossibility is accepted, that is, when it becomes understood that each solution at the level of politics is temporary.[2] Without that insight, new and especially radical challenges to the current order that may be progressive will be either faced with a denial of legitimacy or co-opted by the dominant pattern of interests and processes within a society.[3]
The centrality of the conflict stems from the political, understood by Chantal Mouffe as the dimension of antagonism that is constitutive of human societies. Politics, on the other hand, is "the set of practices and institutions through which an order is created, organizing human coexistence in the context of conflictuality provided by the political".[4] Democracy must seek to tame, not eliminate or eradicate, potential antagonisms in social relations – expectations of the eradicability of conflicts from politics is what leads us to demonize

2 E. Laclau & C. Mouffe, *Hegemony and Socialist Strategy: Towards a Radical Democratic Politics*, Verso, London, 1985, pp. 190-191.
3 A. Schaap, 'Agonism in Divided Societies', *Philosophy and Social Criticism*, Vol. 32, No. 2, 2006, p. 257.
4 C. Mouffe, *On the Political*, Routledge, London, New York, 2005, p. 9.

opponents with whom we are in conflict of no rational solution, and to refuse to accept their demands as legitimate. In pacification of Schmitt's friend/enemy distinction, Mouffe attributes to democracy the responsibility of transforming antagonism into agonism, that is, converting a relation in which "the two sides are enemies who do not share any ground" into "a we/they relation where the conflicting parties, although acknowledging that there is no rational solution to their conflict, nevertheless recognize the legitimacy of their opponents".[5] One of the reasons for citizens' lack of motivation to participate can be seen in the problem of investing too much effort to eradicate what is now perceived and accepted as ineradicable conflict. Likewise, the idealization of an overly demanding regulatory principle of consensus that aims at stability of the polity may have had a similar apathetic effect. The key problem is in the concept of power underlining consensual politics – liberals equate power with a bundle of rights, whereas the discursive conception of the political is communicative rationality. Both understandings of the political are non-political. What they seem to suggest is that only by entering into deliberation respecting certain rules of deliberation can people annul relations of domination among them. Domination can be only exterior to the space of deliberation, but it will more likely be translated into relations of communication as well. To explain what is at stake in allowing citizens to be both citizens and dissidents – by interrogating and upsetting previous political and legal settlements mirrored in institutions – Connolly talks through Foucault. In his 1983 interview Foucault granted that consensus is

> perhaps a critical idea to maintain at all times: to ask oneself what proportion of nonconsensuality is necessary or not, and then one may question every power relation to that extent. The farthest I would go is to say that perhaps one must not be for consensuality, but one must be against nonconsensuality.[6]

Embracing the conflictual nature of politics leads to deeper pluralization of society and opens up a place for authentic political options that could incentivize citizens to participate in politics. For Bonnie Honig, democracy should celebrate, not merely recognize, politics as a disruptive practice that resists the consolidations and closures of administrative and juridical settlement for the sake of the perpetuity of political contest. Celebrating the perpetuity of contest is not trouble-free, but Honig defends it because the "displacement of politics with law or administration engenders remainders that could disempower and undermine democratic institutions and citizens".[7] Rights and law should be part of the political contest rather than the instruments of its closure. Instead of the glorification of universalism and obsession with consensus that characterizes many deliberative

5 *Ibid.*, p. 20.

6 W. Connolly, *The Ethos of Pluralization*, University of Minnesota Press, Minneapolis, 1995, pp. 101-102.

7 B. Honig, *Political Theory and the Displacement of Politics*, Cornell University Press, Ithaca, N.Y., 1993, p. 14.

democrats, we should be addressing imperfect (re)production of universality and consensus and the sociopolitical consequences of such a reproduction.[8]
According to agonists, liberal deliberation has been made possible by depolitization of certain questions – repolitization of the private sphere includes 'remainders' and reassessing existing 'consensuses', thus spreading political space beyond the one licenced by the state.[9] Politics, but also democracy, given the strength of the connection between the two in agonists' writing, should not be politics of securing permanent stability but politics of contestation and contestability. It is necessary to fight illusions of a reconciled society that assures its stability by eliminating conflicts. Morally controversial issues ought not be permanently closed through non-political means such as the judiciary.[10] A fantasy of that kind can lead to totalitarianism, which is probably too dramatic a statement coming from Mouffe.[11] It is this aspect of eternal contestation and retaining some questions in the sphere of the political that is the most controversial element of agonism. It is not easy to accept that conflict should be embraced, and stabilization demonized, although it is far less difficult to accept that the price paid for stability is the unjust settlement of some political issues. The concerns are numerous. More agonistic politics need not always be progressive, just as the more progressive and inclusive society may become so divided that it cannot be sustained. Still, it would be wrong to read agonists as nihilists or revolutionaries seeking revolution and destabilization of the current regime just for the sake of it. They merely point out that besides seeing conflict as a burden that each of us at some point wants to get rid of, it can be seen as an opportunity for change, a product of injustice that should never be stabilized, or simply a fact of political life.
Agonists allow emotions in politics, because they believe that we should not leave the sphere of the emotional only to populists and extremists who use it very frequently and efficiently. It is recognition of the inevitability of conflict that prevents the return of emotions in the form of political extremism. The aim of democratic politics is, as we have seen, to transform antagonism into agonism, not to eliminate negative passions from political life. Politics should not be reduced to rationality – it just points to the limitations of rationality. Unity based on rational consensus is anti-political.[12] Agonists are vulnerable to

8 Bonnie Honig begins her first book *Political Theory and the Displacement* with Nietzsche's words – "[Virtù] rouses enmity toward order, toward the lies that are concealed in every order, institution, actuality – it is the worst of vices if one judges it by its harmful effect upon others". Honig differentiates between political theories founded on virtue (virtue theories of politics), for which she 'accuses' Kant, Rawls and Sandel of representing too well, and virtù theories of politics whose proponents are Nietzsche and Arendt. The former 'displace' conflict in the private domain, equating politics with administration and believing that juridical solutions of problems are tasks of politics and political theory. The latter see politics as disruptive practice that withstands consolidation and closures of the agon completed by administration and courts in order to save perpetuality of the contest. *Ibid.*, p. 2.

9 *Ibid.*, pp. 10-13.

10 *Ibid.*, p. 15.

11 C. Mouffe, *The Return of the Political*, Verso, London, 1993, p. 18.

12 *Ibid.*, p. 115.

critiques that they do not offer institutional solutions for prevention of abuse of emotions and conflicts that may escalate into more aggressive antagonism, but their reasoning is that rationalism, as an element of political liberalism or deliberative democracy, through exclusion of unreasonable and irrational, neglects potentials for fundamentalism of the excluded at its own peril.

I will rely on the three points in showing the nature of agonistic democracy as an ethos. The first concerns the relationship between politics and law, that is, the agonistic ethos that inspires making a decision at a time of both legislation and the application of the law. The second moment deals with the nature of democratic politics as contestation politics, and the third moment points out that the goal of democratic politics is to construct democratic identities (the formation of the democratic subject). The second and third moments suggest that agonists do not consider democracy as a decision-making procedure (although they care about the decisions) nor that they spend enough time designing the institutions that could survive the contestation politics. This remains one of the main criticisms towards the possible success of an agonistic project. However, understood as the conception of democratic ethos and not as a comprehensive democratic theory, agonistic democracy has enough vitality to be considered a significant contribution to contemporary radical democratic theory.

5.3 Realism and Agonism

There is, as William Galston has put it, a dissenting movement in political theory that he labels 'realism.' Although realism is not a unified school of thought, if there is anything that unites the various authors Galson mentions (among whom he includes Connolly, Honig and Mouffe), it is the critique of evasion and displacement of politics by liberalism.[13] He provides evidence for the claim that ethics has been used as a containment of the political. Judith Shklar equated the situation in political theory as legalism since "politics is regarded not only as something apart from law, but inferior to law".[14] Politics, especially as conceptualized in political theory, has been reduced to a servant of the law and ethics. What should be done instead is to defend autonomy of the political so that besides rare moments of the exercise of constituent power even daily discretionary decisions must be imbued with agonistic ethos. The law is limited and does not always inform us of what is to be done. Liberal democracy has been exposed to a constant erosion of the democratic dimension – politics

13 Other 'realists' are Bernard Williams, who actually started using the term realism, then Reymond Geuss, Chantal Mouffe, William Connolly, Bonnie Honig, Judith N. Shklar, Jeremy Waldron, Mark Philp, Stuart Hampshire, John Dunn, Glen Newey, Richard Bellamy, Geoffrey Hawthorne, John Gray, Quentin Skinner, and Stephen Elkin. W. Galston, 'Realism in Political Theory', *European Journal of Political Theory*, Vol. 9, No. 4, 2010, pp. 385-411.

14 *Ibid.*, p. 386.

is reduced to administrative affairs, and citizens are reduced to consumers of government services. The story of the rights of normalized individuals or groups with essentialized identities that is at the core of the liberal conception of the political is actually depoliticizing. These citizen-consumers, 'secured' by rights and the institutions of the rule of law (as if in them lies a force that exists independently of human beings) are poorly prepared to escape from the clutches of various forms of domination in which they can be found, especially in the states of emergency, something that Bonnie Honig writes about in her latest book, *The Emergency Politics: Paradox, Law, Democracy*.[15] The critique of law and rights is not devastating – it is not that the rule of men should completely replace the rule of law, but that the law and rights will not suffice, the binary of rule of men vs. the rule of law does not reflect what is actually taking place during application of so-called 'impartial rules.' Agonists indicate the power and powerlessness of law and emphasize that the role of discretion during daily application of the law has been widely neglected. Precisely those moments of making discretionary decisions are the moments when one conducts oneself responsibly. As an example of agonistic struggle, Honig takes Louis Post, Assistant Secretary of Labour during the administration of President Woodrow Wilson, who, by way of using administrative discretion in interpreting the law, almost anticipated the future rights of non-citizens in the appropriate legal action to prevent deportation of thousands of people who have been exposed to such risk during the first Red Scare. However, Honig showed that the fact that Louis Post had fought against arbitrary although legal deportation measures does not mean he was a proceduralist at any cost. He did not protest when habeas corpus had been suspended by President Grant to break up the Ku Klux Klan. He took the law to be a mechanism for achievement of different progressive political goals.[16] Favoured by radical democrats, a verse from an alternative musician and a feminist icon "any tool is a weapon if you hold it right" finds its place again within this example.

5.4 Deliberation and Agonism

Both deliberative democracy and agonistic democracy aim at further democratization of democracy although what that entails these two conceptions address in different ways, especially with regard to the liaison between constitutionalism and democracy. Instead of Habermas' co-originality thesis, agonists emphasize their agonistic pairing.[17]

15 B. Honig, *Emergency Politics: Paradox, Law, Democracy*, Princeton University Press, Princeton, 2009, p. xv.

16 *Ibid.*, p. 69.

17 Aletta Norval even writes about deliberative democracy and agonistic democracy as two branches of radical democracy, one being inspired by critical theory and the other by post-structuralism. A. Norval, 'Radical democracy', *in* P.B. Clarke & J. Foweraker (Eds.), *Encyclopedia of Democratic Thought*, Routledge, London, 2001, pp. 724-733.

Both deliberative democracy and agonistic democracy engage with the relationship between the two elements of modern constitutional democracy – democracy and constitutionalism. If for liberal democracy this mismatch between the two elements goes in favour of constitutionalism, the deliberative and agonistic approach emphasizes the democratic element. Agonists are not satisfied by how far the democratization of deliberative democracy goes. For deliberativists, the goal of democratic activity is to achieve rational consensus through deliberation, while post-structuralist radicals aim to maintain the disturbing and destabilizing potential of democracy. Since for the agonists irreducibility of relations of power is a fact of modern society, they do not even try to come up with normative preconditions and foundations for unlimited democratic discourse.[18]

The problem, according to the agonists, is that deliberative democrats employ legitimation norms and constitutional restrictions to protect the so-called normative goods from the people whose decisions and practices may endanger these goods. This conflict of constitutionalism with the autonomy of the people, according to Honig, illuminates the paradox of democratic legitimacy and the paradox of constitutional democracy.[19] The first paradox can briefly be summarized in Rousseau's question "whether the general will can err", that is, "what has been decided", so that decisions are not only majoritarian but also just. This is where constitutionalism comes in as a damage controller to distinguish good decisions of the people from bad ones. The paradox of constitutional democracy indicates a problem of obeying the constitution that the currently living citizens have not participated in producing, the constitution being a result of a past generation or simply the legislator. The law, the founding-fathers, the constitution's authors emerge as the rulers of the people, as those who actually make the decisions, as sovereign.

Deliberative democrats believe that the right balance between the two principles reveals that the paradoxes are either false or they can be overcome through practices such as Habermas' 'tappings' or Benhabib's 'democratic iterations.' Responding to Michelman's

18 Taking part in decision making on an equal basis is what constitutes inclusiveness, and that is precisely the first feature of a deliberative ideal. It is not surprising, then, that one of the most intriguing critiques of deliberation was that of difference democrats charging deliberative democracy for exclusion and unfairness. I take this critique to be well intended precisely because authors like Lynn Sanders and Iris Marion Young, in elaborating it, explicitly say that they are not entirely against deliberation, more that they are against deliberation as it is defined now – the rules of deliberation are too restrictive and produce exclusion. When it comes to critique of rational consensus and procedure of ideal deliberation, agonistic critique is similar to that of the difference democrats, although the majority of agonists' positions are often read as incompatible with deliberation. For a different view see A. Knops, 'Debate: Agonism as Deliberation – On Mouffe's Theory of Democracy', *The Journal of Political Philosophy*, Vol. 15, No. 1, 2007, pp. 115-126. For difference democrats' critique of deliberation see I.M. Young, 'Communication and the Other: Beyond Deliberative Democracy', *in* S. Benhabib (Ed.), *Democracy and Difference*, Princeton University Press, Princeton, 1996, pp. 120-136; L. Sanders, 'Against Deliberation', *Political Theory*, Vol. 25, No. 3, 1997, pp. 347-376.

19 B. Honig, 'Between Decision and Deliberation: Political Paradox in Democratic Theory', *American Political Science Review*, Vol. 101, No. 1, 2007, p. 1.

remark about the infinite regress of constitutional practice, which states that the Constituent Assembly cannot vouch for the legitimacy of the rules according to which it itself has been formed, and that the democratic process governed by the constitution is in a vicious circle of infinite regress, Jürgen Habermas shifts the problem of legitimacy into the field of future generations. According to him, a democratic constitution is "a tradition-building project with a clearly marked beginning in time" and "all the later generations have the task of actualizing the still-untapped normative substance of the system of rights laid down in the original document of the constitution".[20] Future generations need to implement these rights more successfully than the first generation, but this is not a struggle between past and present, constitutionalism and democracy, but rather, the two principles – constitutional and democratic – are co-original, each depending on the other. This is a different statement from Mouffe in her book *The Democratic Paradox*, where she writes that

> liberal democracy results from the articulation of two logics which are incompatible in the last instance and that there is no way which they could be perfectly reconciled. Or, to put it in a Wittgensteinian way, that there is a constitutive tension between their corresponding 'grammars,' a tension that can never be overcome but only negotiated in different ways.[21]

Seyla Benhabib defines democratic iterations as characteristic culturally and politically induced adoptions of universal and cosmopolitan norms (the mediation between universal norms and the will of democratic majorities). Benhabib uses this concept to relax Hannah Arendt's paradox of rights – the right to have rights – believing that citizens will more and more internalize cosmopolitan norms and, for instance, accept migrants as citizens.[22] Iterations are normative and institutional solutions to the paradox of democratic legitimacy. The expression of the democratic will must be measured from a moral point of view. Otherwise, democracy is reduced to decisionism, which does not justify the principles it represents.

Honig addresses this issue in response to Seyla Benhabib's treatment of the question "whether the general will can err". If it errs, writes Rousseau, it is not the general will, but the will of all, because the general will always tends to the public advantage.[23] How to prevent the people, even the good people, from being fooled? How to discern the general

20 J. Habermas, 'Constitutional Democracy: A Paradoxical Union of Contradictory Principles?', *Political Theory*, Vol. 29, No. 6, 2001, pp. 773-774.

21 C. Mouffe, *The Democratic Paradox*, Verso, London, 2000, p. 5.

22 S. Benhabib, *The Rights of Others: Aliens, Residents and Citizens*, Cambridge University Press, Cambridge, 2004; S. Benhabib, *Another Cosmopolitanism*, Robert Post (Ed.), Oxford University Press, Oxford, 2005.

23 J.-J. Rousseau, 'The Social Contract, Book II, Chapter III', *in* J.-J. Rousseau, *The Social Contract and The First and Second Discourses*, edited and with an Introduction by S. Dunn, Yale University Press, 2002, p. 172.

will and not align with the will of all? Benhabib rejects both Rousseau's solutions. The first is the arithmetic solution:

> There is often a great deal of difference between the will of all and the general will; the latter regards only the common interest, while the former has regard to private interests, and is merely a sum of particular wills; but take away from these same wills the pluses and minuses which cancel one another, and the general will remains as the sum of the differences.[24]

For Benhabib, this is not really a solution because it is not at all clear what the removal and addition of individual wills means.[25]
The second of Rousseau's solutions is the introduction of a new player within this game – a legislator. Benhabib also rejects this solution because a legislator represents an idealized rationality, not deliberative rationality, and by accepting such a solution a deliberativist would surrender the idea of legitimacy.[26] Honig almost bids in its counter-reading of Rousseau: perhaps Rousseau via arithmetic solution actually expresses the hopelessness of knowing for sure when we have our hands on the general will and not the will of all.[27] Or perhaps Rousseau suggests that it is not easier to identify a good legislator from the general will. Because, first of all, even if the legislator knows the right answer to the question of the good law, the very fact of his presence destroys the autonomy of the people. But even if we accept that a people is never a single protagonist of its own (hi)story, but often also of someone else's, which is something Rousseau understood, it is still the decision of the people to accept or reject the good laws that the legislator proposes. The people need to respect the legislator who must be recognized as the embodiment of the general will.[28] The problem here doubles. What Honig is trying to do with this example is to show that it is the Rousseauian legislator who can be a symbol of democratic politics as contestatory politics, since it can always be argued that the legislator is not the proper legislator but a charlatan. The decision of the people on the matter of who the legislator is and whether, how and to what extent the people will follow the legislator demonstrates ways of people building (nation building). This decision has to be made by the people, even if it causes division among them.[29]

24 *Ibid.*, p. 172.
25 S. Benhabib, 'Deliberative Rationality and the Models of Democratic Legitimacy', *Constellations*, Vol. 1, No. 1, 1994, p. 29.
26 *Ibid.*, p. 30.
27 Honig, 2007, p. 4.
28 *Ibid.*, pp. 5-7.
29 Honig argues against reading of Rousseau as a theorist of too unified conception of the people. Because of the paradox of politics – the will of the people to accept or reject legislator's law, the people who are not yet a people – the people are "never fully captured" by the legislator's law, that is, the people are never fully formed or united. I am not convinced that Honig's reading of Rousseau is correct, although it has been correctly used for agonistic utilization of the paradox of politics. *Ibid.*, p. 7.

Bonnie Honig asserts that deliberative democrats prefer to deal with the paradox of democratic legitimacy and constitutional democracy because it is the people who, according to them, are a problem, and the rules (laws) are solutions – either cosmopolitan norms to be adopted through democratic iterations, or the constitution whose rights are to be tapped. There is, however, a more fundamental Rousseauian paradox. This is what most authors call the paradox of politics. William Connolly is the first among agonists to remind us of this paradox, accusing Rousseau of both revealing the problem and concealing it.[30] The famous formulation goes like this:

> In order that a newly formed nation might approve sound maxims of politics and observe the fundamental rules of state-policy, it would be necessary that the effect should become the cause; that the social spirit, which should be the product of the institution, should preside over the institution itself, and that men should be, prior to the laws, what they ought to become by means of them. Since, then, the legislator cannot employ either force or reasoning, he must have recourse to an authority of a different order, which can compel without violence and persuade without convincing.[31]

The paradox elucidates the question of the beginning and the founding of a general will – how did any particular norms or the constitution come into being, how can any constitution be democratically legitimate if it is constituted by the people who were supposed to legitimate the constitution itself?

What is the purpose of these paradoxes? It seems to me that by way of their illumination agonists tend to protect the presence of the people as the subject of democratic politics, a subject that is often absent in constitutional democracy. Contestatory politics reformulate key issues in such a way that, instead of binary logic offering dichotomies (either rule of law or rule of the people, law or violence, unified people or multitude, the general will or the will of all, deliberation or decision), we encounter a vicious circle that leads to a temporary decision, but permanent indecisiveness. Simply, agonists do not believe in love of democracy and constitutionalism, happy endings for future generations whose time will reconcile current tensions, nor in the devastating marriage of two principles as Carl Schmitt would have it. Rather, they believe that there is an unsolvable productive tension that can only temporarily stabilize the pragmatic negotiations between the political forces in which one manages to establish hegemony over the other. Moreover, the tension between constitutionalism and democracy should take the form of contamination since "once the articulation of the two principles has been effectuated – even if in a precarious way – each of them changes the identity of the other".[32] This readiness to accept the

30 Connolly, 1995, p. 137.

31 Rousseau, 2002, Book II, Chapter VII, p. 182.

32 Mouffe, 2000, p. 10.

risks – a 'bad' decision of the people, or a precarious change of principles via their contamination – is precisely a democratic virtue, since without it, democracy as a project of experimenting and innovations would not have been possible.
I find it hard to imagine that agonistic politics can ever be the guiding model/principle of institutions that have the imperative of efficiency as well as the desire for self-preservation and stability. That is why democratization of the laws, democratization of the people, new even if wrong decisions, can only be inspired by the agonistic ethos coming outside of mainstream institutions. Connolly's version of the Rousseauian paradox is that "democratic virtue presupposes a democratic way of life, while that way of life in turn presupposes the virtues it should precede".[33] The paradox of politics returns here with the question where this agonistic ethos comes from – how do we cultivate it? Institutions would have crushed it even if we could imagine their functioning according to such principles.

5.5 Construction and Articulation of Democratic Identity

Economic democracy is based on the process of aggregation of given preferences through aggregation of interests expressed in the elections, while deliberative democracy seeks transformation of preferences through deliberation aiming at collective decision by way of consensus. At the core of agonistic democracy is a process of construction and the articulation of interests and identities, but also agonistic contestation of articulated identities, and not a proposition of new decision-making procedures. This appears to be a much broader goal, in the spirit of a radical democratic ethics and not institutional politics. It is this emphasis on the formation of democratic subjects that agonists add as new quality to democratic theory, and it comes as a consequence of the postmodern character of agonism. The postmodernity of agonistic democracy is conditional – Mouffe claims that radical democracy is modern when it comes to emancipatory struggles for equality, but postmodern with regard to overcoming the epistemology of Enlightenment.[34] In her own words – "it is not a question of moving from a 'unitary unencumbered self' to a 'unitary situated self'; the problem is with the very idea of the unitary subject".[35] There is no undifferentiated rational subject whose actions are a direct translation of his or her identity, as people are always and at the same time multiple subjects situated at the intersection of different communities that they belong to, with different articulations of their diverse identifications.
Agonists insist on an understanding of agent's identity as one that is not fixed. The openness and vagueness of the ways in which different agents' positions become articulated are

33 W.E. Connolly, *Identity/Difference: Democratic Negotiations of Political Paradox* (expanded edn.), University of Minnesota Press, Minneapolis, London, 2002, p. 193.
34 C. Mouffe, 'Radical Democracy: Modern or Postmodern?', *Social Text*, No. 21 (Universal Abandon? The Politics of Postmodernism), 1989, pp. 32-33.
35 Mouffe, 1993, p. 20.

features of postmodern agents as a subject of democratic politics. The postmodern subject is much more complex than the liberal individual understood as utility maximizer, a Marxist person determined by his class membership or communitarian agent whose goals have been constituted by his community.[36]

So, if an agent's identity is not pre-given nor fixed, political practice should not be reduced to the defence of cemented identities nor should power be understood solely as an external relationship of the two pre-defined identities. On the contrary, power and political practices constitute and reconstitute identities. It follows that democratic politics should not be invested in futile attempts at removing power and eradicating conflicts that arise because of the differences, but should instead promote forms of power that are consistent with democratic values – liberty and equality – subject to various interpretations.[37] It is important to note that some differences arise as a consequence of domination rather than as expressions of emancipatory pluralism. Agonistic politics contest fixation of such identities and their demands for recognition. As an alternative to the concept of representation of identities, Mouffe (together with Laclau) introduces the concept of articulation:

> To deny the existence of an a priori, necessary link between subject positions does not mean that there are not constant efforts to establish between them historical, contingent and variable links. This type of link, which establishes between various positions a contingent, unpredetermined relation, is what we designated as 'articulation.' Even though there is no necessary link between different subject positions, in the field of politics there are always discourses that try to provide an articulation from different standpoints. For that reason every subject position is constituted within an essentially unstable discursive structure, since it is submitted to a variety of articulatory practices that constantly subvert and transform it. This is why there is no subject position whose links with others is definitively assured and, therefore, no social identity that would be fully and permanently acquired.[38]

The concept of articulation testifies that there is more to contestatory politics than a mere game of disturbing settled identities and interests within institutions. Articulation is a notion that is closest to procedural notions such as deliberation. It should be used as a means for egalitarian struggles, but it never denies the necessity of contestation of the works of articulation.

Rather than seeking to determine the basic principles that should govern democratic deliberation, agonistic democrats aim to understand democracy primarily in terms

36 Mouffe, 1989, p. 35.
37 Mouffe, 1999, p. 753.
38 Mouffe, 1993, p. 78.

of an ethos that affirms the contingency and openness of political life. For them, any kind of political identity is a thorny, delicate issue and contingent on achievement of political action.

While calling for contestatory politics, agonists also cherish the cultivation of a corresponding ethos appropriate for late-modern life in a world of deep pluralism and one that allows the creation of new identities in an uncertain and paradoxical process.

Connolly proposes two civic virtues critical for such an ethos. The first is agonistic respect, as he says, "the kissing cousin of liberal tolerance". The idea of tolerance has been widely criticized as demeaning for the minorities and marginalized who are merely tolerated by those who are the centre, majority, the 'normal' ones. Agonistic respect is a more appropriate version for recognition that we live in a world where adversaries are mutually interdependent but they do not accept the consolidation of the positions of those who may only tolerate or who may only be tolerated. It entails that "you absorb the agony of having elements of your own faith called into question by others and you fold agonistic contestation of others into the respect that you convey towards them".[39]

The interest in emerging powers and identities results with an introduction of the notion of a politics of becoming by Connolly. The second civic virtue – critical responsiveness – is appropriate for the politics of becoming while it is still under way. The politics of becoming is not a solution of the paradox of politics, but a warning against its concealment, something that previous conceptions of democracy are guilty of. This is the

> paradoxical politics by which new and unforeseen things surge into being, such as a new and surprising religious faith, a new source of moral inspiration, a new mode of civilizational warfare, a new cultural identity unsettling an existing constellation of established identities, a new collective good, or the placement of a new right on the existing register of recognized rights.[40]

In order for the politics of becoming to bring into being new things (new rights, such as the right of doctor-assisted suicide, or new identities, such as the political identity of agonistically re-democratized nation) critical responsiveness needs to be cultivated. It requires presumptive generosity on the part of citizens when confronted with new demands, but this responsiveness to life and requests of others is never fully predetermined. Critical responsiveness is critical precisely because of the fact that no constitution, legislation or moral code can tell us in advance which demands are justified or progressive. There are no universal prescriptions for identification of differences agonists should accept or contest.

39 W. E. Connolly, *Pluralism*, Duke University Press, Durham, 2005, pp. 123-124.
40 *Ibid.*, p. 121.

5.6 Conclusion and a Declaration

Agonistic democracy is not a model without any social vision except for one prioritizing contestation.[41] It primarily aims at mobilizing disappointed democrats and leftists, who should establish an alliance in pursuit of a common struggle just as articulation can create a specific type of connection between our various individual identifications. However, the point is not that the democratic alliance wins at any cost since the sheer victory may bring unbearable losses, [42] the goal is to modify the identities of these groups, so that, for instance, interests of the workers are not defended at the cost of interests of women or the interests of immigrants. It is necessary to respect the principle of equivalence of these struggles if they are to be truly democratic.[43] Such an alliance would not solve the problem of exclusion and alienation of certain individuals and groups, but the added value is in understanding that any consensus exists only as a temporary result of a provisional hegemony, as stabilization of power, and that it always leads to some forms of exclusion.[44] These forms of exclusion will be contested, and not frozen, as moral standards condensed from past political struggles often tends to be.

The future of democracy, its survival really, is seen by agonists in uncertainty, experiment, contestation, struggle against remainders of politics of universalism and hegemony. It is appropriate to understand current efforts in development of agonistic conceptions of democracy as attempts to strengthen the democratic ethos of permanent openness of political life brought into being by agon, so that those excluded, either deliberately or accidentally, either characterized as unreasonable, irrational, unskilled for proper deliberation or emotional, can be returned to the political sphere and have their identities transformed and politicized. Postulation of any finality is what agonistic doubt works against. They point out how important it is to make a decision when there is no rule to be followed, or sometimes precisely when there is a rule to be followed but it is not clear what following that rule entails. At the same time, the indecisiveness agonism brings to us may be frightening as there is no way to know for sure whether we have elected charlatans or proper legislators (or we could have elected only among charlatans!). There are no guarantees that the politics that defends contingency as much as agonistic politics does will actually be a proper response for the crisis of democracy. As Connolly admits, "there is no guarantee, certainly, that the contingent politics of assemblages will proceed in the desired way. There never are guarantees of this sort".[45]

---

41 Connolly, 2002, p. xxvi.

42 With regard to feminist politics, Hannah Arendt asked, "What will we lose if we win?" This is the motive repeatedly used by Honig in her book Emergency Politics. Honig, 2009, pp. 66 and 130.

43 Mouffe, 1993, p. 19.

44 Mouffe, 1999, p. 756.

45 Connolly, 1995, p. 96.

With this, we reach the limits of agonism. To differentiate itself from constitutionalism, democracy must acknowledge our ability to learn and equip us for risk-taking. Proposed civic virtues point in the right direction, but how do we cherish them? Why would people respect their adversaries and their differences, or worse, allow potentially new adversaries and their differences to come into play? How to reach that moment when they do? The question is a recurrence of Rousseau's paradox of politics, which has not been solved philosophically, but it may be soothed politically by an alternative declaration of independence pledged by all of us:

Let's feign these truths to be self-evident: that each individual needs an identity; that every stable way of life invokes claims to collective identity that enter in various ways into the interior identifications and resistances of those who share it; that no god created humanity so that contending claims to identity will coalesce into some harmonious whole or be dissolved into some stable, recognizable, and transcendent principle; that the singular hegemony of any set of identities requires the subordination or exclusion of that which differs from them. How is one to respond to this condition? How are we to respond if – affirming connections to others through ties of identity as well as the abundance of lives not exhausted by the identities that form us – we reject the clean, consistent stance of subjugating difference merely because it is at odds with identities we live and endorse? Here a twofold refusal may be needed: (i) if the identities installed in us achieve social hegemony, we resist repressing difference merely because its existence threatens our self-assurance; (2) if dispositions branded into us are marginalized or repressed by hegemonic identities, we refuse to plot a future revenge in which we vindicate ourselves through simple reversal of the present. This is part of the declaration of independence needed.[46]

46 Connolly, 2002, pp. 158-159.

Part II
Human Rights (Culture): Revisiting Doctrines on Foundations

6 Rawls on Human Rights and Political Justification

David M. Rasmussen

In his *Idea of Human Rights* Charles Beitz states, "The doctrine of human rights is the articulation in the public morality of world politics of the idea that each person is a subject of global concern".[1] However, the problem is how to justify them. Jacques Maritan, one of the participants in the construction of the Universal Declaration of Human Rights (1948), put it this way

> I am quite certain that my way of justifying belief in the rights of man and the ideal of liberty, equality, fraternity is the only way with a firm foundation in truth. This does not prevent me from being in agreement on these practical convictions with people who are certain that their way of justifying them, entirely different from mine or opposed to mine [...] is equally the only way founded upon truth.[2]

It is one thing to articulate a doctrine of human rights as the post-world war history of human rights discourse indicates. It is another thing to justify them. The problem of justification emanates from the realization that the pluralistic culture of our day begins with the frank acknowledgement of a plurality of ideas of justice and a multiplicity of conceptions of the good. This fact, the fact of pluralism as Rawls called it, problematizes universalistic claims that have traditionally been the basis for the justification of human rights. So much is commonplace. Given that context, Rawls, who spent little time in his early (*The Theory of Justice)* and his middle (*Political Liberalism*) periods, turned directly to the problem of human rights in his *Law of Peoples,* where he adapted a minimalist strategy framed by the concept of the political. Those influenced by Rawls have more or less followed in his footsteps, sticking with essentially minimalist claims regarding human rights. Whether Rawls should have devoted more time to the development of a human rights doctrine during his pre-*Law of Peoples* work is an open question.[3]

---

1 C. Beitz, *The Idea of Human Rights*, Oxford University Press, Oxford, 2009, p.1.

2 From the Introduction to *UNESCO, Human Rights: Comments and Interpretations,* Allan Wingate, London, 1949, pp. 10-11; cited *in* C. Taylor, *Conditions of an Unforced Consensus in Human Right*, presented at Bangkok Workshop, March 1996, at <www.iilj.org/courses/documents/CharlesTaylor.pdf>.

3 It is necessary to qualify this statement by stating that what Kant would have called the doctrine of right is central to his early work. Hence, primary goods could be understood in the sense of rights, *i.e.*, as legitimate entitlements that should be provided to subjects in the theory of justice. Also, the notion of right is central to the idea of the congruence between the right and the good that is the preoccupation of the third and final section of *The Theory of Justice.* Also, it could be claimed that certain rights are presupposed in the construction of the Original Position. However, my sense is that Rawls did not choose to contribute to the human rights discourse as such until his later work.

In the following essay I will begin by first developing the foundations for Rawls' theory of rights in the *Law of Peoples.* Second, I will examine the case for justificatory minimalism. Finally, I will move the argument for justification of human rights beyond justificatory minimalism.

6.1 Human Rights and The Law of Peoples

The task of *The Law of Peoples,* a treatise on international law, is to construct a framework for understanding non-liberal descent peoples. Clearly, this move from the national to the international scene was framed by a number of developments in Rawls' thought beginning with his outline of the problem of stability in the third part of *The Theory of Justice.* Centring his political philosophy on the development of a theory of social cooperation formulated in the social contract tradition initiated by Hobbes, Rawls would come to realize that the fact of pluralism would significantly affect the very possibility of achieving 'stability', as he would begin to put it, "for the right reasons". Clearly, the problem of stability forced him to reconsider the entire project he developed in *The Theory of Justice* and, although I cannot go into detail regarding the manner in which his project changed, allow me to list six consequences of what he came to see as the fact of pluralism. They are: (1) the turn from the metaphysical to the political, (2) the distinction between the comprehensive and the political, (3) the idea of overlapping consensus, (4) the subordination of reason to reasonability, (5) the elaboration of the domain of the political and (6) the development of the idea of public reason. Taken together, the consequences of taking seriously the fact of pluralism in relation to the problem of stability would shape the Rawls' approach to human rights on the international level. The first major transition from his earlier work was marked by the publication of the paper 'Justice as Fairness: Political not Metaphysical',[4] that constituted a point of departure from the epistemological justification of justice as fairness, the principal idea of *A Theory of Justice.* His realization was that given diversity, one could only sustain the idea of justice as fairness on the basis of an interpretation of democratic culture. However, having succumbed to diversity how could he account for unity sufficient for social cooperation? Rawls' answer to this question depended upon a division of labour between the comprehensive and the political. Indeed, there is a significant conflict between comprehensive doctrines in democratic culture, but his assumption was that acquiescing to the domain of the political could accommodate conflict. To be sure, comprehensive views as in the case of various religious or secular orientations can be incommensurable. However in

4 Rawls states: "Briefly, the idea is that in a constitutional democracy the public conception of justice should be, so far as possible, independent of controversial philosophical and religious doctrines. Thus, to formulate such a conception, we apply the principle of toleration to philosophy itself: the public conception of justice is to be political, not metaphysical. Hence the title." J. Rawls, *Collected Papers* (Edited by Samuel Freeman), Harvard University Press, Cambridge, 1999, p. 388.

most cases they have reconciled themselves to the emerging domain of the political. How is this done? The answer is overlapping consensus. Rawls always intended that overlapping consensus should not be understood as a mere overlapping of similar elements within various comprehensive doctrines, but rather as an inclusion of the values of the political within comprehensive doctrines. However, what remains to be explained is how comprehensive doctrines could or should be tolerated in a democratic culture. The answer to this question occurs in terms of the distinction between pluralism and reasonable pluralism, based on the distinction between the reasonable and the rational. To be rational is to be concerned with one's own good, while to be reasonable is to take the other into account. A reasonable person is one who can simply understand and articulate the claims of a comprehensive doctrine not her own[5]. A reasonable comprehensive doctrine is one that has accommodated itself to the domain of the political. To say that pluralism exists simply means the modern culture is characterized by having a multitude of comprehensive doctrines. To say that reasonable pluralism exists is to say that comprehensive doctrines exist that have accommodated themselves to the domain of the political and can be conceived as reasonable. As a consequence, subjects within a modern culture characterized by diversity who can distinguish between the reasonable and the rational are able to view other comprehensive doctrines as not necessarily true but as reasonable.

Now, the integration of these new elements within the Rawlsian scheme results in a special form of justification. First, justification, heretofore the property of moral theory and epistemology, would hereafter be confined to the freestanding political domain. Second, political justification would seek a wide berth, *i.e.*, it would constitute a forum for the public in which agreement or disagreement could be expressed. Finally, justification would occur in accord with the liberal principle of legitimacy that Rawls articulated in the following manner:

> our exercise of political power is fully proper only when it is exercised in accordance with a constitution the essentials of which all citizens as free and equal may be reasonably be expected to endorse in light of principles and ideals acceptable to their common human reason.[6]

Finally, public reason contextualizes political justification by creating a public discourse in which political justification can be expressed.

5 To be sure the concept of reasonability does a lot of work for Rawls. The idea is that a reasonable person is able to look at the point of view of another person without dismissing that point of view on metaphysical or epistemological grounds based on a conception of truth. Hence, according to Rawls, one should be able to look at another person's comprehensive doctrine without dismissing it as false but rather perceiving it as legitimate or in these terms reasonable.

6 J. Rawls, *Political Liberalism*, Columbia University Press, New York, 1993, p. 137.

Now, turning to *The Law of Peoples* directly, we can see how all these factors come into play. First of all, non-liberal societies are essentially societies that subscribe to comprehensive doctrines in which political activity is thought to be the expression of an idea of the good that is shared by all the members of that society. They can be well ordered but not necessarily well ordered in the sense of a liberal democratic society. Second, they can be characterized as having a consultation hierarchy. Although they do not subscribe to the liberal principle of legitimacy, they do provide for representation. Their criterion for legitimacy contrary to the claims of liberal democracy is that they provide representation on the basis of membership. For an appropriate model of representation, Rawls cites the Millet system of the Ottoman Empire that gave representation although not the right of governance to Christians and Jews. Third, although there is no rule of law as in the context of a liberal democracy, it is fundamental that there be a system of law as well as a judiciary to interpret it. Some think Rawls was somewhat prophetic in imagining a society, Kasanistan,[7] which incorporates these three phenomena: a consultation hierarchy, a mode of representation and a rule of law.

Clearly, Rawls conception of the law of peoples is very much determined by basic characteristics of his post (*Theory-1971)* development. In particular, the differentiation between the comprehensive and the political is fundamental to his interpretation of international politics because it would mean that minimal political structures, consultation hierarchy, representation and rule of law would be singled out. The one basic implication of this constraint is that one need not confront non-liberal cultures on the level of comprehensive doctrine. In so doing, it would be possible to escape the battle of the titans, or the clash of civilizations, *i.e.,* confronting the international community with liberalism as the supreme comprehensive position. Indeed, his critique of cosmopolitanism[8] would give the clue to his relatively consistent position. If one were to take liberalism as a comprehensive doctrine that from an epistemological perspective would have to be justified as true, we could interpret non-liberal societies as moving on a Hegelian evolutionary scale towards the end of history. It would also be possible to turn comprehensive liberalism into the basis for critique. Then the next step would be an attempt to redeem the world on the bass of our cosmopolitan vision. Clearly, Rawls does not want to go there.

---

7 Rawls lists six guidelines that the consultation hierarchy of Kasanistan should follow, which I paraphrase here: Every group must be consulted, everyone must belong to a group, some members of each group must be included in the decision-making body, the body that makes the final decision must weigh the claims of each of the bodies represented, decisions should be made in accord with the special priorities of Kasanistan, one of which should be respect for minorities, and finally the special priorities should fit into a scheme of cooperation. J. Rawls, *The Law of Peoples*, Harvard University Press, Cambridge, 1999, p. 77.

8 Rawls objects to cosmopolitanism on essentially two grounds. First, cosmopolitan interpretations by positing universal equality do not grant legitimacy to non-liberal forms of society discounting them in advance and postulating an ultimate triumph of liberal doctrines. Second, as he states: "The ultimate concern of a cosmopolitan view is the well-being of individuals and not the justice of society." *Ibid.*, p. 119. By making this second point, one can see that Rawls is still concerned with the stability problem that he took up in the third part of *The Theory of Justice.*

Having made the distinction between the comprehensive and the political and having singled out the emerging domain of the political, it is the idea of toleration that governs Rawls' perspective on the society of peoples. The central assumption is that liberal peoples can tolerate non-liberal peoples without forcing them to conform to their standards. In short, toleration functions in the international context as a principle of justice. The focus on toleration is a way of siphoning out negative reasons that liberal societies may have for judging a society of peoples either from an idealized utopian perspective (cosmopolitanism) or from a myopic nationalist perspective (ethnocentrism) which claims that human rights are exclusively the property of well-ordered democratic societies. Rawls' modest claim is that the basic criterion for justifying the legitimacy of law of peoples is a mutual respect for urgent rights. Whatever one may conclude from this minimalist view, and I admit there are many criticisms of it, is that since the criteria for legitimacy have been recognized and established, there is no need or basis for intervention if urgent rights are respected. Quite simply, intervention on the basis defined beyond this limit would be illegitimate, meaning that when urgent rights are not respected there is a basis for intervention.

6.2 Justificatory Minimalism

Following Hobbes, Rawls thought stability could be achieved if one could resolve the isolation and assurance problems. The first problem occurs when individual decisions taken in isolation produce an outcome that is worse for everyone even though the decisions were entirely rational. The assurance problem centres on each person's willingness to cooperate depending on the assurance that all will cooperate.[9]

Rawls' task at the end of *TJ* was to address the problem from the moral, as opposed to Hobbes' instrumental, point of view. The major transition in Rawls' thought occurred when he addressed the fact of pluralism, as we have seen. The recognition of pluralism led to the realization that while there was a plurality of comprehensive positions that were potentially incommensurable, the emergence of the political realm constituted a value sphere that was freestanding. As a consequence, the cooperation necessary for stability could be achieved within the emerging realm of the political. Now when Rawls turns to international law in *The Law of Peoples,* he is still concerned with the stability problem and its political justification and the ongoing development of the realm of the political. Without going into the threefold model constructed for reflection on the society of peoples, suffice it to point to the two criteria for decent hierarchical societies that specify political rules that cut across comprehensive barriers in order to assure stability. Those rules or laws change the way political societies or states have conceived of themselves since the Treaty of Westphalia (1648). It is to the dramatic shift in international law that has

9 J. Rawls, *The Theory of Justice* (2nd edn), Harvard University Press, Cambridge, 1971, pp. 237-238.

occurred since World War II that has become much more demanding than in the past that Rawls first turns as a kind of preliminary statement to establishing the two criteria.

> We must reformulate the powers of sovereignty in light of a reasonable law of peoples and get rid of the right to war and the right to internal autonomy, which have been part of the (positive) international law for the two and a half centuries following the Thirty Years' War, as part of the classical states system.
> Moreover, these ideas accord with a dramatic shift in how international law is now understood. Since World War II international law has become far more demanding than in the past. It tends to restrict a state's right to wage war to cases of self-defense (this allows collective security), and it also tends to limit a state's right to internal sovereignty. The role of human rights connects most obviously with the latter change as part of the effort to provide a suitable definition of, and limits on, a government's internal sovereignty, though it is not unconnected with the first.[10]

Essentially, then, post-World War II international law, among other things, affects the right to war and internal sovereignty. The first constraint is tangentially related to human rights in that states no longer have the right to declare war, or, to put it in another way, they have limited justification for declarations of war. Obviously, the rights of citizens are affected in that, at least in theory, states no longer have reason to demand that citizens go to war if those wars are wars of aggression. However, it is the second criterion that has the most significant association with human rights.

> [A] decent hierarchical people's system of law, in accordance with its common good idea of justice, secures for all members of the people what have come to be human rights. A social system that violates these rights cannot specify a decent scheme of political and social cooperation.[11]

The least we can expect of non-liberal peoples is an acceptance of a list of urgent rights. The important point here is that urgent human rights are not a standard imposed by liberal societies on non-liberal societies, but rather a standard accepted by liberal and non-liberal societies alike as conditions of membership in a society of peoples. As I would like to put it, these are rules that come with the emerging domain of the political on which there should be an overlapping consensus.

---

10 J. Rawls, 'The Law of Peoples', *in Collected Papers*, Harvard University Press, Cambridge, 1999, p. 535.

11 J. Rawls, *The Law of Peoples (with The idea of Public Reason Revisited)*, Harvard University Press, Cambridge, 1999, p. 65.

> Among the human rights are the right to live (to the means of subsistence and security); to liberty (to freedom from slavery, serfdom, and forced occupation, and to a sufficient measure of liberty of conscience to ensure freedom of religion and thought); to property (personal property); and to formal equality as expressed by the rules of natural justice (that is, that similar cases be treated similarly).[12]

Clearly, Rawls has developed a distinctive justification for human rights, a political justification.[13] A political justification can be distinguished from justifications based on natural law, justifications based on appeals to morality, cosmopolitan justifications and purely functional justifications. The problem with natural law justifications is that they are based on universal comprehensive assumptions about anthropology as in the French Rights of Man or the American Declaration of Independence or theology in the case of the natural law doctrine such as that of Aquinas. Equally, both moral and cosmopolitan justifications can be said to rely on comprehensive doctrines, thus denying the fact of pluralism. At the same time, functional justifications, in his view, would not get beyond a modus vivendi. As the domain of the political is freestanding, so political justification is singular. The advantage of this political form of justification is that "Human Rights [. . .] cannot be rejected as peculiarly liberal or special to the Western tradition".[14]

At the same time, political justification can claim universality on political rather than comprehensive grounds.

To be sure, this form of justification rests on a kind of minimalism. However, he still believes human rights can be justified philosophically, moving us beyond a modus vivendi. For Rawls, as there can be a distinction between pluralism and reasonable pluralism, there can be a distinction, as we have seen, between stability and stability for the right reasons. To achieve stability at the level of a modus vivendi, a balance of forces, would mean the achievement of stability on the basis of mere self-interest. Rawls, who eschews political realism, preferring to describe his orientation as one based on a 'realistic utopia',[15] wants stability

12 *Ibid.*

13 For Rawls a political justification avoids the pitfalls of comprehensive doctrines. He states: "These rights do not depend on any particular comprehensive religious doctrine or philosophical doctrine of human nature. The Law of Peoples does not say, *e.g.*, that human beings are moral persons and have equal worth in the eyes of God; or that they have certain moral and intellectual powers that entitle them to have rights. To argue in these ways would involve religious and philosophical doctrines that many descent hierarchical peoples might reject as liberal or democratic, or in some way distinctive of Western political tradition and prejudicial to other cultures." *Ibid.*, p. 68.

14 *Ibid.*, p. 65.

15 Rawls states: "I said that political philosophy is realistically utopian when it extends what are ordinarily thought of as the limits of practical political possibility. Our hope for the future rests on the belief that the possibilities of our social world allow a reasonably just constitutional democratic society living as a member of a just Society of Peoples. An essential step to being reconciled to our social world is to see that such a Society of Peoples is indeed possible." *Ibid.*, p. 124.

for the right reasons. The major point about the two criteria is that they can be affirmed by peoples who are capable of not only acting in their own interests but also taking account of each other. Hence, we can say that there are reasons, public reasons, reasons shared by the society of peoples for endorsing human rights. When this is possible one can say that we have stability for the right reasons.

6.3 Beyond Justificatory Minimalism

Rawls has been criticized for holding a position on human rights that while going beyond the claims of a functionalist position fails to be sufficiently broad to incorporate a range of rights. Certainly, the functionalist argument has something in its favour, at least from an historical point of view. An historical overview of human rights doctrine would conclude that not only were the two criteria regarding war and constraints on internal sovereignty developed after World War II but also a significant expansion of human rights doctrine itself. Among these developments, one must include the Universal Declaration of Human Rights, which Rawls refers to by the way, the conventions on political, civil and racial discrimination, as well as the rights of women, the rights of the child, torture, genocide and apartheid. Every society, liberal or non-liberal, inherits this modern tradition of human rights even though they may adapt to it in different ways. As we have seen, Rawls, in order to meet the dual charges of ethnocentrism on the one hand and imperialism on the other, limits his justification of human rights to the narrow range of urgent rights. At this point we may question whether the two criteria are adequate from a contemporary perspective. A lot has happened in the period since *The Law of Peoples* was written. Allow me to cite a number of developments that challenge the minimalist interpretation.

1. The nation state no longer plays the role it once did, with the result that the line between the national and the global has become less visible.
2. The ethos of democratic culture that Rawls pointed to in his notion of the emergence of the political has continued to develop.
3. The political discourse of public reason has continued to develop beyond national borders in ways he barely detected in *The Law of Peoples.*
4. In the age of social media the culture of democracy may be seen as less of an imposition of a liberal imperialism and more as the object of desire for those oppressed by the tyrannies of oligarchies and dictatorships.
5. Democracy, challenged on the one hand by the contradictions of globalization and oppressed by neo-liberal hegemony on the other, may itself be in jeopardy.

Rather than criticize Rawls for his justificatory minimalism, I embrace the framework he established while attempting to move beyond it. The framework began with his distinction between the comprehensive and the political in which the political was seen as an emerging phenomenon that developed in relationship to overlapping consensus developed into the two-stage theory in the context of the argument for stability and was used to establish the two criteria in *The Law of Peoples*. Contrary to the agonistic critics of Rawls, the political is part of the emerging ethos in which the values of tolerance on the one hand and democracy on the other go hand in hand. This development, contrary to the claims of the cosmopolitans and through the iterations of global justice, provides the basis for a political justification of human rights that avoids the charge of empty universalism as well as naïve ethnocentrism. However, given the development of a world culture, the justificatory claims of the political and the cosmopolitan are coming closer on the very basis of the development of the emerging domain of the political.

7 Human Rights: A Dworkinian View

Dragica Vujadinović

7.1 Introduction

Ronald Dworkin[1] – one of the greatest contemporary political and legal philosophers – has pursued his comprehensive liberal theory for nearly four decades, beginning with the field of philosophy of law in his books *Taking Rights Seriously*,[2] *A Matter of Principle*[3] and *Law's Empire*,[4] followed roughly two decades later by his book *Justice in Robes*.[5] Along the way, Dworkin developed a liberal political theory of justice based on an 'equality of resources' account of justice, set out in the book *Sovereign Virtue – the Theory and Practice of Equality*[6]. In his latest work, *Justice for Hedgehogs*,[7] Dworkin intends to solidify the philosophical foundations of his theory, and especially to illustrate the unity of ethical and moral values as well as more fully develop his conception of the integrity of law, politics and morality.

The concept of human dignity, or the foundational values of equal concern for each human being and equal respect for each individual's attempt to create his own life, have been at the centre of his legal, political and philosophical considerations from the beginning and up to the final articulation of his theory.

His legal and political theories are based on and derived from a moral perspective, in the sense that human dignity is the measure of an appropriate legal and political system. There is a direct correlation between the liberal democratic state's respect for human dignity, as expressed through human rights protection, and its political legitimacy. However, the question of justice must also be taken into account. Dworkin's 'equality of resources account of justice' is another essential component for protecting human dignity, although the political regime could be legitimate even while being to a certain extent unjust. The book *Sovereign Virtue* is devoted to the issue of just economic policy and politics in general. There he recognizes a legitimate government as one that ensures the just redistribution of

1 Ronald Dworkin died on 14 February 2013 at the age of eighty-one. He was widely regarded as one of the most influential philosophers of law and political philosophy of the post-war era of the 20th century, but also of the 21st century.

2 R. Dworkin, *Taking Rights Seriously*, Gerald Duckworth & Co Ltd, London, 1977.

3 R. Dworkin, *A Matter of Principle*, Harvard University Press, Cambridge, Massachusetts, 1985.

4 R. Dworkin, *Law's Empire*, Harvard University Press, Cambridge, Massachusetts, 1986.

5 R. Dworkin, *Justice in Robes*, Harvard University Press, Cambridge, Massachusetts, 2006.

6 R. Dworkin, *Sovereign Virtue – the Theory and Practice of Equality*, Harvard University Press, Cambridge, Massachusetts, London 2000.

7 R. Dworkin, *Justice for Hedgehogs*, Harvard University Press, Cambridge, Massachusetts, London, 2011.

resources; the sovereign is treated as the moral agent (the term also used in other books such as *Law's Empire* and *Freedom's Law)* who is responsible for justice. In other words, the virtue of the sovereign is justice; a government is legitimate when it is just, when it treats citizens from the vantage point of 'the equality of resources account of justice', *e.g.*, when it creates economic and social policy, as well as the legislature in general, in accordance with the principle of justice. In his last book *Justice for Hedgehogs*, he somewhat changes his focus, by pointing to the fact that legitimacy and justice are different virtues. Justice is necessary for the legitimacy of political power, and an extremely unjust distribution of resources combined with extreme poverty can significantly erode political legitimacy. In addition, a*laissez-faire* economy can never be fully just, but as justice is a matter of degree, political legitimacy can also survive in combination with a *laissez-faire* economy – which further implies that a regime can be legitimate even if not and when not fully just.[8]

In accordance with the 'equality of resources account of justice', the sovereign power or coercive political government must secure the just distribution of resources. To be just, the distribution must be "endowment insensitive", or independent from any differences of the individual with regard to social status, natural talents or handicaps on the one hand, and "ambition-sensitive" to personal choices on the other.[9]

According to his book *Sovereign Virtue,* instead of affirming inequalities as legitimate, and instead of accepting the lessening of inequalities as a goal (starting from a realistic view of the actual state of affairs), Dworkin insists upon a utopian ideal of full equality of resources as a legitimate goal for liberal governments and liberal communities.[10] As he says, "[t]his book argues that equal concern requires that government aims at a form of material equality that I have called equality of resources".[11]

In his other books, including the last one, *Justice for Hedgehogs,* the legitimacy of sovereign power has been treated primarily as a question of the quality of legal and political order, which by rule have to be framed in accordance with the requirements of constitutional democracy. However, the measure of overall achievement of any political community aiming to be a constitutional democracy must be the quality of protection and affirmation of basic human rights and, accordingly, the fundamental value of human dignity.

According to Dworkin, political legitimacy is also a matter of degree. The issue is determined by the extent to which constitutional democracy in all its institutional segments functions in favour of protecting human rights and insofar as it affirms the human dignity of each individual citizen. The context of his analysis of political legitimacy is the nation state (US federal states and their federal units are an even more narrow context of analysis). However, this does not suggest that his focus was parochial. Rather, we could

8 Dworkin, 2011, pp. 351-353.

9 Dworkin, 2000, pp. 65-119.

10 *Ibid.*, p. 3.

11 *Ibid.*

assume that Dworkin attempted to present his conception of political legitimacy as an ideal-typical sample for all political communities, which tend to accomplish the form and content of a constitutional democracy. His legal and political theory have been contextually linked with the liberal tradition and constitutional democracy, *e.g.*, the institutional framework of the rule of law and constitutional guarantees against the misuse of the majoritarian will for purposes that are counter to the equal concern and equal respect for each individual or citizen. However, on the other hand, it could be remarked critically that the issue of globalization, and especially of the genesis of the current centrality of human rights within international law, have not been fully considered in Dworkin's theory of political legitimacy.

When speaking about Dworkin's conception of human rights, it has already been mentioned that he considered human rights from the viewpoint of political legitimacy, and starting from the conception of human dignity. He continued developing this conception from his first book *Taking Rights Seriously* until closing the circle of his opus in the last book *Justice for Hedgehogs.* His conception of human rights could be viewed as belonging to the foundationalist/traditionalist conceptions of human rights. These kinds of conceptions understand human rights as expressions of essential features of the human being. The essence of humanity, of being human, is interpreted differently – as human dignity or autonomy of man; also, as linked with basic capabilities of men, basic capacities for acting, or with basic interests.[12]

Dworkin wrote *Taking Rights Seriously* in 1977. That year is interesting because some authors, like Samuel Moyn[13] (Charles Beitz[14] similarly), link the year 1977 with a breakthrough shift in the meaning of human rights and international law. Moyn identifies Carter's presidential inaugural speech in 1977 as the moment in which human rights were designated as crucially relevant for foreign affairs and international politics and law for the first time. Carter's words were: "Because we are free we can never be indifferent to the fate of freedom elsewhere [...] Our commitment to human rights must be absolute". Moyn also mentions that in 1977 the founder of Amnesty International received the Nobel Prize. He argues that this was the beginning of the process of making human rights a global issue in international law, a global social movement, and the focus of widely shared public awareness. This in turn started the process of making human rights the source of justification for humanitarian intervention, and its becoming the new or the last 'utopia'.[15]

A critical approach towards Dworkin's theory of human rights is in the background of this analysis, in the sense that although Dworkin grasped at the mentioned time the centrality

12 *See* J.L. Cohen, 'Rethinking Human Rights, Democracy and Sovereignty in the Age of Globalization', *Political Theory*, Vol. 36, No. 4, 2008, pp. 578-606.

13 S. Moyn, *The Last Utopia: Human Rights in History*, Harvard/Belknap Press, Cambridge, 2010. *See also* S. Moyn, 'Human Rights in History', *The Nation*, 30 August/6 September 2010.

14 C. Beitz, *The Idea of Human Rights*, Oxford University Press, Oxford, 2009.

15 Moyn, 2010, p. 2.

of human rights, he did not, however, catch the novelty of contemporary human rights and international law. The Westphalian concept of the nation state and the system of nation states persisted in Dworkin's view as the framework for human rights considerations. In contrast, other relevant authors, such as the aforementioned Moyn and Beitz, argue that a great shift happened in considering human rights from the 1970s and on. They state that not only the rights of man (as understood in the 18th century) but also universal human rights from the post-World War II era (as expressed in UNDHR, 1948) are primarily conceived as pertaining to domestic rights in the context of the nation state. Further, the UNDHR – despite its international framework and affiliations – kept the focus on the legitimacy of the nation state without a real anticipation of the new transnational political order, or 'supranational governance through law'. Only in the 1970s did international law start fully articulating its focus on individual and human rights-transforming into an area of international concern.[16]

Moyn explains this outburst of interest in human rights in the 1970s as a response to the collapse of universalistic schemes of post-war liberalism and socialism, according to which the construction of human rights exploded as a 'persuasive moral alternative' and the 'last utopia'.[17]

Beitz also insists on the novelty of contemporary human rights, and says that what distinguishes contemporary human rights from earlier conceptions of rights is the idea that 'each person is a subject of global concern'.[18]

I will first present Dworkin's conception of human rights and political legitimacy. Then I will try to place this inherent interpretation into the comparative context of some of the relevant contemporary interpretations and justifications of human rights, in order to delineate achievements and previously mentioned limits of his view on human rights, and of his understanding of the interrelation of human rights and political legitimacy.

16 "In any case, 'human rights' meant something different in the 1940s. Despite its new international significance, its core meaning remained as compatible with the modern state as the older tradition of the domestic rights of man had been. Both were the background principles of nations united by them. In this sense, if in few others, 'human rights' preserved a memory of the 'rights of man and citizen' more than summoning a utopia of supranational governance through law." (*Ibid.*, p. 4). A different opinion on the character and implications of UNDHR is offered by Ari Cohen, in a sense of the continuity of the meaning of human rights and human dignity from the post-World War II era up until nowadays. According to this opinion, the mere practice of building the text of UNDHR showed consensus among representatives of different cultures about the notion of human dignity; the concept of human dignity for all humanity is a very recent development, which stands in the centre of the International Bill of Rights (A. Cohen, *In Defense of Human Rights*, NT: Routledge, London, 2007, pp. 67 and 84)

17 Moyn explains the causes of this shift with certain elements of the new historical context: "To be sure, there were a number of catalysts for the explosion: the search for a European identity outside cold war terms; the reception of Soviet and later Eastern European dissidents by Western politicians, journalists and intellectuals; and the American liberal shift in foreign policy in new, moralized terms, after the Vietnam catastrophe. Equally significant, but more neglected, were the end of formal colonialism and a new view toward the third world. Empire was foreclosed, yet romantic hopes for decolonization were also smashed and the era of 'failed states' was opening." (Moyn, 2010, p. 6.)

18 Beitz, 2009, p. 1.

7.2 Dworkin's Conception of Human Rights and Political Legitimacy

From his first book on human rights, *Taking Rights Seriously*, until now, Dworkin connects the issue of human rights to the issue of political legitimacy (of constitutional democracy).[19] The meaning of taking rights seriously here and in later books is that, in order to be considered legitimate, governments must treat each citizen with equal concern:

> Anyone who professes to take rights seriously, and who praises our Governments for respecting them, must have some sense of what that point is. He must accept, at the minimum, one or both of two important ideas. The first is the vague but powerful idea of human dignity. This idea, associated with Kant [. . .] supposes that there are ways of treating a man that are inconsistent with recognizing him as a full member of the human community, and holds that such treatment is profoundly unjust.[20] The second is the more familiar idea of political equality. This supposes that the weaker members of a political community are entitled to the same concern and respect from their government as the more powerful members have secured for themselves.[21] [. . .] The institution of rights is therefore crucial, because it represents the majority's promise to the minorities that their dignity and equality will be respected [. . .] If the Government does not take rights seriously, then it does not take law seriously either.[22]

In his last book, *Justice for Hedgehogs*, Dworkin most comprehensively theoreticized human rights, and again put the focus on the importance of human rights for nation-state legitimacy.

In his book *Sovereign Virtue – The Theory and Practice of Equality*, Dworkin bases the legitimacy of government behaviour on the so-called two cardinal principles of humanity – equal concern and special responsibility. The first principle, equal concern, requires a government to adopt laws and policies that ensure its citizens' fates do not depend on their economic and social background, gender, race, individual skills or handicaps. The second principle, special responsibility, requires that a government work to connect the individual fates of its citizens to the choices that they have made.[23]

---

19 Dworkin opts for representative democracy, which is constitutional democracy, and not for majoritarian democracy. He also calls it the partnership conception of democracy. According to this conception of democracy, unelected judges and judicial review are not anti-democratic; elected officials and constitutional judges protect individual rights from the majority will. Majoritarian democracy is defective. Legitimacy of the representative government requires a distribution of political power that reflects an equal concern and respect that the community must have for each citizen. The partnership conception is much better from the standpoint of dignity and legitimacy than the crude mathematics of majority rule. (Dworkin, 2011, p. 394).

20 *Ibid.*, p. 198.

21 *Ibid.*, p. 199.

22 *Ibid.*, p. 205.

In *Justice for Hedgehogs*, Dworkin again considers two fundamental principles of humanity, but this time he formulates them as two ethical principles (*i.e.*, principles of individual ethics): the principles of self-respect and of authenticity. The author translates political principles into their ethical analogues. In doing so, he emphasizes that we have an ethical responsibility to create something of positive value out of our lives, and that this ethical responsibility is an objective one. In addition, he argues that our various responsibilities and obligations to others flow from the above-mentioned personal responsibility for our own lives.

These two principles together offer a conception of human dignity. Dignity requires self-respect and authenticity, and dignity helps in identifying the content of personal morality (how we should treat others). As Dworkin says, acts are wrongful if they insult the dignity of others. The principle of dignity demands that we be responsible not only for the success of our lives but also for the lives of others (relational responsibility).

There is an internal connection between individual ethics, personal morality and political morality. Human dignity connects them, and he calls it the 'Kantian principle'.

When Dworkin addresses ethics and personal morality, he studies them through the concept of responsibility, *i.e.,* duties, obligations. From self-respect as the central concept of individual ethics, he turns towards the central concept of personal morality – our duty to aid others and not to harm them, as well as our special duties as individuals towards friends and relatives and the promises that we make to them. Thereafter, in *Justice for Hedgehogs* Dworkin turns back to political morality and political obligations, as a distinct department of value, where impartiality is necessary and where certain individuals have special roles and powers to act on behalf of the community as a whole. Human dignity also expresses two fundamental principles of equal concern and special responsibility, and insofar as is central for political morality and political legitimacy. In addition, closing the circle in this argumentation leads to the concept of human rights.

When speaking about justification, for Dworkin, human rights do not require any justification. They are derivatives of human dignity, and human dignity lies in the basic philosophical foundations of his legal and political theory. Human dignity is, according to him, incontestable; it sums up fundamental principles of humanity, *e.g.*, the intrinsic value of human life, the sacredness of the human being.[24]

In accordance with his theory of an objective truth in the field of values,[25] Dworkin claims absolute truth for the theory of human rights. Basic human rights and human dignity have

23 Dworkin, 2000, pp. 5-6.

24 Ari Cohen puts into question Dworkin's conception of the intrinsic value of the human being, 'secular sacredness' of human dignity, *e.g.*, philosophical and not religious conception of the sacredness of human life and human dignity. (Cohen, 2007, p. 67.) The so-called secular sacredness is contested essentially: "The non-religious foundation that Dworkin proposes, however, is flawed for a variety of reasons, not the least of which is that it misunderstands the concept of sacredness on which it is based." (*Ibid.*, p. 84).

25 R. Dworkin, 'Objectivity and Truth: You Should Better Believe', *Philosophy & Public* Affairs, Vol. 25, No. 2, 1996, pp. 87-139.

a quality of objective truth; they are not true by definition, nor do they follow from some immutable laws of human nature, or Divine law. They should be accepted as uncontested without justification, even though many people disregard them as substantive and objectively true values. The point is that we must accept them because what makes them true for us is our humanity, the fact that we have life to live and to live well, and death to face.[26] Their pivotal position should be accepted as axiomatic.They are universal, but not universally endorsed. However, Dworkin fails to pose the question of what the foundations are for this concept of human dignity.

When compared with the open issues and attempts for justification given in other relevant theories, Dworkin's pledge for the axiomatic character of human dignity and objective truthfulness of human rights does not seem an acceptable position. It seems dogmatic and almost theological, and lacks the capacity to capture different and multiple dimensions of the contemporary practice and theory of human rights.

7.2.1 Political Legitimacy

As already mentioned, justice and human rights are two compatible and complementary dimensions of his considerations of the legitimacy issue. According to *Sovereign Virtue*, justice is a matter of sovereign responsibility to treat each person with equal concern and respect.

When Dworkin comes back to political morality and political legitimacy in *Justice for Hedgehogs*, he puts the focus on human rights and on obligations of the sovereign to secure full respect for the rights of citizens. He says that when it comes to political morality and political legitimacy, rights plainly provide a better focus than duties and obligations, because "individuals have political rights, and some of these rights, at least, are matched only by collective duties of the community as a whole rather than of particular individuals". There is a deep connection between the pivotal idea of political legitimacy, two principles of human dignity and human rights.[27]

According to Dworkin, the principle of legitimacy is the most abstract source of political rights. He sums up the rights-based and morally founded conception of legitimacy:

> Government has no moral authority to coerce anyone, even to improve the welfare, well-being, or goodness of the community as a whole, unless it respects those two requirements [of human dignity]person by person. The principles of dignity therefore state very abstract political rights: they trump

26 R. Dworkin, Keynote Address, Boston University School of Law Symposium, *Justice for Hedgehogs*: A Conference on Ronald Dworkin's Forthcoming Book, September 2009, *Boston University Law Review*, p. 476.

27 Dworkin, 2011, p. 330.

> government's collective policies. We form this hypothesis: All political rights are derivative from that fundamental one. We fix and defend particular rights by asking in much more detail, what equal concern and respect require.[28]

Principles of dignity are directly expressed in political and human rights. The first principle of dignity – the principle of self-respect – is supported by paradigmatic human rights: the rights not to be tortured, discriminated and exposed to blatant prejudices, not to be punished when innocent and the right to due process. These human rights derive from the first principle of human dignity (the principle of self-respect, equal value and equal concern). The rights of free speech and expression, and the rights to conscience, political participation and religious belief, support the second principle of dignity – the principle of authenticity and personal responsibility.

All political rights are trumps of political legitimacy, but no nation turns all political rights into constitutional rights or even ordinary legal rights, and not all political rights represent basic human rights. Dworkin poses the question: what differentiates human rights from other political rights?[29] He concludes that the most basic human right is the right to human dignity, which is in a way the right to an attitude, *e.g.*, "a right to be treated *as* a human being whose dignity fundamentally matters".

> We must therefore insist that though people do have a political right to equal concern and respect on the right conception, they have a more fundamental, because more abstract, right. They have a right to be treated with the attitude that these debates presuppose and reflect – a right to be treated *as* a human being whose dignity fundamentally matters. The more abstract right – the right to an attitude – is the basic human right. Government may respect that basic human right even when it fails to achieve a correct understanding of more concrete political rights – even when its tax structure is, as we think, unjust.[30]

According to him, human rights are those which most fundamentally and most abstractly express and protect human dignity. More concretely, the rights whose violation implies the barbaric endangering of human dignity are basic human rights.

---

28 *Ibid.*, p. 330.

29 Dworkin says: "But how shall we then distinguish human rights from other political rights that also act as trumps? It seems widely agreed that not all political rights are human rights. People who all accept that government must show equal concern for all its members disagree about what economic system that requires. An unfettered free market? Socialism? Redistribution according to some standard or goal? Which standard or goal? Egalitarians, libertarians, and utilitarians each present their opinion as indispensable to genuine freedom and equality. But almost none of them would suggest that the many nations that disagree with his opinion are guilty of human rights violations: libertarians argue that taxation is theft, but few claim that it is a violation of a human right. Why not? Human rights are widely thought to be special and, according to most commentators and to political practice, more important and fundamental. In what way?" (Dworkin, 2011, p. 332).

30 *Ibid.*, p. 335.

Dworkin considers legitimacy a matter of degree. This means that a nation state can be built upon policies and laws that demonstrate a good faith attempt to protect the dignity of a citizen, including *e.g.*, the rule of law, established democracy, judicial review as the constitutional test, free speech and press, adequate police service, etc., and still not be fully legitimate. It can happen that some discriminatory or oppressive laws be enacted (discriminating against minorities, *e.g.*) that can stain the state's legitimacy without destroying it altogether, inasmuch as the political avenues of correction are available (civil disobedience, *e.g.*). However, if the stain is so dark, widespread and resistant to cleansing, legitimacy lapses entirely, and then citizens must contemplate not just civil disobedience but actual revolution.[31]

Dworkin introduces the prospect of revolution into his discourse as a response to the extinguished political obligation in "terrible circumstances [. . .] when a government in power is no longer a legitimate government".[32]

Dworkin also introduces the possibility of international intervention as a legitimate response to barbaric acts and certain drastic cases of human rights violations by nation states.

7.2.2 Human Rights and International Law

Drastic cases of endangering human rights and human dignity include barbaric acts of genocide based on blatant racist prejudices, systemic rapes and torture of victims for contempt or even just for amusement, and other crimes that represent violations of the first principle of dignity (equal human value, equal concern). He says that nations and lawyers disagree about what the first principle of dignity requires, but some judgments do match the world's consensus about the most basic human rights violations.[33] He accepts that when it comes to the second principle of dignity – personal responsibility, different political cultures and states can arrive at different conclusions about how best to secure personal responsibility of individuals. However, governments that punish blasphemy and heresy, or deny, in principle, the right to free speech or of the press, apply torture (which reduces the victim to an animal), allow for punishment without due process, legally forbid a woman's right to property, profession and political participation clearly violate human rights. He concludes:

> Some such acts may be sufficiently serious as to require formal economic and even, if barbaric, military intervention provided the two crucial conditions I described earlier are met. In less grave and more controversial cases the proper forum of enforcement is not an economic or military battleground but the chambers of international courts and tribunals that rely on treaties, international law, or more informal international pressure to secure compliance.[34]

31 *Ibid.*, pp. 321-322.

32 *Ibid.*, p. 321.

33 R. Dworkin, 'Human Rights and International Law', Manuscript, p. 8.

34 Dworkin, 2011, p. 337.

Dworkin makes important comments, mostly in the footnotes, related to concrete authors of relevant conceptions different from his own. For example, he mentions Charles Beitz and James Griffin, who signify the representatives of mutually opposed conceptions (Beitz, together with Rawls, represents the political conception of human rights; Griffin represents the substantive, foundational conception of human rights).
Dworkin implicitly tries to put his own substantive conception of human rights into comparative perspective with the political conception represented by Beitz and Rawls.[35]
According to Dworkin, unpromising are Beitz's attempts to specify human rights from the point of view of interpreting the 'discursive' practice of human rights (that now includes claims in treaties and other international documents, claims of political officials, international associations of states, judicial bodies, non-governmental organizations, and academic discussants, and to distinguish them from the viewpoint of certain principles (*e.g.*, the principle of urgency). Dworkin says that

> interpretation of that kind requires general principles that can fix the best justification of the raw data of that practice, and these must be 'top-down' principles of the kind Beitz wants to avoid.[36]

He agrees with Beitz, that classification of human rights cannot be arbitrary, but must be based on certain standards that would justify an international intervention/sanction in the case of their violation.[37]
The trump-over-sovereignty conception is the name that he gives to the classificatory strategy of the representatives of the so-called political conception of human rights. According to that conception (of Rawls and Beitz), human rights are only those rights which are important enough to trump national sovereignty. In other words,

> if those who claim authority over any territory violate these human rights of people in their power, then other nations are permitted to attempt to stop them by means that would otherwise not be permitted – by economic sanctions or even military invasion.[38]

35 *Ibid.*, p. 333.
36 *Ibid.*, n. 5, pp. 329-335.
37 *Ibid.*
38 "A number of writers have suggested the following classificatory strategy. Human rights are those that trump not merely collective national goals but also national sovereignty understood in a particular way. (This is often called the Westphalian conception of sovereignty because it was prominent in the understanding of the system of nation-states that the Treaties of Westphalia achieved). According to this conception, one nation or group of nations must not interfere in the internal affairs of another nation . . . These writers suggest that we should classify as human rights only those rights important enough to trump national sovereignty on that conception. If those who claim authority over any territory violate these human rights of people in their power, then other nations are permitted to attempt to stop them by means that would otherwise not be permitted – by economic sanctions or even military invasion." (*Ibid.*, p. 333).

Dworkin critically concludes that this trump-over-sovereignty argument sets too high a bar, because international law documents have greatly inflated the category of human rights. He also criticizes the conception as trying to classify human rights as convenient for licensing sanctions according to their substantive content, importance and urgency. He says that this conception implies arbitrariness concerning the merits of substantive importance.

Dworkin suggests a different strategy for differentiating human rights from other political rights, one based on the standards of political legitimacy, namely, respect for the two principles of dignity, respect for an abstract right to an attitude.

However, in the conceptions of both Dworkin and Beitz – which start at opposite poles according to their presuppositions – the consequence is that only those rights that are important enough to trump national sovereignty and to justify international (humanitarian) intervention, do represent human rights proper.

After his last book, *Justice for Hedgehogs,* Dworkin released the article 'Human Rights and International Law',[39] which he had previously not authorized for quoting and left unpublished. In this text, however, he mostly repeats his ideas from *Justice for Hedgehogs*, from chapters on 'Legitimacy'[40] and 'Political Rights and Concepts'.[41] What is different in this text compared with *Justice for Hedgehogs* is that he moves the footnoted comments on Griffin and Beitz into the main text.

It is worth mentioning that this unpublished text, in spite of its almost unchanged content when compared with *Justice for Hedgehogs*, through its new title 'Human Rights and International Law' probably indicates Dworkin's intention (though unrealized and, unfortunately, unrealizable any more) to locate his own conception more interactively with and closer to current discussions about human rights as the focus of the international law.

In contrast to the above-mentioned political theories of human rights, Dworkin still considers human rights in the context of the so-called Westphalian model of nation states. From *Taking Rights Seriously* to*Justice for Hedgehogs,* he considers human rights primarily from the point of view of nation-state legitimacy. The violation of human rights leads primarily to the conception of civil disobedience and, in the last instance, revolution. Dworkin does consider in his last book the issue of barbaric acts as causes of justified international intervention; however, he does not do it substantially, *i.e.,* he does it without ever substantially reconsidering his nation-state framework of analysis.

39 Dworkin, *supra* note 33, pp. 2-3. *See also* Dworkin, 2011, pp. 321-322.

40 Dworkin, 2011, pp. 321-322.

41 *Ibid.*, pp. 332-344.

7.3 The Nature and Justification of Human Rights – Comparative Approach

7.3.1 Classification of Theories of Human Rights

Rainer Forst describes the various grounds of justification for human rights: he differentiates between ethical justification (Griffin's), political–legal (Earls, Beitz) and 'justificatory minimalism' – intercultural toleration (Raz, Joshua Cohen, Vincent).[42] According to his classification, Dworkin's conception belongs within the scope of the ethical justification.

Joseph Raz speaks critically about ethical doctrine, which includes in itself some theories that manifest a traditionalist approach – which consider human rights as important rights that are grounded in our humanity. Dworkin's conception would obviously fit this type well. He remarks that some theories of this nature offer a way to understand human rights, which "is so remote from the practice of human rights as to be irrelevant to it".[43]

Charles Beitz differentiates – in contradistinction to his political conception of human rights – 'naturalistic' and 'agreement' theories about what human rights are, assuming that both views seek to understand human rights as expressions of certain abstract ideas.[44] He calls into question the naturalistic conceptions, according to which human rights are entitlements that belong to people 'by nature' or 'simply by virtue of their humanity'. Obviously, Dworkin's conception fits here as well. Beitz also criticizes theories according to which human rights are objects of agreement among diverse moral and political cultures.[45] He defines, in contrast to both theories, human rights as

> an emergent discursive practice consisting of a set of norms for the regulation of the conduct of governments and a range of actions open to various agents for which a government's failure to abide by these norms supplies reasons.[46]

---

42 R. Forst, 'The Justification of Human Rights and the Basic Right to Justification: A Reflexive Approach', *in* C. Coraddetti (Ed.), *Philosophical Dimensions of Human Rights – Some Contemporary Views*, Springer, Dordrecht/Heidelberg/London/New York, 2012, pp. 3-21.

43 J. Raz, 'Human Rights Without Foundations', *in* S. Besson & J. Tasioulas (Eds.), *The Philosophy of International Law*, Oxford University Press, Oxford, 2010, pp. 321-337.

44 Beitz, 2009, p. 48.

45 *Ibid.*, p. 10.

46 Beitz adds: "To put the point generally, human rights not only function as standards to which the international community may hold each country's institutions accountable. They also operate as goals of political change for nongovernmental actors and as a global analog of the public conception of justice found in well-ordered domestic societies. [. . .] No analysis of human rights that did not capture this aspirational aspect would be faithful to the hopes of the framers of modern human rights doctrine or the roles that human rights have come to play in the discourse of global politics today." (*Ibid.*, p. 44.).

Beitz defines human rights by founding them in the practice of contemporary international law.

Jean Cohen[47] counterposes 'traditional' and 'political' conceptions of human rights. The first construes human rights as moral rights that all people have due to some basic feature of interests, which are deemed intrinsically valuable.[48] The traditionalist ones could function until the end of 1980s, but from 1989 onwards human rights discourse acquired a new function, related to the justification of sanctions, military invasions and enforcement of international law against violators of human rights.

Jean Cohen accepts the 'political' conception of human rights; however, she develops that conception differently from the way Rawls and Beitz do. She introduces a distinction between internal and external legitimacy. She insists on a dual system of international law, including, on the one hand, the language of human rights addressed to domestic politics through citizens' struggles, and on the other the discourse of enforcement linked to specific human rights, which can attain the status of hard international legal norms that suspend sovereignty in certain cases.[49]

Cohen would certainly classify Dworkin as belonging to the traditional conception, with the consequence that his theory does not manage to explain new meanings and functions of human rights discourse. In addition, his conception of political legitimacy could grasp neither theoretically nor practically Cohen's differentiations between internal and external legitimacy.

7.3.2 The Issue of Founding Human Rights

According to Dworkin, human rights express (morally, legally, politically) the basic value of human dignity, and they represent the main criterion, the "trump" of political legitimacy of the given sovereign, nation-state government.

Beitz wants to capture the novel aspects of the contemporary meaning and practice of human rights. The most important novelty of contemporary human rights, according to him, is the idea that "each person is a subject of global concern".[50] He starts with contemporary human rights practice as we find it and tries to clarify the normative discipline implicit in the practice. He maintains that human rights should be understood in terms of "a public normative practice with global scope" whose central concern is to protect individuals against the inconvenient actions of their governments. He also finds novel the

47 J. Cohen, "Rethinking Human Rights, Democracy, and Sovereignty in the Age of Globalization", *Political Theory*, Vol. 36, No. 4, 2008, pp. 578-606.

48 *Ibid.*, p. 578.

49 *Ibid.*, p. 588.

50 Beitz, 2009, p. 1.

"normative breadth of provisions included in the various postwar human rights documents".[51] He defines human rights as functioning not only

> as standards to which the international community may hold each country's institutions accountable. They also operate as goals of political change for non-governmental actors and as a global analog of the public conception of justice found in well-ordered domestic societies [. . .] No analysis of human rights that did not capture this aspiration aspect would be faithful to the hopes of the framers of modern human rights doctrine or to the roles that human rights have come to play in the discourse of global politics today.[52]

Beitz refuses foundationalist considerations, which attempt to posit a certain moral order that exists independently from current international doctrine and practice. Beitz would certainly have placed Dworkin in this foundationalist, naturalistic framework.
He criticizes naturalistic theories as inconvenient for capturing the contemporary practice and discourse of human rights. Griffin, with his idea of human dignity and personhood, as well as Martha Nussbaum and Amartya Sen, with their ideas about human rights as protections of 'basic human capabilities' all belong to this group.[53] One of the problems with these doctrines, according to Beitz, is that their normative content falls short of the list of protection actually found in international human rights doctrine.
Beitz also criticizes the 'common core' theory (of Walzer, with thick and thin moralities), and 'overlapping consensus' theories (of Martha Nusbaum, Charles Teylor and Daniel Bell), as well as theories about the 'progressive convergence' (as the basis of intercultural agreement).[54] Beitz declares himself a follower of Rawls' political conception of human rights, as articulated in *Laws of the Peoples*.[55] He says that reasoning analogously with Rawls' conception of justice,

> one might think that although people disagree about the content of human rights, they may agree about the role of human rights in practical reasoning about the conduct of global political life. The role defines the concept of human right. As Rawls understands them, human rights are standards whose satisfaction guarantees a society against external intervention and is necessary for acceptance as a cooperating member of the Society of Peoples.[56]

51 *Ibid.*, pp. 1, 14 and 212. *See also* J. Flynn, 'Human Rights in History and Contemporary Practice: Source Materials for Philosophy', *in* Coraddetti, 2012, pp. 11-12.

52 Beitz, 2009, p. 44.

53 *Ibid.*, pp. 47-72.

54 *See*, *ibid.*, p. 87.

55 *Ibid.*, pp. 97-102.

56 *Ibid.*, p. 100.

Beitz concludes that in Rawls, and generally in the political conception, human rights function as a standard of international legitimacy.[57]
Beitz, however, remarks that Rawls' view of the practical role of human rights is far more limited than what is observable in practice.

> The difficulty is that this view of the practical role of human rights is so much more limited than what we observe in present practice. For example, Rawls does not describe human rights as entitlements enforceable in national constitutions, as they are sometimes regarded in the regional human rights courts and as they were imagined by some of the framers of the declaration. There is no provision for practices of international monitoring, reporting and censure (though perhaps there might be). He notices but does not incorporate the broad array of non-coercive political and economic measures used by states and international organizations to influence the internal affairs of societies where human rights are threatened. He does not represent human rights as justifications for individuals and nongovernmental organizations to engage in reform oriented political action.[58]

He concludes that human rights are standards for domestic institutions whose satisfaction is a matter of international concern.[59] In addition,

> since human rights are supposed to be capable of guiding political action by agents external to the societies in which they are breached, it must be shown that any candidate human right is a suitable object of international concern.[60]

According to Beitz, the practice of human rights is part of the global normative order (including laws like norms, background norms and principles, and international treaty law).[61]
As already remarked, Dworkin does not capture this specific character of contemporary human rights as trans-national, as a matter of global concern supported by the changed character of international law in comparison with the Westphalian model.
James Griffin[62] identifies the grounds for human rights within historical tradition in the "the dignity of the human person", with the basic idea that human rights mean securing and protecting the high value we place on 'personhood', and that having rights stems from being human. Kantian resonance is present in the concept that the 'dignity of our status' as human beings is tied to our capacities for reason and freedom. He defines personhood in

57 "Adherence to human rights is necessary for a society to be a member of the Society of the Peoples and sufficient to guarantee a society against reform oriented intervention." (Beitz, 2009, p. 100).
58 *Ibid.*, p.101.
59 *Ibid.*, p. 128.
60 *Ibid.*, p. 140.
61 *Ibid.*, pp. 209-212.
62 J. Griffin, *On Human Rights*, Oxford University Press, Oxford, 2008.

terms of the need to protect our autonomy, liberty and welfare, and he further derives specific rights from these highest-level values. Griffin admits a certain shift in the meaning of human rights and tries to meet the challenge of relating his theory to contemporary practice; however, he does not grasp the connection between the changing content of human rights, social movements and struggles. He also lacks an explanation for discontinuities in the politics of human rights (about which Beitz and Moyn talk).[63]

Dworkin speaks about human dignity in a foundationalist way similar to Griffin. Therefore, Dworkin is vulnerable to the same objections. Dworkin also undermines social struggles as a referential framework for human rights development.

For Habermas, there is continuity between social struggles for human dignity in 18th-century revolutions and contemporary international dimensions of human rights. Struggles for human dignity make violations of dignity visible and push the protection of human rights forward within nation states as well as beyond national boundaries. Therefore, there is historical continuity as in Griffin, but – contrary to Griffin – he also links human dignity with the dynamic character of human rights and their development through struggles.[64]

Habermas argues[65] that the changing post-World War II conditions and the enactment the UNDHR put human dignity and the worth of each human being into the centre of international law and national constitutions.[66] He further argues that appealing to human dignity made it easier to reach an overlapping consensus during the founding of the UN and during negotiations for human rights agreements and international legal conventions.[67] Habermas remarks that these changing historical conditions made us aware of something that was inscribed in human rights from the outset, and that is the normative substance of the equal dignity of every human being, which only human rights addresses explicitly.

Habermas also specifies a modern meaning of human dignity as very much different from the pre-modern status-dependent human dignity. The modern one becomes universal human dignity, and universalization is accompanied by individualization. Dworkin would certainly agree with this explanation.[68]

Habermas says: "Human dignity, which is one and the same everywhere and for everyone, grounds the indivisibility of all categories of human rights",[69] a statement that Dworkin would affirm.

---

63 *See* Flynn, 2012, pp. 13 and 17.

64 *See, ibid.*, p. 17.

65 J. Habermas, 'The Concept of Human Dignity and the Realistic Utopia of Human Rights', *in* Corradetti, 2012, pp. 63-81.

66 *Ibid.*, p. 64.

67 *Ibid.*, p. 65.

68 *Ibid.*, p. 66.

69 *Ibid.*, p. 67.

Dworkin does mention the post-World War II era and the role of the UN in founding the importance of human rights,[70] but more often speaks about human rights either abstractly (seemingly in a timeless way) or in a sense of locating them within the liberal context in general.
Habermas discusses the 'Janus face' of human rights, in a sense that human rights have a moral as well as a legal dimension, *e.g.*, that they contain a moral promise of equal respect, which is also spelled out in concrete legal terms. He says that human rights circumscribe that part of morality which *can* be translated into the medium of coercive law and become political reality in the robust shape of civil rights.[71]
Dworkin might not agree with the 'Janus-face' characterization of this duality, but he would fully agree that moral and legal dimensions are indivisible in human rights; even more, in Dworkin's conception, all legal norms have been part of political morality. Habermas insists, and Dworkin would concur, that it is important to retain the connection between the moral basis of human rights and its legal expression in civil rights, which is preferable to the minimalist approach to human rights justification (the one given in political terms, differently but in the same matrix of thought by Rawls, Beitz, Raz, etc.).[72]
Habermas adds a dynamic dimension into his analysis of human rights, namely the fact of human rights emerging as a result of pressure from social violent and revolutionary struggles, but also initiated by civil movements/civil society.
This dynamic dimension of human rights has, however, been, put aside in Dworkin's case. It could be explained with Dworkin's insisting on the integrity approach, which might contribute a bit to the hermetic and static outcomes of his thought.
Rainer Forst,[73] like Habermas, rejects the idea of a philosophical derivation of the substantive content of human rights. He favours the approach that stresses the importance of political participation ("deeper normative grammar of human rights"), and which connects the French Declaration of 1789 and the Universal Declaration of Human Rights of 1948. Concerning social struggles, he puts into question the focus on external interventions related to human rights violations, and rehabilitates the importance of the internal perspective as well.

70 "Human rights have had good press since the Second World War. Dozens of human rights conventions and treaties have been signed, among them the Universal Declaration of Human Rights enacted by the United Nations General Assembly in 1948, the European Convention on Human Rights, and the Cairo Declaration of Human Rights. Hundreds of books, monographs, and studies on the subject have been published. Some people and some institutions use the phrase casually and even hyperbolically [...] I use the phrase in a stronger way that matches the strong sense of a political right: to designate a trump." (Dworkin, 2011, p. 332).

71 *Ibid.*, p. 68.

72 There is one more similarity between Habermas and Dworkin's conception that equality and liberty equally represent main/indivisible liberal principles. Habermas warns about dangers related to the world trend (not only existent in the USA, Great Britain and Europe but elsewhere) of squaring an autonomous life of citizens primarily through guarantees of economic liberties; he says that this trend leads to destroying the balance between different categories of basic rights.

73 Forst, 2012, pp. 81-106.

As already mentioned, Forst elucidates the different grounds of justification of human rights. He differentiates the ethical justification (Griffin's), political–legal (Earls, Beitz) and 'justificatory minimalism' – intercultural toleration (Raz, Joshua Cohen, Vincent).
Forst says that he wants to promote a fourth approach, which is more appropriate than the first foundationalist approach – which highlights the normative core of human rights as protecting basic human interests – or the second, which prioritizes their role in international law, or the third approach, which claims to be universally justifiable across different cultures and ethical ways of life. He connects human rights as an expression of human dignity with the basic right to justification, *e.g.*, with the republican pledge for political participation in favour of protection and grounding of autonomy, and with the reflexive quality of mutual respect (practical implications) and normative implications (moral justification of human rights).[74]
According to Forst,[75] human rights are not claims to certain substantive 'goods' but to a certain social and political standing of persons as 'norms-givers'. He adds that

> the notion of 'dignity' that lies at the heart of such a conception of human rights is not metaphysical or ethical one, combined with a doctrine about the good life. Rather, dignity means that a person is to be respected as someone who is worthy of being given adequate reasons for actions or norms that affect him or her in a relevant way.[76]

Dworkin could have accepted such an approach to justification if he had wanted to conduct justification. While he did not at all intend to provide justification for human rights other than related to the political legitimacy of the nation state, and based on principles of human dignity, his conception fits the first group of theories of human rights, which Forst calls foundationalist and oriented towards an ethical justification, and which Jean Cohen calls 'traditionalist'.
Forst's conception of human dignity, and of justification of human rights through reflexive discursive practice and through political expression of the right to justification could have resonated with Dworkin's ideas, and could have served to push Dworkin to capture better and more comprehensively the challenges of the contemporary theory and political practice of human rights.
However, Jeffrey Flynn critically remarks that both Habermas and Forst, by focusing too much on an internal perspective, risk missing "something essential about the

74 "[T]he main *function* of human rights is to guarantee, secure and express each person's status as an equal given his or her right to justification. The republican meaning of human rights I alluded to above locates their legal and political role in that protection and in the grounding of political autonomy – or 'sovereignty'[. . .]." (*Ibid.*, p. 100.).

75 *Ibid.*, p. 99.

76 *Ibid.*, p. 100.

contemporary meaning of human rights: the external perspective that captures the idea that 'the world is watching'".[77] The same kind of critique applies to Dworkin as well.
Flynn also tries to retain the historical connections of the rights of man from the 18th century with universal rights established in the mid-20th century, on the one hand, with contemporary human rights which attained a global, trans-national dimension and linkage with humanitarian interventionism, on the other.
He asks:

> Is it possible to develop a conception of human rights that captures the dynamic elements of an 'emergent global practice' (Beitz) without losing sight of the 'historical notion' (Griffin) of human rights?

He says that the struggle for human rights has to be captured in the philosophical theory of human rights as related to both external and internal perspective (in the 18th century, in the 20th and in the future).[78]
He also insists on the need to distinguish humanitarianism from human rights.[79] The point is, "Viewing human rights strictly through a humanitarian lens runs the risk of viewing others merely as objects of suffering and not as subjects of rights".[80] Moreover,

> When the status of those internal agents is taken seriously, this form of activism keeps in view the idea that the ultimate aim must be to go beyond viewing others as merely objects of concern or pity to viewing them as subjects of rights.[81]

Ari Cohen argues more in a historical than philosophical manner that common convictions among different traditions that arose during deliberations of the UN representatives from different countries and different religious and cultural backgrounds during the Universal Declaration drafting process clearly demonstrated that "there is substantial cross-cultural agreement on the idea of human rights upon which the UDHR could be built".[82]

77 Flynn adds: "Do Habermas and Forst give enough credence to the extent to which the global human rights movement is central to the meaning and practice of human rights today and that this global movement is defined as much (if not more) by struggles *on behalf of the rights of others* as it is by those struggling for their own rights?" (Flynn, 2012, p. 19).

78 *Ibid.*

79 Forst does not accept Beitz's approach, which starts from the given political practice, including humanitarian interventionism. He proposes first finding out or constructing a justifiable set of human rights that a legitimate political authority has to respect and guarantee. According to him, only *then* can we ask what kinds of legal structures are required at the international level; only *after* we have to think about and set up legitimate institutions of possible intervention (as measures of last resort). "Human rights do not serve primarily to limit internal 'autonomy' or 'sovereignty' (Rawls uses both terms) but to ground internal legitimacy. The claim to external respect depends on internal respect based on justified acceptance; however, one can not infer the legitimacy of intervention [. . .] directly from a lack of internal acceptance." (*Ibid.*, p. 93).

80 *Ibid.*, p. 20.

81 Flynn, 2012, p. 21.

82 Cohen, 2007.

The author adds that "it is more than this cross-cultural understanding that human beings have dignity that grounds the contemporary human rights regime":

> And yet, I also want to argue that for the notion that human beings possess dignity seems to open the door to yet another question; that is, one must wonder from where we have acquired this dignity.[83]

Ari Cohen discusses whether the concept of dignity – like its religious coeval, sacredness – can be understood in the absence of a religious cosmology:

> [I] want to argue that the Universal Declaration represents a much greater achievement. It is not simply that no single tradition was victorious in setting out the foundation of human rights that others could accept, though it is true that none was; instead, the Declaration's virtue is that everyone was able to agree upon and endorse a *common* foundation: the dignity of the human person.[84]
> I want to argue that that it is the experience of coming to consensus on the question of foundation of human rights that provides the concept's grounding.[85]

Cohen concludes:

> The nations of the world may disagree on a great many things – philosophical as well as practical – but they have all agreed on this important point: every human being is entitled to the rights enshrined in the Universal Declaration by virtue of the inherent dignity that is common to us all [. . .] In constructing this consensus, then, we have succeeded in establishing a practical non-religious foundation upon which the idea of human rights can rest.[86]

7.4 Conclusion

Just to repeat with critical implications, Dworkin – in contrast to those who make an effort to justify the concept of human dignity – takes for granted the concept of human dignity and has been building on it his entire theoretical construction of the integrity of law, morality and politics. He considers human rights to be universal, timeless, abstract and founded in human dignity.

83 *Ibid.*, p. 138.
84 *Ibid.*, p. 144.
85 *Ibid.*, p. 145.
86 *Ibid.*, p. 151.

We can critically remark that this, so to say, no-need-for-justification argument, represents a serious manifold of Dworkin's conception of human rights and human dignity. He gives a static character to human rights, while undermining social struggles as a referential framework for human rights development. In his considerations, human rights and human dignity are not related to emerging political practices and dynamism either in the context of the nation state or in the global context.

Dworkin does not grasp the shift in the meaning of human rights, *e.g.* their becoming a matter of global concern. He does recognize the centrality of human rights in contemporary political history and does "take human rights seriously" from the 1970s and during more than 40 years of his fruitful theoretical work. However, his books – right from *Taking Rights Seriously* to *Justice for Hedgehogs* – do not resonate fully and substantially with the shift to centrality of human rights from the nation-state context to the international one, as well as the shift in the meaning of internal legitimacy and its relation with the external one. The Westphalian perspective of international law persists in his theory of human rights.

He does not properly consider a difference between internal and external legitimacy; he primarily focuses on the internal legitimacy of the liberal-democratic state, and does not offer a theoretical framework for understanding human rights from the current perspective of international law.

Dworkin's integrity of law, politics and morality approach brings with itself qualities of an admirably coherent and inherently rounded off position; however, it also bears the danger of becoming a conception that is too hermetic (self-satisfied and self-sufficient) to really resonate with the most lively contemporary discussions and current changes in the present practice.

Through his long-lasting and constant attempt to develop a comprehensive and integrated conception of the most relevant concepts of political and legal philosophy, Ronald Dworkin became one of the most relevant political and legal philosophers of the 20th century and beginning of the 21st century. On the other hand, paradoxically, his constant insistence on interpretative coherence and integrity became – quite contrary to Dworkin's intentions – a limitation for the comprehensive capacities of his theory, including his conception of human rights and political legitimacy.

Even a modest attempt to present the theoretical results of Ronald Dworkin, alongside a comparative analysis of his and other relevant authors' conceptions of human rights, could help to envision the contemporary relevance of the Dworkinian perspective, as well as to open up space for critical considerations of the inherent limitations of his theoretical legacy.

8 Legal Claims, Side Constraints and the Principle of Liberty: A Libertarian Perspective on Human Rights

Axelle Reiter

8.1 Introduction

This chapter is meant to provide an analytical understanding of the concept of rights, which matches that embodied in international human rights norms and the international 'constitutionalization' process. Any analytical examination of what constitutes a right needs to dwell on several key questions, whose answers make up the formal components of the concept. First, who are the holders or the beneficiaries of the rights? And what does it mean, theoretically and practically, to hold a right? Then, what are right-claims; namely, what is their structure, their nature, their function, their scope and their content? Third, who are the addressees of those claims? And what are the corollary duties obliging each of them? Besides, additional issues ought to be tackled when dealing with legal rather than moral rights. Chiefly, what is the connection, if any, and the relation between the two; *i.e.*, between purely positivistic and meta-legal rights? What is the legal source of the rights invoked? And, finally, how are they sanctioned and by which means of enforcement? All these queries must be addressed in order to understand the meaning of human rights and their impact on the evolution of the international system.
In view of the contemporary entrenchment of human rights norms in general public international law, the following analysis builds on the liberal and cosmopolitan vision of democracy present in the United Nations Charter. This implies the primacy of individual entitlements over majoritarian preferences and the authority of the international community as a whole over its member states. Such a context requires a neutral and rights-based approach to law and justice, which entails in turn a deontological conception of human rights as side constraints on personal actions. Basic rights are, subsequently, defined as individual spheres of power or choice, priority of which overwrites all other concerns. This allows to escape their instrumentalization and the risks of utilitarian trade-offs, as well as paternalist and moralist encroachments upon people's exercise of their liberty. The issue of the co-possibility of human rights and of the adjudication of conflicts among rights is raised next. It is argued that such clashes are to be avoided by an appropriate

characterization of the competing claims and a strict hierarchy between the various liberties protected. As a result, individual freedoms are only limited by the symmetric rights of others, in cases where they are abused for liberticidal purposes. As a matter of principle, any departure from this general rule of liberty is unjustifiable.

8.2 Neutrality, Liberal Sovereignty and Cosmopolitanism

Legal cosmopolitanism is characterized by its individualism, universality and generality. First, it is concerned with individual human beings, rather than any more overreaching entity. Second, it considers every single person equally, independent of their attachment to a particular group. Third, the rights and obligations that arise from the respect due to human beings bind all legal actors, be they individual or collective agents. Interestingly, classical liberalism and libertarianism are built on a similar defiance from state power as cosmopolitanism. It is ultimately founded on a fervent and all-encompassing individualism.[1] The self is insulated from the political, and epistemologically or conceptually prior to it, and the allegiance of individuals to any supposedly shared enterprise they did not actually consent to is strongly contested. This results in a rejection of both the impersonal determination of what is valuable and the belief in an objective moral order.[2] Hence, "what is good is good ultimately because it is preferred, and it is good from the standpoint of those and only those who prefer it".[3]

Liberal philosophy takes seriously on "the dual challenge of value subjectivity and the need for normativity".[4] In the absence of an objective or non-relativistic determination of morality, state authorities are supposed to remain rigorously neutral when faced with clashing conceptions of the good life. This implies some absence of public bias towards any single one of the competing projects and aspirations held in the country.[5] It leads directly to a general principle of strict neutrality, whose violation also breaches a wider commitment to justice.[6] Liberal neutrality transposes the need for a consensus on the question of 'what is correct' from the substantial level to a higher plane, and it provides an answer to this question at the stage of identification of who holds the ultimate power of decision, in "agreeing to let people decide for themselves".[7] Nothing is held intrinsically valuable, aside from

1 N. P. Barry, *On Classical Liberalism and Libertarianism*, McMillan, Houndmills, 1986, p. 4.

2 *See*, on the incompatibility between free will, or individuality, and the mere notion of an objective morality R. Nozick, *Philosophical Explanations*, Clarendon, Oxford, 1981, pp. 354-355 and 448.

3 D. Gauthier, *Morals by Agreement*, Oxford University Press, Oxford, 1986, p. 59.

4 E. Mc Donald, *Framing the Legal within the Post-Foundational: International Law and Ethics after the Critical Challenge* (Ph.D. Thesis, European University Institute, Florence, 2006), p. 83.

5 Etymologically, the idea of 'neutrality' comes from the laws of war, where it designated the abstentionist position of third parties to the conflict. Accordingly, the notion of non-intervention or non-interference lies at the very core of the concept, which forbids meddling in the legitimate concerns of others.

6 R. Nozick, *Anarchy, State, and Utopia*, Basic, New York, 1974, pp. 33 and 272-273.

7 D. Schmidtz, *Elements of Justice*, Cambridge University Press, Cambridge, 2006, p. 6.

the subjective value individuals attach to it. In the absence of any objective or rational way to determine the good, and in the presence of ideological clashes and differences of opinions, the only open avenue to prevent the development of countless irresoluble feuds remains that of letting each person determine for herself the meaning of it all, or lack of it. Normativity then re-emerges at the level of the protection of personal choices and, indeed, free will. It becomes a question of power sharing and of defending individuals from coercive attempts at superimposing a pre-established vision of the good over their own.

By recognizing her equal moral agency, liberal neutrality leaves to each human being a private sphere of action, which is shielded from the demands of majoritarian interests or public moralism, and where she can develop her own personal conception of the good life. Thereby, far from undercutting freedom, it reconciles subjectivism and justice through the consecration at a meta-level of a principle of equal liberty, which becomes the keystone of the entire social edifice; where each person is equally free to find out value and meaning on her own terms. Although justice is not associated with any substantive or material requirement, it is not empty or content free but it relies on "the actual preferences expressed by actual people".[8] Definite content is provided by each individual for herself, and social cohesion is reached by relying on common rules on a secondary plane, that of the attribution of various prerogatives and competences. So adjudication depends on the respect of second order norms and the division of power into various spheres of sovereignty. Besides, "all interferences require special justification while respect for individual liberty is justified by itself".[9]

The methodological individualist analysis of social interactions in terms of individual actions leads to the ethical individualistic claim that "all social, economic, legal, and political relations must be reconstructed in terms of agreements based on reciprocal consent or contract".[10] This might explain why so many liberal theorists are starting from situations akin to the state of nature and use mechanisms such as the social contract, in an attempt to provide some legitimacy – derived from the foundational value of individual consent and, thus, ultimately from the premises of voluntarism – to the institutional structure that they finally advocate. From this position, the polity cannot validly claim any other competences than those which result from the aggregation of previously existing rights transferred to it by their individual holders.[11] No entitlements or obligations exist at the societal level, unless they are derived from rights and duties held in the first place by individuals. Just institutions, both at the trans-national and at the municipal level, emerge from the antecedent rights of individuals.

---

8 W. Sadurski, *Moral Pluralism and Legal Neutrality*, Kluwer, Dordrecht, 1990, pp. 90 and 165.

9 *Ibid.*, pp. 89-90.

10 C. Chwaszcza, *Moral Responsibility and Global Justice: A Human Rights Approach*, Nomos, Baden-Baden, 2007, pp. 55-58 and 148.

11 Nozick, 1974, pp. 89-90, 115, 118 and 133-134.

At the international level, the possibility emerges for unmediated individual claims addressed directly to the international community, leading to a new concept of liberal sovereignty, where states' "sovereignty is not absolute and includes respect for its legal limitations",[12] and of legitimacy. Incontestably, "sovereignty is only a name given to so much of the international field as is left by law to the individual action of states".[13] As peremptory international norms or *ius cogens*, together with the interdiction of aggression, fundamental rights determine the limits of law's legitimacy and the democratic character of the polity. They "serve as constraints on which institutions we should have"[14] and as standards of legality of municipal organs. A legitimate state is a rights-respecting state, and democratic institutions are institutions protective of basic rights. In this perspective, human rights constitute a sort of Hartian rule of recognition of the international legal order; namely, they serve as criteria for the validity at the supranational level of each and every legal provision otherwise adopted.

8.3 Individual Spheres of Power, ius in rem and erga omnes Obligations

Right-based theories are usually contrasted with those that root the foundations of political philosophy in a set of goals or duties. Right-based philosophies are built on the consecration of some form of private sovereignty and are concerned with the autonomy of individual actions rather than with their conformity to external standards. Crucially, they protect the value of each individual's independent thought, free choice and voluntary agency.[15] In consequence, "the concept of a right is primitive in theories where it has the special role of defending people's freedom to hold and implement different, often mutually incompatible", visions of what is good, right or just. Conversely, theories that do not either give precedence to personal liberty over all other values or set apart individual moral sovereignty are essentially duty-based and not right-based.[16] Furthermore, because of their consecration of the principle of self-sovereignty, right-based theories empower each and every individual with a veto over those acts and measures that interfere with his or her personal choices; which denotes an attachment to unanimity, rather than majority, as a requirement for social or political decisions. Intrinsically, a right is "a claim that gives its possessor a kind of veto power". Provided everyone holds the right, it "places a condition

12 D. Türk, 'Reflections on Human Rights, Sovereignty of States and the Principle of Non-Intervention', *in* M. Bergsmo (Ed.), *Essays in Honour of Asbjorn Eide: Human Rights and Criminal Justice for the Downtrodden*, Nijhoff, Leiden, 2003, p. 765.

13 H.L.A. Hart, *The Concept of Law*, Clarendon, Oxford, 1961, pp. 215-216 and 256.

14 R.G. Frey, 'Act-Utilitarianism, Consequentialism and Moral Rights', *in* R.G. Frey (Ed.), *Utility and Rights*, Blackwell, Oxford, 1985, p. 63.

15 R. Dworkin, *Taking Rights Seriously*, Duckworth, London, 1977, p. 172; R. Dworkin, 'The Original Position', 1973 *University of Chicago Law Review*, p. 523.

16 A. Ingram, *A Political Theory of Rights*, Oxford University Press, Oxford, 1994, p. 10.

of unanimous acceptability, in this respect, on action".[17] In view of this, a general right to liberty knows no other limits than the liberty of others. Hence, the recognition of broad human rights eventually entails an adhesion to John Stuart Mill's 'principle of liberty' or 'harm principle'.[18] More radically, this logically leads to the connection, exposed by Robert Nozick, between the acknowledgement that "individuals have rights, and there are things no person or group may do to them without violating their rights", and the question of philosophical anarchism.[19]

While goal-based theories are teleological and duty-based theories deontological, both are concerned with the drafting of primary content-loaded norms, in the sense that they define the good or the right in accordance with a set of general social concerns. By opposition, right-based theories define justice or the right through the elaboration of 'secondary' rules, which are content-free and deal solely with the boundaries of personal powers and the adjudication of competing claims. Metaphorically, they settle the confines of permissible interpersonal actions by drawing a "line (or hyper-plane)" that "circumscribes an area in moral space" around each person.[20] They enclose individual liberty in a perimeter of protection, from which any type of interference or restriction is barred.[21] In so doing, they allocate "spheres of action" and "fix the limits within which a subject is entitled to freely exercise her will".[22] Accordingly, one needs to understand "rules for rights as prescriptions for realising a certain interpersonal distribution of freedom".[23] Basically, rights consist in the set of principles that sanction and legalize the appropriate allocation of freedom and control among individual human beings and its preservation. They are secondary norms in the Hartian sense of the term; that is to say, 'second order' rules that "confer powers, public or private".[24] Even though they could and have been characterized as a set of substantive secondary dispositions,[25] they more accurately fit the definition of rules of competences. They endorse a conception of justice that is empty of any other content than the respect and protection of a generalized freedom of action. They essentially organize

17 T. Nagel, *Mortal Questions*, Cambridge University Press, Cambridge, 1979, pp. 114 and 116.

18 J.S. Mill, *On Liberty*, 1859, Chapter 1.

19 Nozick, 1974, preface, p. ix and p. 4.

20 L.E. Lomasky, 'Rights Without Stilts', *Harvard Journal of Law and Public Policy*, No. 12, 1989, p. 801; J. Narveson, 'Anarchy, State, and Utopica' [sic], 1977 *Dialogue*, pp. 305-306; Nozick, *supra* note 6, p. 57.

21 H.L.A. Hart, 'Legal Rights', *in* H.L.A. Hart, *Essays on Bentham: Studies in Jurisprudence and Political Theory*, Clarendon, Oxford, 1982, p. 173; L.E. Lomasky, 'Compensation and the Bounds of Rights', *in* J. W. Chapman (Ed.), *Compensatory Justice*, New York University Press, New York, 1991, p. 26; J.T. Sanders, 'Projects and Property', *in* D. Schmidtz (Ed.), *Robert Nozick*, Cambridge University Press, Cambridge, 2002, p. 45.

22 J. Habermas, *Between Facts and Norms: Contributions to a Discourse Theory of Law and Democracy*, 1992; translation by W. Rehg, MIT, Cambridge (Mass.), 1996, pp. 82-85.

23 H. Steiner, 'The Natural Right to Equal Freedom', *Mind*, Vol. 83, 1974, p. 208.

24 H.L.A. Hart, 'Lon L. Fuller's *The Morality of Law*', 1965 *Harvard Law Review*, p. 1292; Hart, 1961, pp. 78-79, 91-92 and 237-238.

25 Chwaszcza, 2007, pp. 22 and 124.

the distribution and extent of the legal capacities of rival actors and determine the scope of individual self-sovereignty.

Each and every person is a right-holder, simply by virtue of her humanity, and a commitment to a radical form of cosmopolitanism of the 'interactional' sort obtains. Since all human beings are 'equally' human, they all possess the same human rights; which means that basic rights are, by definition, universal. In effect, denying someone such rights is denying his or her humanity. Once the owners of human rights have been identified to be all individual human beings *qua* human beings, there still remains to determine the quintessence of the rights they hold and the addressees of the consequent obligations. In this respect, the universal characterization of the concept of rights plays both ways, in connection with their holders as well as their addressees. In consequence, "a right is properly basic if and only if it is a claim owed to everyone and held against everyone". Besides, "because the relationship in which rights-holders stand to each other is reciprocal, it is also symmetrical" and "there are no separate classes of givers and receivers, but rather what each gives to others is also received from them".[26] It leads again to Mill's principle of liberty, as the most faithful expression of the limits of human rights.

In view of this, human rights embody a general right or *ius in rem*, by opposition to *ius in personam*. Basic rights are constitutive of a set of real obligations, which their holder can oppose *erga omnes* and not solely against specific debtors. They stand out against purely personal obligations, arising from contracts or liability rules and interpersonal or relational claims contingent on people's interactions with each other or their participation in a given polity. They precede any social relation, and duties are derivative from rights, rather than the other way around. Broadly speaking, a general right entrenches an "equal right of all men to be free in the absence of any of those special conditions which constitute a special right to limit another's freedom". In consequence, "the assertion of general rights directly invokes the principle that all men equally have the right to be free", whereas "the assertion of a special right [. . .] invokes it indirectly".[27]

8.4 Procedural Justice, Choices and Side Constraints on Action

Rights theories are not only deontological but also procedural, in the sense that they do not look at the outcomes of given acts and measures but rather at their historical record or pedigree. A pure procedural model of justice requires a complete absence of consequentialism at all levels of analysis. This means that a 'purer' theory of rights has to follow a historical entitlements' model, like the one developed by libertarians, and to conceive them as side constraints. Analytically, to characterize rights as 'side constraints', 'trumps'

26 L.E. Lomasky, 'Liberalism Beyond Borders', *Social Philosophy and Policy*, Vol. 24, 2007, p. 212.
27 H.L.A. Hart, 'Are There Any Natural Rights?', *Philosophical Review*, Vol. 64, 1955, p. 188.

or 'shields' implies that they are both privileged and personalized claims. They are conceived of as the expression of each person's autonomous control and power over his or her own life and self. Subsequently, "rights are typically conceived of as *possessed* or *owned by* or *belonging to* individuals", so that they form "a kind of moral property of individuals to which they are as individuals entitled".[28] They are attached to the individual right-bearer and belong to her, in the sense that she owns them and can dispose of them as (and whenever) she wishes to; she is entitled to decide at will whether to invoke, trade, waive or renounce them. This implies an adhesion to the 'choice' or 'will theory' rather than the 'benefit' or 'interest theory' of rights. Indeed, one of the main criteria to tell the two theories apart lies in the empowerment of the right-holder with the ultimate decision over the (non-)enforcement of his or her rights or lack of control upon the matter.

Rights actually draw a line between, on the one hand, what the powers that be and the majority in any given society have some amount of discretion over and, on the other hand, what they should never be allowed to do. In effect, they trace an unbridgeable frontier between the individual sphere of liberty and policy considerations of a utilitarian or otherwise instrumental nature, aimed at fostering particular interests, preferences or visions of the good. To be sure, "there are some actions we would forbid even if a majority wanted them [and] if a utilitarian calculation supported these actions". Hence, "rights stand as barriers to maximising utility and, indeed, to satisfying the preferences of the people in a society".[29] As such, they are a safeguard against both majoritarian and aggregative demands. They "do not determine a social ordering but instead set the constraints within which a social choice is to be made".[30] They impose, thus, limits on political legitimacy and the extent of acceptable public intervention. Essentially, legal rights are absolute side constraints on other laws and regulations. Moreover, depriving a person of his or her rights in the interest of the community or a greater number of people denies him or her, at the same time, any claim to autonomy and a meaningful or value-filled existence. This implies that rights are considered to be fundamental, in the sense that their respect and protection are seen as ultimately valuable in themselves; independently of both external effects and the advancement of alternative goods that the defence of rights may help to promote.

The recognition of basic human entitlements as side constraints on personal action consecrates the passing from a Hobbesian or purely negative notion to a Lockean or positive conception of freedom and procedural justice, where consideration for the rights of others is built into the structure of liberty and circumscribes it. It implies that rights work

28 *Ibid.*, p. 182; H. Steiner, 'Working Rights', *in* M.H. Kramer, N.E. Simmonds & H. Steiner (Eds.), *A Debate over Rights: Philosophical Enquiries*, Clarendon, Oxford, 1998, pp. 269-270.

29 R. Nozick, 'Commentary on Symposium: Equality and Efficiency; What is the Optimum Equality in Incomes?', *in* C.D. Campbell (Ed.), *Income Redistribution*, American Enterprise Institute for Public Policy Research, Washington, 1977, p. 54.

30 Nozick, 1974, p. 166.

as some sort of objective quasi-ethical criteria,[31] against which yardstick all actions are measured. The concept of liberty is thereby moralized, instead of being amoral and totally neutral, and it becomes 'justice-based'. Yet, since moral agents and their rights epistemologically precede the construction of the state and political authority, we assist to a reconciliation of both concepts of liberty that circumvents the hazards raised by Isaiah Berlin. For Berlin, the totalitarian threat inherent to the moralizing of freedom materializes when passing from an individualistic liberal notion of autonomy and self-determination to the republican idea of political or collective self-determination, with the result that individuals lose their right to self-ownership and personal freedom in the process.[32] But the pivotal libertarian idea of 'strong (self-)ownership' puts forward that individual moral rights and responsibilities are detached from politics and that they normatively precede it.[33] To make sense of the issue at stake here, one needs to look at the sharp dissimilarities existing between two contrasting visions of what constitutes positive liberty or autonomy.

On the one hand, right-based theories moralize freedom in order to determine the sphere of privacy and personal sovereignty over which each individual has control and in which he or she exercises freedom in a totally unfettered fashion. In consequence, his or her freedom is only limited by the equal liberty and self-sovereignty of other individuals. In a word, because rights theories obtain from voluntarism, they identify autonomy with unencumbered self-sovereignty. On the other hand, autonomy has contrastingly been equated with self-mastery and rationality. In this latter view, attention is paid not only to external constraints on liberty but also to so-called 'internal constraints', and it is claimed that this new type of constraints on autonomy ought to be minimized, in spite of the agent's reluctance to do so. This results in the counter-intuitive and rather absurd situation where the person is coerced into becoming 'free'. Depending on whether the self-styled internal constraints are determined subjectively on the basis of second order desires or 'objectively' by the powers that be, we end up at best with an apology of paternalism or otherwise with a justification for legal moralism and full-blown authoritarianism. This is precisely the type of fallacious nonsense that Isaiah Berlin denounces as an upshot of a positive concept of liberty.[34] The right-based approach never falls prey to such excesses, nor does it ratify liberticidal consequences, since the "imposition of terms by third parties who foist their own interests and ideals on unwilling others is the epitome of injustice".[35]

In particular, Nozick's moralized conception of freedom being pre-political and thoroughly atomistic sidesteps this danger easily, in the sense that his vision of positive liberty

31 Barry, 1986, p. 135.

32 I. Berlin, 'Two Concepts of Liberty', *in* I. Berlin, *Four Essays on Liberty*, Oxford University Press, Oxford, 1969.

33 S.R. Perry, 'The Distributive Turn: Mischief, Misfortune and Tort Law', *in* B. Bix (Ed.), *Analysing Law: New Essays in Legal Theory*, Clarendon, Oxford, 1998, p. 149.

34 Berlin, 1969.

35 Lomasky, 2007, p. 223.

is based on a simple equalization of negative liberty, by distributing freedom between all individuals and translating the requisite absence of coercion into universal rights. Autonomy is not identified with rationality, which would necessarily entail some paternalistic encroachments on liberty. Instead, it is tied to an 'endorsement constraint', namely to "the idea that nothing is non-instrumentally good for a person without their endorsement of it". This implies that irrational and even self-destructive choices remain legitimate, "insofar as they are sincerely one's own choice", because "dignity is *imbued in the very act of making a choice*".[36] Autonomy is just reinterpreted as a principle of equal negative liberty and protection from coercion.

8.5 Spontaneous Cooperation, Enforceable Claims and International Public Order

In this libertarian perspective, individual entitlements are adequately identified with the invariant functional core of ethics, in the sense that they constitute a necessary precondition to the possibility of any social life. Nozick identifies *the* invariant social purpose of ethics to be the facilitation of "coordination and cooperation to mutual benefit". He suggests a basic norm "closely intertwined" with that purpose as one example of how its function can be adequately fulfilled. The principle put forward, as the core of ethics, only "makes mandatory the widest voluntary cooperation to mutual benefit". By opposition, it outlaws "interactions that are not to mutual benefit, unless these are entered into voluntarily by all parties" or retort "to previous violations of the principle or to preparations to violate it". In a word, it boils down to a principle of voluntary cooperation, tightly linked to the 'ethics of respect' articulated by the recognition of absolute rights of non-interference as side constraints upon human action. Only this functional core invariantly mandates coercive sanctions, whereas 'higher' ethical layers are a matter of personal determination, left to the free will and the development of each individual.[37] In a similar fashion, David Gauthier, Loren Lomasky and Jan Narveson derive morality directly from the rationality of cooperation.[38] In particular, the fact that constrained maximization and altruistic strategies prevail over straightforward maximization "in the indirect combat for evolutionary survival in a world of limited resources".[39] In this sense, evolutionary game theory demonstrates on purely mathematical grounds the necessity of morals and justice.

---

36 D.F. Murray, *Nozick, Autonomy and Compensation*, Continuum, London, 2007, pp. 112-114.

37 R. Nozick, *Invariances: The Structure of the Objective World*, Harvard University Press, Cambridge (Mass.), 2001, Chapter 5, pp. 240-253, 259, 268-274 and 280-282.

38 Gauthier, 1986, Chs. 5 and 6, pp. 113-189; L.E. Lomasky, *Persons, Rights and the Moral Community*, Oxford University Press, Oxford, 1987, pp. 68-75; Murray, 2007, pp. 103-104; J. Narveson, *The Libertarian Idea*, Temple University Press, Philadelphia, 1988, pp. 140-147.

39 Gauthier, 1986, pp. 188-189.

This rejoins the idea of a spontaneous order, which progressively emerges from the decentralized actions of multiple agents. Borrowed from the structure of classical liberal economics, this type of invisible hand explanation of the evolution of the legal order is particularly useful for the analysis of international law. Indeed, the current international system is largely the result of a long process of codification or crystallization of essentially customary rules, which have spontaneously developed over time through the un-concerted acts posed at different levels by the various actors that compose the international community. The main distinctiveness of the international legal order consists in its absence of a centralized law-making authority. Typically, all subjects of international law are able to participate in the elaboration of the supranational norms that will then bind them.[40] As such, the role played at the global level by the human rights paradigm might usefully be portrayed as the growth of a nucleus of public rules in a wider regulatory framework otherwise mostly akin to private law. In that, Nozick's explanation for the emergence of the minimal state out of the state of nature is interesting not only at the normative but also at the purely descriptive level, as an approximation of the development of the international legal order. His focus on individual rights as the only appropriate moral concerns to be guaranteed by the law is also in line with the recent evolution of the international system, grounded in the concept of a right-based international public order.

In this respect, one cannot ignore the specificity of working with legal rights as enshrined in international instruments, in contrast with purely natural rights as the basis for an ideal theory of justice. In the former case, unlike the latter, one is bound to rely on a conception of fundamental rights that fits the description and principal characteristics of human rights in these treaties. Attention needs to be paid here to the traditional division between basic human rights, understood as natural rights, and fundamental legal rights. Yet, such a distinction only makes sense in cases where both sets of rights would differ or, at least, where some externalities would be acknowledged in the treatment and settlement of legal rights claims. If a Nozickean conception of rights is accepted, this differentiation becomes futile and void of any tangible meaning: both concepts present an identical structure and refer to the same set of individual entitlements. It has been advanced that Nozick is actually dealing in legal rather than moral rights.[41] This seems to be a pretty fair assessment of his project, in the light of his definition of rights as mostly *enforceable* claims[42] and eventually as the only appropriate object of enforcement. Although this approach has been criticized for using a moral right as a basis for a legal right, thereby creating some "confusion between nature rights and society rights",[43] it is actually one of the interesting properties of Nozick's rights theory that it tries to bridge the classical rift between natural and legal rights.

40 P.-M. Dupuy, *Droit international public* (9th edn), Dalloz, Paris, 2008, pp. 18-19.

41 A. Halpin, *Rights and Law: Analysis and Theory*, Hart, Oxford, 1997, p. 250, n. 99; H.L.A. Hart, 'Between Utility and Rights', *Columbia Law Review*, Vol. 79, 1979, p. 834.

42 Nozick, 1974, pp. 10-12, 108-110, 118 and 132-133; Nozick, 2001, pp. 281-282; Nozick, 1981, pp. 499-500.

43 Halpin, 1997, pp. 243-244 and 246.

The main advantages of adopting a Nozickean view of rights are its closeness to the conception developed by the international human rights system and the fact that Nozick's entire political philosophy is basically constructed on the idea of inviolable individual entitlements. By providing a detailed specification of the rights held by all human beings, international human rights law allows to pass from the philosophical analysis of the core features of basic rights to the actual entrenchment of particular legal rights. It merely gives a more fully fledged substance to the enounced rights. It foresees mechanisms for their enforcement, by means of legal remedies, and it organizes some supranational control over their respect in front of various supervisory organs. Hence, passing from an analytical to a purely legal understanding of rights does not entail any shift in the essence of what rights claims are fundamentally about or modify the nature and intrinsic properties of those rights. It only provides them, in practice, with an institutional frame of protection, which guarantees their effectiveness and enforcement.

8.6 Coherence, Co-Possibility and Normative Hierarchy

Human rights have been posited, both at the ethical and at the legal level, as primordial values whose respect can never be endangered in the name of competing goals or in order to escape unwanted outcomes. It means that rights are *always* trumping non right-based considerations and that they are never to be weighed, balanced and traded off, in order to promote utility, the general welfare or majority preferences. Yet, the ensuing model still needs to be coherent and able to deal with concrete cases in an appropriate manner. A clear verdict of (il-)legitimacy, which derives directly from the application of the relevant rules of validity in a normative model, is required so that one can afford not to look at the consequences of specific actions when one assesses their acceptability. But, in reality, only for absolute norms, because they are "by definition infinitely stringent and cannot be overridden", is the simple fact of their applicability fully conclusive and 'action-determinative'.[44] This entails that the rules in question be sufficiently precise and that they do not clash against one other. In turn, it implies a logically coherent set of fundamental norms; here, a logically coherent set of basic human rights.

Nozick's analysis of rights as negative absolute side constraints on individual action allows building up a set of co-possible legal rights, which can be enforced concomitantly. In this view, the usual mechanisms of checks and balances are purely redundant. Nothing needs to be balanced since individual rights are co-possible and the state has no legitimate public function, safe for that of protecting these rights. No other consideration needs to be taken into account at the level of adjudication than that of the (in-)existence of the claimed rights, and a verdict on the (in-)appropriateness of restricting people's liberty in a given case

44 F. Schauer, *Playing by the Rules: A Philosophical Examination of Rule-Based Decision-Making in Law and in Life*, Clarendon, Oxford, 1991, p. 115.

obtains from a strict application of this basic rule. This requires that rights be conceived as personal choices derived from a general entitlement to personal autonomy, whose only limits are those of the ban on aggression implied in Mill's harm principle. In such a thoroughly non-prudential perspective, rights do not need to be weighed or balanced, since they never clash, and the practical consequences of actions are disregarded as immaterial to the question of their legal validity. As a result, most of the restrictions, exceptions and other qualifications affecting fundamental freedoms and entitlements can be dismissed as unnecessary and illegitimate. Yet, this all hangs on the internal consistency of the proposed rights matrix, and the co-possibility of Nozick's set of absolute choice rights depends both on their purely agent-relative and mostly negative character. Indeed, positive rights are hardly co-possible. Most crucially, the trouble does not lie so much in the difficulty to accommodate these rights in a libertarian framework as in the irreconcilability of positive rights among themselves and their necessary restricting of negative rights.

This poses a problem since a substantive theory of rights needs to account for the entire range of rights enshrined in international documents, which includes typically positive rights; chiefly, procedural rights and those protected by the International Covenant on Economic, Social and Cultural Rights. In the absence of an internally coherent set of rights, the only way to escape unwanted trade-offs resides in an *a priori* hierarchy of clashing entitlements. The most primordial rights – the rights to life, physical integrity and personal liberty – could be entrenched unconditionally, while lesser ones would merely constitute trumps on competing claims and considerations that are not right-based and give way in inter-rights conflicts. Core rights protected as inalienable in international conventions, like *habeas corpus* and the ban on torture, should remain absolutely immune from any kind of bargaining and trade-offs. Besides, the positive aspects of both procedural and social rights cannot be invoked for further restrictions than those encroachments on individual property that are strictly necessary to their financing. This solution might be criticized for its lack of neatness. But it reduces the amount of legal uncertainty otherwise generated by the *ad hoc* balancing of competing claims, and it corresponds to the division of fundamental rights into derogable and non-derogable ones, in the emergency clauses of international human rights treaties, as well as to the recognition of a hierarchy of rights in the case law of the European Court of Human Rights.[45]

8.7 Human Rights, Non-Aggression and the Emergence of a Global Minimal State

To sum up, in essence, human rights are the rights held by each and every human being, in his or her quality of human being. As such, any human right is a *ius in rem* opposable *erga omnes*.

45 *Streletz, Kessler & Krenz v. FRG*, 22 March 2001, paras 87 and 94.

The role of supervising the respect of these fundamental freedoms and entitlements is ultimately entrusted to the whole international community; *i.e.*, all subjects of public international law in their capacity of trans-national actors and subjects of a cosmopolitan legal order. The enforcement of these norms is, accordingly, equally entrusted to the entire international community; more specifically, to domestic courts and tribunals in the first instance and with an appeal before international monitoring bodies. At the end, human rights constitute at the same time constraints on the individual actions of every agent and standards for the evaluation of the legitimacy of political structures and the validity of laws. The recognition of negative rights conditions the legitimacy of all human actions and imposes, thus, a general duty of non-interference on all types of agents, be it individuals, other private actors or public officials. Conversely, the positive obligations that derive from the necessity to guarantee procedural and social rights only hold against states. Finally, the role of the international community is to guarantee the protection of both classes of rights by their addressees and enforce their respect whenever they fail to do so.

The radically cosmopolitan and libertarian conception of rights that underlies international human rights law and *ius cogens* is the sole paradigm that allows to evade altogether the likelihood of state-promoted abuses, by conferring on individuals an unassailable sphere of self-sovereignty. The entrenchment of personal autonomy and free will as preconditions for the construction of a truly cosmopolitan world incidentally permits the peaceful coexistence of radically different conceptions of society and the meaning of life. The control effectuated by the international community is comparable to that of Robert Nozick's libertarian minimal state as a framework for utopias, under which totally dissimilar societies can develop side by side as long as they abide by the basic requirement of mutual respect for the freedom of others.[46] Contemporary developments in public international law are inspired by a similar ideal, and many facets of the actual system confirm the thesis that we are in the presence of an emerging global minimal state of such a type. In fact, the libertarian utopian framework captures to a large extent the peculiarities of the international legal regime and rests on comparable foundations.

First of all, it displays the notable quality not to focus on specific domestic experiences but rather on a philosophical vision of rights applicable to a wide variety of societies, including the global one. This ensures the adaptability of the model at the international level, without having to face the usual problems of translation that municipally grounded social democrat alternatives encounter. Its denunciation of established national borders and conservative approaches to citizenship, because they cannot be reconciled with a serious commitment to individual freedom, reinforces this universal feature of the theory.[47] Secondly, in a libertarian context, law does not take responsibility for

46 Nozick, 1974, especially pp. 297-334.

47 S. Cvijić, *Democracy Beyond the Demos: Bringing the Immigrants (Back) In* (Ph.D. Thesis, European University Institute, Florence, 2005), pp. 67-130, especially pp. 108-110.

the final configuration of society. It is only concerned with providing a formal legal frame, within which individuals can live their own lives according to their personal projects and preferences, and, aside from basic freedoms and entitlements, it solely recognizes the general principles of private law as legitimate rules. Likewise, international law is often characterized by its private nature.[48]. It frequently resorts to the use of reprisals, the instrument of private justice by excellence, and remains heavily decentralized, even if put at the service of the international public order.[49] Thirdly, the libertarian definition of rights as side constraints on action, spheres of liberty and specific facets of a general principle of non-aggression fits well into the legal frame created by the Charter of the United Nations, whose main object and purpose consists in protecting global peace and universal rights. The identification of the material scope of *ius cogens* with the interdiction of aggression and the respect of international human rights and humanitarian law strengthens the endorsement of such a conception of individual rights. Nozick ends his defence of the cosmopolitan utopia with these words:

> Treating us with respect by respecting our rights, it allows us, individually or with whom we choose, to choose our life and to realize our ends and our conception of ourselves, insofar as we can, aided by the voluntary cooperation of other individuals possessing the same dignity. How *dare* any state or group of individuals do more. Or less.[50]

The international legal order attempts to seriously engage in this challenge by assigning a peremptory status to basic human rights, effectively entitling every human being to imagine his or her own ideal life and live it freely.

48 D. Anzilotti, *Cours de droit international*, Sirey, Paris, 1929, pp. 44-45 ; O. Quirico, *Réflexions sur le système du droit international pénal: La responsabilité 'pénale' des états et des autres personnes morales par rapport à celle des personnes physiques en droit international* (Ph.D. Thesis, Université Toulouse I Sciences Sociales, Toulouse, 2005), p. 513.

49 P.-M. Dupuy, *L'unité de l'ordre juridique international*, Cours général de droit international public, 2002. *Recueil des Cours de l'Académie de Droit International de La Haye*, Vol. 297, pp. 390-391.

50 Nozick, 1974, p. 334.

Part III
Identity, Political and Human Rights Culture in Transitional Countries of Eastern Europe

9 Human Rights Culture in Serbia – The Case of Sexual Minorities

Miodrag Jovanović & Ivana Krstić

9.1 Introduction

If one googles the phrase 'human rights culture', or the similar one – 'culture of human rights' – one gets surprised at the insignificantly small number of received hints that are actually related to the intended subject of search. The furthest that most of the suggested hints reach is to reinvigorate the ongoing debate on the universality of human rights, by raising the question whether this concept can be equally well entrenched in all parts of the world, due to the specificities of the general cultural patterns of some societies. For instance, until recently, there was no particular word in the Chinese Mandarin language to denote the concept of human rights. When finally construed (Rén Quán), this phrase slowly entered into all areas of the public and official language. It is also interesting to note that the word (Quán) is being used only in the last three decades to refer to the concept of subjective legal right, even though when literally translated, its more precise meaning is 'power'. Our experience of teaching the very topic of universality of human rights at the universities in midland China assured us that not only has this notion become rooted in the present-day vocabulary of this society, but also that new generations do not seriously bite the famous 'East Asian values' argument against the universality.[1] At the same time, discussions with Chinese professors and students clearly vindicated cultural sensitiveness in interpreting the concept of human rights, by laying emphasis on economic, social and cultural rights.[2]

If the aforementioned episode vindicates Donnelly's words that irrespective of "their past practice, nothing in indigenous African, Asian, or American cultures prevents them from endorsing human rights now",[3] it does not yet tell us more about what a particular 'human rights culture' would amount to, and especially whether it can be fully developed outside of the mainstream liberal democratic political culture. This chapter has no ambition of addressing all the intricate problems hidden behind these more general questions. It will, nonetheless, argue that human rights culture can only be part of a larger political culture, which is principally supportive of human rights. In that respect, 'human rights culture' is understood

1 *See* O. R. Bauer & D.A. Bell (Eds.), *The East Asian Challenge for Human Rights*, Cambridge University Press, Cambridge, 1999.

2 Donnelly argues, I believe rightly, that universality of human rights is reconcilable with their culturally sensitive implementation. J. Donnelly, 'The Relative Universality of Human Rights', *Human Rights Quarterly*, Vol. 29, No. 2, 2007.

3 *Ibid.*, p. 291.

as *the totality of attitudes towards and practices related to human rights*, at the personal, societal and institutional levels. By focusing on Serbia, as a transitional society, the chapter will try to show how the robust and effective implementation of human rights at the institutional level, or lack of it, is vital for reinforcing, or benumbing, the human rights culture at the personal and societal levels. To be sure, these processes are mutual, insofar as institutions, including courts, tend to behave in a way that will meet the general approval of public opinion, especially in sensitive matters upon which the given society is largely divided.[4]

One such issue in the transitional Serbia concerns the protection of human rights of sexual minorities. Although one may argue that Serbia has a satisfactory legal framework for the protection of the LGBT population against discrimination, this regime is not fully implemented. Moreover, an overall institutional support for the exercise of their constitutionally guaranteed rights is largely lacking, as blatantly evidenced by several consecutive cancellations of the Belgrade Pride. The then conducted public polls have revealed that this attitude was grounded in the prevalent sentiment of the Serbian society towards this event. The reason why the authors focus on the case of sexual minorities lies in the fact that any investigation on the state of affairs of the human rights culture in one society needs to take into account the most vulnerable group of people. It is the overall institutional and societal treatment of such groups that should serve as one of the prime parameters in assessing how well entrenched is human rights culture in the given society.

9.2 What Is 'Human Rights Culture'?

As already indicated in the Introduction, human rights culture is a concept that cannot exist on its own, *i.e.*, without being part of a larger political culture. In that respect, one may define political culture, along with the *International Encyclopedia of the Social Sciences*, as

> the set of attitudes, beliefs and sentiments which give order and meaning to a political process and which provide the underlying assumptions and rules that govern behavior in the political system. It encompasses both the political ideals and operating norms of a polity. Political culture is thus the manifestation in aggregate form of the psychological and subjective dimensions of politics. A political culture is the product of both the collective history of a political system and the life histories of the members of the system and thus it is rooted equally in public events and private experience.[5]

When the aforementioned highlighted relations between legal norms and political ideals/values, as well as between institutional and societal actors are reconstructed at the level

4 This is so even in most liberal societies. For one such analysis of the relation between the U.S. Supreme Court and the U.S. public opinion, *see* G.E. White, 'The Supreme Court's Public and the Public's Supreme Court', *in Patterns of American Legal Thought*, The Michie Company, Charlottesville, 1978.

5 *International Encyclopedia of the Social Sciences*, Macmillan, New York, 1968, Vol. 12, p. 218.

of a human rights culture, as a segment of a larger political culture, one may argue that a strong human rights culture is the necessary underpinning of an effective regime of human rights. That culture itself cannot take significant hold unless the political culture is supportive of human rights.[6]

On European soil, at least, this larger political culture goes roughly along the lines of liberal-democratic principles, such as tolerance,[7] critical thinking[8] and civic responsibility.[9]

One of the rare definitions of human rights culture, which one may come across in the literature, states that this culture is "a 'lived awareness' of the human rights principles, particularly, the Universal Declaration, but also its progeny".[10] This picturesque statement, however, does not fully capture all the important ingredients of such a culture. Hence, when decomposed, the starting definition of a human rights culture, as *the totality of attitudes towards and practices related to human rights*, contains several elements. Namely, at the individual level, this culture consists of one's:

(a) awareness of possessing exercisable rights and liberties;
(b) readiness to recognize and respect someone else's rights and liberties;
(c) ability to identify violations of one's own and someone else's rights and liberties and
(d) determination to use all disposable legal, and when necessary political, means to protect one's own and, in certain cases, someone else's rights and liberties.

This understanding of 'human rights culture' essentially follows classical Almond and Verba's usage of the notion 'political culture', which denotes "the specifically political orientations – attitudes toward the political system and its various parts, and attitudes toward the role of the self in the system".[11] One of the key findings of their study is to reject simplifications in terms of treating particular political cultures as homogeneous and

6 R. Falk, 'Taking Human Rights Seriously at Home', *Political Quarterly*, Vol. 68, No. 2, 1997, p. 179.

7 Arblaster defines it as "the duty, on the part of state, society or the individual, of allowing and not interfering with activities and beliefs which, although they may be disliked or even disapproved of, do not in themselves make any infringement on the equal right of others to act and believe as *they* choose." A. Arblaster, *The Rise and Decline of Western Liberalism*, Basil Blackwell, Oxford, 1984, p. 66.

8 It can be defined as "the careful and deliberate determination of whether to accept, reject, or suspend judgment about the claim." B.N. Moore & R. Parker, *Critical Thinking – Evaluating Claims and Arguments in Everyday Life*, Mayfield Publishing Company, Palo Alto, 1986, p. 4.

9 In a classical treatise on citizenship, Heater discusses the concept of civic virtues, arguing that " the ideal good citizen must be a paragon of multiple virtues, who brings to the fore different qualities according to circumstances." Although, generally speaking, basic virtues to be developed are "loyalty, responsibility and respect for political and social procedural values," it is important to bear in mind that "each of these virtues contains a complex cluster of personal qualities, positive attitudes and beneficent behavior." D. Heater, *Citizenship: The Civic Ideal in World History, Politics and Education*, Longman, London and New York, 1990, p. 193.

10 J. Wronka, 'Creating a Human Rights Culture Implications for Peace', *Peace and Conflict Studies*, Vol. 2, No. 1, 1995, p. 40.

11 G.A. Almond & S. Verba, *The Civic Culture – Political Attitude and Democracy in Five Nations*, Sage, London, 1989, p. 12. At yet another place, they underline that they "employ the concept of culture in only one of its many meanings: that of psychological orientation towards social objects. When we speak of the political culture of a society, we refer to the political system as internalized in the cognitions, feelings, and evaluations of its population." *Ibid.*, p. 13.

unified. Consequently, the 'citizen' is a mix of participant, subject and parochial ideal types of political culture,[12] just as "the civic culture is a particular mix of citizens, subjects, and parochials".[13] This, furthermore, implies that although the prevalence of the participant political culture is the most conducive societal setting to the development of a robust human rights culture, this does not necessarily exclude manifestations of what was already in the 1940s coined as 'the authoritarian personality.' Adorno, Frenkel-Brunswik, Levinson and Sanford's work on the authoritarian personality[14] has been harshly criticized in the contemporary literature in political psychology for its alleged methodological flows,[15] but its everlasting contribution is in elucidating the traits of such a personality even in individual cases which can otherwise be well categorized under the rubric of 'participant political culture'. In the preface to the *Studies in Prejudice* which, together with the study on the authoritarian personality, belongs to the same series of treatises, Horkheimer classifies this work as "a book about social discrimination". However, unlike other empirical studies of the time, the central theme of this work is "a relatively new concept [. . .] the authoritarian type of man". This novelty of the concept is summarized in the following way:

> In contrast to the bigot of the older style he seems to combine the ideas and skills which are typical of a highly industrialized society with irrational or anti-rational beliefs. He is at the same time enlightened and superstitious, proud to be an individualist and in constant fear of not being like all the others, jealous of his independence and inclined to submit blindly to power and authority.[16]

Authoritarian elements in the political culture of a society are primarily manifested through prejudice towards 'others', where 'otherness' is sometimes defined in terms of the skin colour or ethnic group membership, sometimes in terms of religious beliefs or class status, and at times in terms of the sexual orientation and dispositions. Since these elements are, to a greater or lesser extent, present in each society, a more robust version of human rights culture would require the existence of some counterbalancing forces reflected in the ability to identify cases of someone else's rights violations, as well

12 *Parochial* political culture is a type in which no clear differentiation of specific political roles and expectations exists among actors, *i.e.*, political specialization is minimal. *Subject* political culture is one in which institutional and role differentiation exists in political life, but towards which the citizen stands in largely passive relations. Finally *participant* political culture is one in which the relationships between specialized institutions and citizen opinion and activity are interactive. *Ibid.*, pp. 16-18.

13 *Ibid.*, p. 19.

14 T.W. Adorno *et al.*, *The Authoritarian Personality*, Harper & Brothers, New York, 1950.

15 One such review of the fifty years' legacy of this work states that it "is probably the most deeply flawed work of prominence in political psychology." J. Levi Mar, 'The Authoritarian Personality, 50 Years Later: What Questions Are There for Political Psychology?', *Political Psychology*, Vol. 22, No. 1, 2001.

16 M. Horkheimer & S.H. Flowerman (Eds.), *Studies in Prejudice*, Harper & Brothers, New York, 1949, p. ix.

as in the determination of individual and societal actors to use all the available legal and political resources in order to protect the human rights of members of the most vulnerable groups.

However, we are of the opinion that a more robust version of human rights culture depends largely on attitudes and practices of institutional actors, especially state, and that it could hardly be fully developed and strengthened without adequate institutional support. For example, if discrimination or human rights violation is the consequence of actions of state bodies, particularly those belonging to the executive branch of government, this, then, sends a potentially powerful negative message to the rest of society, which can only be partially remedied by subsequent courts' decisions in individual cases. The same applies to public speeches of political parties' officials or MPs, whose inflamed rhetoric directed towards vulnerable groups in the public discourse could also have detrimental effects on strengthening human rights culture. For this reason, it would be highly inappropriate to reduce the research of human rights culture to the individual level, when it operates at the institutional level as well. This point will be proven in the rest of the paper on the case of Serbia, where the attitudes and actions of institutional actors towards sexual minorities reinforce the social stigma of the members of these groups, thereby hindering the development of a more robust version of human rights culture.

9.3 Sexual Minorities in Serbia: Between Law and Reality

The position of the LGBT population in Serbia illustrates the interconnection between the human rights protection and human rights culture. Although the position of sexual minorities is better with time, it must be said that they belong to one of the most vulnerable groups in Serbia.[17] This is nothing new, as millions of people across Europe are discriminated, stigmatized and exposed to violence because of their actual or perceived sexual orientation.[18] The primary reason for their vulnerability in the Serbian society can be found in the dominant perception of nation, religion and traditional values concerning gender, sexuality and the family roles.[19]

---

17 *See, e.g.*, European Commission, Serbia 2012 Progress Report, Brussels, 10 October 2012, p. 16.

18 *See more* at *Discrimination on grounds of sexual orientation and gender identity in Europe*, 2nd edition, Council of Europe, 2011, available at <www.coe.int/t/Commissioner/Source/LGBT/LGBTStudy2011_en.pdf> (last accessed16 March 2013).

19 *E.g.*, 70% of 975 interviewees said that homosexuality is a sort of illness, 51% agreed that public institutions should actively work on combating homosexuality, while 50% perceived homosexuality as a threat to society. Gej Strejt Alijansa, Predrasude na videlo – homofobija u Srbiji, Izveštaj o istraživanju javnog mnjenja o LGBT populaciji [Gay Straight Alliance, The Report on the Survey of Public Opinion on LGBT], CeSID, February/March 2008, available at <http://gsa.org.rs/wp-content/uploads/2012/03/istrazivanje_ljudska_lbgt_2008_za_gsa_cesid.pdf> (last accessed 19 March 2013).

9.3.1 LGBT's Rights: One Step Forward, Two Steps Back

As for the legal framework regulating the status of the LGBT population in Serbia, it is generally satisfactory, insofar as it provides solid legal grounds for their protection.[20] Article 21 of the Serbian Constitution[21] proclaims that "[a]ll are equal before the Constitution and law", and that "[e]veryone shall have the right to equal legal protection, without discrimination". Under the Constitution,

> [a]ny direct or indirect discrimination on any grounds, particularly on race, sex, national origin, social origin, birth, religion, political or other opinion, property status, culture, language, age, mental or physical disability shall be prohibited. (Art. 21, para. 3).

This provision contains an open-ended clause that stipulates the prohibition of discrimination on any ground, not just those explicitly mentioned in Article 21, and covers sexual orientation as well.

In March 2009, the comprehensive anti-discrimination law was adopted. The Law on the Prohibition of Discrimination (LPD)[22] is an important milestone in securing basic human rights in Serbia. The LPD prohibits direct and indirect discrimination, violation of the principle of equal rights and obligations, the prohibition of calling to account, association for the purpose of discriminating, hate speech, disturbing and humiliating treatment and severe forms of discrimination. Thus, it prohibits a wide range of discriminatory actions (Article 5). Also, Article 2, para. 1 prohibits discrimination based on the grounds of

> race, skin colour, ancestors, citizenship, national affiliation or ethnic origin, language, religious or political beliefs, gender, gender identity, sexual orientation, financial position, birth, genetic characteristics, health, disability, marital and family status, previous convictions, age, appearance, membership in political, trade union and other organizations and other real or presumed personal characteristics.[23]

---

20 This legal framework provides grounds for the prohibition of discrimination against sexual minority groups on any basis. S. Đorđević-Lukic (Ed.), *LGBT populacija i reforma sektora bezbednosti u Republici Srbiji*, [*LGBT People and Security Sector Reform in the Republic of Serbia*], OSCE, Belgrade, 2011, p. 20.

21 *The Official Gazette of the Republic of Serbia*, no. 98/2006.

22 *The Official Gazette of the Republic of Serbia*, no. 22/2009.

23 This long list of prohibited grounds is criticized by some, as it may bring a range of unintended scenarios that may destabilize the effectiveness of the LPD. *See*, *e.g.*, OSCE/ODIHR Comments on the Draft Law on Prohibition of Discrimination Law of the Republic of Serbia, Warsaw, 19 March 2009, para. 10.

In other words, the LPD explicitly prohibits discrimination based on gender identity and sexual orientation, but the express inclusion of these two grounds of discrimination directly influenced its later adoption.
Drafting of the LPD lasted for four years before it was submitted to the Parliament. It received wide support from the Government, relevant ministries and the Parliamentary committees.[24] Nevertheless, the adoption of the LPD was accompanied by heavy debate in the Parliament, which eventually led to the withdrawal of the final draft law from the procedure due to the public opposition of the Church.[25] Moreover, many politicians and members of the 'intellectual elite' were also against a broad definition of discrimination. One of them explained his opposition to equal protection of sexual minorities in the following words:

> In the next step, anti-discrimination will not be enough anymore. They will require equality. After the legal equality is obtained, they will go further and request the recognition of social equivalence. And in a few years we will be required to officially declare homosexuality to have the equal value as heterosexual orientation.[26]

As a compromise, some provisions of the initial draft were changed, demonstrating the power of the Church to influence this process.[27] The Law was finally passed with a narrow majority. Despite all, two provisions of the LPD particularly address discrimination based on sexual orientation. Thus, Article 13, para. 1 defines causing and inciting inequality, hatred and enmity on the grounds of sexual discrimination as a severe form of discrimination. Article 21 states that sexual orientation is a private matter, and that every person has

24 *Politika online*, 'Vlada povukla Predlog zakona protiv diskriminacije' ['The Government Withdrawn the Draft Law on the Prohibition of Discrimination'], 5 March 2009, available at <www.politika.rs/rubrike/Politika/Vlada-povukla-Predlog-zakona-protiv-diskriminacije.lt.html> (last accessed 16 March 2013).

25 The Serbian Orthodox Church and seven 'traditional religious communities' protested against religious freedoms given in Art 18, as well as against inclusion of gender equality in Art. 21. In addition, a reference to transsexuals was intentionally omitted from the final version of Art. 21, which provides prohibition of discrimination based on sexual orientation. *See more* at Beogradski centar za ljudska prava, *Ljudska prava u Srbiji u 2009: Pravo, praksa i međunarodni standardi ljudskih prava*, [Belgrade Center for Human Rights, *Report on Human Rights in Serbia in 2009: Law, Practice and International Standards of Human Rights*], Belgrade, 2010, pp. 57-58.

26 *See* S. Antonić, 'Tolerancija nije dovoljna' ['Tolerance Is Not Enough], *Politika*, 19 March 2009, text available at <www.politika.rs/pogledi/Slobodan-Antonic/TOLERANCIJA-NIJE-DOVOLJNA.sr.html> (last accessed 23 March 2013).

27 The Holy Assembly of Bishops of the Serbian Orthodox Church emphasized that there is no scientific evidence that sexual orientation is an inborn trait, adding that "a number of eminent scientists deem transsexuality to be a mental disorder." *See* I. Stakić, 'Homophobia and Hate Speech in Serbian Public Discourse: How Nationalist Myths and Stereotypes Influence Prejudices against the LGBT Minority', *The Equal Rights Review*, Vol. 7, 2011, p. 55, available at <www.equalrightstrust.org/ertdocumentbank/ERR7_isidora.pdf> (last accessed 25 March 2013).

the right to declare his/her sexual orientation, while discriminatory treatment on account of such a declaration is forbidden.

Many other laws prohibit discrimination, and some of them explicitly refer to sexual orientation as a ground of discrimination.[28] However, the enforcement of anti-discrimination provisions is inconsistent owing to a very low human rights culture. The reasons should be found in a still widespread homophobia and prejudice against the LGBT population that very often leads to victimization not only of those who belong to this group, but also of those who are associated with them or perceived as belonging to sexual minorities. For that reason, it is very important that Article 21 of the LPD covers real and presumed characteristics as grounds of discrimination.[29] This attitude is particularly visible during campaigns against the organization of Gay Pride.[30] The first attempt to organize this event back in 2001 was unsuccessful as some participants and supporters were beaten by the right-wing groups.[31] The second Gay Pride was cancelled by the organizers in 2004 due to the violent March riots in Belgrade and Niš.[32] After several years of delay, the next Pride was scheduled for September 2009, but was cancelled as the Ministry of Interior recommended holding the event at an alternative location, which was safer, but also less attractive. This decision of the Ministry of Interior violated the organizers' right to assemble, as the Constitutional Court decided at the end of 2011.[33] Although the Court did not establish discrimination towards the LGBT population, it reasoned that the freedom of assembly was violated as the gathering was reported well in advance, the decision on

28 The Labour Law in Art. 18 prohibits discrimination in the area of employment, *The Official Gazette of the Republic of Serbia,* no. 24/2005, 61/2005 and 54/2009; The Law on Higher Education in Art. 8 guarantees the right to higher education to everyone with secondary school diploma without any distinction, *The Official Gazette of the Republic of Serbia,* no. 76/2005, 100/2007 – authentic interpretation, 97/2008, 44/2010 and 93/2012; The Law on Youth in Art. 5 prohibits discrimination, *The Official Gazette of the Republic of Serbia,* no. 50/2011; The Broadcasting Law in Art. 21 prohibits information inciting discrimination, hatred or violence, *The Official Gazette of the Republic of Serbia,* no. 42/2002, 97/2004, 76/2005, 79/2005 – subsequent law, 62/2006, 85/2006, 86/2006 - corr. and 41/2009; Public Information Law in Art. 38 prohibits publishing of ideas, information and opinions that incite discrimination, *The Official Gazette of the Republic of Serbia,* no. 43/2003, 61/2005, 71/2009, 89/2010 – Constitutional Court decision US and 41/2011 - Constitutional Court decision.

29 This was documented in the report by the Human Rights Commissioner of the Council of Europe on his visit to Serbia from 12 to 15 June 2011, available at <https://wcd.coe.int/ViewDoc.jsp?Ref=CommDH(2011)29&Language=lanEnglish&Ver=original&Site=COE&BackColorInternet=DBDCF2&BackColorIntranet=FDC864&BackColorLogged=FDC864> (last accessed 16 March 2013).

30 *See more* on this issue in M. Radoman, 'Istraživanje stavova LGBT populacije o sektoru bezbednosti' ['Survey on the Views of LGBT Population Towards the Security Sector'], *Filozofija i društvo,* XXIII (1), 2012.

31 According to some sources, more than 40 persons were physically attacked. *B92,* 'Razbijanje Gay Parade' ['Breaking the Gay Pride'], 30 June 2001, Belgrade, available at <www.b92.net/specijal/gay-parada/gay-saop.phtml> (last accessed16 March 2013).

32 These events were triggered by the massive human rights violations of Serbs in Kosovo. *See* Human Rights Watch, 'Kosovo/Serbia: Protect Minorities from Ethnic Violence', 19 March 2004, available at <www.hrw.org/news/2004/03/18/kosovoserbia-protect-minorities-ethnic-violence> (last accessed 16 March 2013).

33 Constitutional Court, decision Už br. 1918/2009, 22 December 2011.

reallocation of the Gay Pride was brought a day before the scheduled event, and, hence, it was unlawful.

The Pride was rescheduled for 10 October 2010 and finally organized, but with devastating results, as the right-wing groups demolished Belgrade, and some 132 policemen and 25 citizens were injured.[34] In 2011 and 2012, Gay Pride was banned by the Ministry of Interior due to the alleged security threats. In October 2011, the Council for National Security banned the Pride on grounds that it might "obstruct public transport, endanger the health, public morale or security of people and property".[35] At the same time, the Patriarch requested the ban of a "parade of shame" and called its participants a deviant group. As a reaction, some NGOs openly advocated that the Serbian criminal law has to penalize "hate crimes",[36] bearing in mind a number of reported incidents of this sort.[37] They claimed that the penalization of 'hate crime' as a distinctive criminal offence would contribute to the efficient processing of cases against persons charged for committing violence and other crimes against the LGBT population, as hate crimes are commonly motivated entirely or in part by the fact or perception that a victim is different from the perpetrator.[38]

In December 2012, 'hate crime' was incorporated into amendments to the Criminal code in the following manner: if a criminal act is based on hatred of another person's race, religion, national or ethnic background, gender, sexual orientation or gender identity, the court shall treat it as an aggravating circumstance, unless it is stipulated as an element of a criminal offence.[39] A hate crime presents a more severe form of each criminal act, for which more serious penalties are stipulated. Although a hate crime is not incorporated as a special criminal offence, but as a special fact that is relevant for assessment of sentence for an offence committed out of hatred, it will significantly contribute to the efficient prosecution of those suspected of violence and other crimes against LGBT persons.

The powerful tool for proper protection of victims of discrimination in the LPD is found in the special court procedure and the establishment of an independent, specialized body,

34 *B92*, 'Demoliranje Beograda, još jednom' ['Demolition of Belgrade, Once Again'], 10 October 2010, available at <www.b92.net/info/vesti/index.php?dd=10&mm=10&nav_category=16&nav_id=464314&yyyy=2010> (last accessed 16 March 2013).

35 ILGA-Europe's submission to the European Commission's 2012 Progress Report on Serbia, Brussels, 11 May 2012, p. 1.

36 *See, e.g.*, Gej strejt alijansa, *Korak po korak: Godišnji izveštaj o stanju ljudskih prava LGBT osoba u Srbiji za 2010* [Gay Straight Alliance, *Step by Step, 2010 Report on the State of Human Rights of LGBT Persons in Serbia*], Belgrade, 2011, p. 9.

37 In one such case, a woman was wearing a T-shirt with LGBT symbols. She was attacked in Belgrade city centre, beaten up and stabbed. During this attack, she was constantly asked if she was a lesbian. As a result, her finger ligaments were cut, and she suffered concussion, scratches and bruising. *Supra* note 35, p. 2.

38 For more on hate crime *see* P. Iganski, 'Why Make "Hate" a Crime?', *Critical Social Policy*, August 1999; S.D. Johnson & B.D. Byers, 'Attitudes Toward Hate Crime Laws, *Criminal Justice*, Vol. 31, No. 3, May-June 2003; R.J. Dittman, 'Policing Hate Crime. From Victim to Challenger: A Transgendered Perspective', *Probation Journal*, Vol. 50, No. 3, 2003.

39 Art. 54a, *The Official Gazette of the Republic of Serbia*, no. 121/2012.

the Commissioner for the Protection of Equality (CPE),[40] who can also initiate strategic cases before the court. However, a small number of cases taken before the court are legally qualified as discrimination against LGBT persons, even though this form of discrimination is widespread in different areas of life, such as health care, education, access to goods and services.[41] The reasons for this state of affairs can be found in the recently introduced anti-discrimination legislation, in the lack of capacity and knowledge of public institutions, especially prosecutors, judges and attorneys to deal with this matter, but also in the lack of public awareness, especially of actual or potential victims of discrimination. Sometimes they are not aware of their status of victim, but more often they do not believe that they will receive adequate remedy for the suffered discrimination. The reasons should also be seen in inactivity of some NGOs to fill lawsuits, but also in frequent wrong interpretation of Article 85, para. 1 of the Civil Procedure Code[42] from the judges. This Article significantly diminishes choices for representation in civil matters to parties and their attorneys. However, the LPD is a *lex specialis,* and its Article 46, para. 1 expressly permits NGOs to submit claims.

Nevertheless, in 2011, ten complaints were submitted to the CPE for discrimination on this ground, and only four were submitted by individuals, while others were filed by NGOs. However, in 2012, only eight complaints were submitted, indicating a reduction in the number of complaints despite existing widespread discrimination. Mostly, cases concern the hate speech towards sexual minorities,[43] and they illustrate that when there is a will for consistent enforcement of an existing piece of legislation, it can provide adequate protection to those in need. This issue was particularly raised before the Constitutional Court, which ordered the prohibition of activities of the right-wing organization 'Obraz' and its deletion from the registry of associations.[44] In this case, the Constitutional Court found that members not just tolerated, but supported unconstitutional activities of the organization that were based on a discriminatory attitude towards sexual minority groups. These activities

40 For more on the CPE *see* N. Petrušić, 'Procesni položaj poverenika za zaštitu ravnopravnosti u antidiskriminacionim parnicama' ['Procedural Position of the Commissioner for the Protection of Equality in Antidiscrimination Proceedings'], *Pravni život,* Vol. 11, 2012. Different states have established governmental or quasi-judicial bodies, but in some states they operate as fully independent bodies. For more on these bodies *see in* Equinet, *Equality Bodies and National Human Rights Institutions – Making the Link to Maximise Impact,* The European Network of Equality Bodies, Brussels, 2012.

41 *E.g.*, at the beginning of 2011, one young man was unable to donate blood at the Institute for transfusion in Belgrade, because he wrote in the questionnaire that he was a homosexual. Eventually, he was disqualified as a blood donor because of his sexual orientation. In another case, one woman requested a confirmation from the local municipality that she was not married. She needed this certificate to get married to another woman in Spain, but she was refused without any explanation. She got this certificate after the support of the organization working on LGBT rights. *See* D. Vučković, 'Disriminacija nad lezbejkama i gejevima u Srbiji' ['Discrimination of Lesbian and Gay Population in Serbia'], Labris, available at <www.labris.org.rs/labris/aktivnosti/edukacija-i-lobiranje/1690-diskriminacija-nad-lezbejkama-i-gejevima-u-srbiji.html> (last accessed 23 March 2013).

42 *The Official Gazette of the Republic of Serbia,* no. 72/11.

43 *See also Vejdeland and Others v. Sweden,* ECtHR, Application no. 1813/07, 9 February 2012.

44 Constitutional Court of Serbia, Case VIIU-249/2009, 12 June 2012.

were manifested in hate speech, harassment and degrading treatment, with the aim of violating the constitutionally established rights and freedoms, the rule of law, principles of democracy and commitment to European principles and values, as well as the fundamental principles underlying the constitutional order of the Republic of Serbia. The Court particularly noticed that the Republic of Serbia has relatively recently gone through a very difficult period in history, burdened by war, and that it is still loaded with many prejudices that have deep roots in the Balkans history. Thus, of particular importance is the protection of social values by all means and in a timely manner in order to prevent phenomena that can create an atmosphere of uncertainty and fear among members of entire social groups.[45]

There is another judicial decision worth mentioning. A Belgrade lower court rendered its first judgment pursuant to Article 11 of the LPD, which prohibits hate speech. In this case, the court reasoned that readers' homophobic comments on an article, published in July 2009 on the website of the daily *Press*, constituted an instance of the hate speech against sexual minorities. It was found that the daily discriminated against this vulnerable group by allowing the posting of such comments. The court set up a temporary measure, by prohibiting the publication of the impugned comments on the website and ordered the publication of judgment in its entirety, but rejected compensation.[46] This decision was affirmed by the Appellate court in February 2012. The Belgrade Appellate court confirmed that freedom of expression in media is limited by the prohibition of publication of ideas and opinions that incite discrimination. The court reasoned that the defendant was responsible as the moderator of the website, insofar as it did not prevent readers from posting ideas that could have unforeseen harmful consequences for democratic processes and development of society, although they were removed ten days after they were posted.[47] Most of the 80 posts contained insults, namely that people who belong to the sexual minority are 'perverse', 'sick', and 'immoral', that they are 'bastards', who should be placed in 'ghetto', and 'isolation'. Not only is this one of the first judgments decided pursuant to the LPD, but it

45 The Constitutional Court had in mind that the authorities of the Republic of Serbia – Ministry of Interior, the competent public prosecutor's office and the courts have taken a series of measures and activities against illegal actions of members of the association. The group became known in 2001 for their attack on the first Gay Pride in 2001, which left several people injured. Also, the Serbian Ministry of Interior dubbed Obraz in 2005 a clerical-fascist organization. Furthermore, Serbia's Public Prosecutor in September 2009 filed a motion for the ban on all extremist organizations, including Obraz. Finally, in April 2011, a Belgrade court jailed Obraz's leader Mladen Obradović for two years for organizing riots during the October 2010 Gay Pride, in which about 140 people were injured. In March 2012, he was sentenced to 10 months in prison for spreading hatred and inciting violence against LGBT people ahead of Belgrade Pride 2009. *See* B. Barlovac, 'Serbia Bans Far-Right Organization "Obraz"', *Balkan Insight*, 12 June 2012, available at <www.balkaninsight.com/en/article/serbia-bans-far-right-obraz> (last accessed 19 March 2013).

46 Belgrade Center for Human Rights, *Human Rights in Serbia*, Belgrade, 2011, pp. 265 and 266.

47 Gay Straight Alliance, 'Court of Appeal in Belgrade Confirmed that Hate Speech Against LGBT Population cannot Be Justified by Freedom of Speech and Information, 16 February 2012, available at <http://en.gsa.org.rs/2012/02/court-of-appeal-in-belgrade-confirmed-that-hate-speech-against-lgbt-population-cannot-be-justified-by-freedom-of-speech-and-information/> (last accessed 19 March 2013).

also sends the clear message that it is important to focus on banning dissemination of hate speech and intolerance towards LGBT persons, often contained in online editions of the print media and other web portals.[48]

In some other cases, courts established the responsibility of politicians for acts of hate speech against the LGBT population. For example, in November 2011, an MP, who is also the president of one of the ruling parties and the mayor of a municipality, was found guilty of hate crime on account of his offensive speech during the preparations for the Belgrade Pride in 2011. On this occasion, he was reported saying:

> The position of my party, and my own position is that we are against any gathering, whereby homosexuals would walk the streets of Belgrade and try to present something that is an illness as something that is normal.[49]

The list of politicians who believe that "homosexuality is immoral", akin to pedophilia, and that it "should be medically treated" is rather long.[50] Similarly, the Orthodox Church and its religious dignitaries very often use hate speech against homosexuals. One of them said for the Gay Pride:

> Yesterday we watched the stench poisoning and polluting of the capital of Serbia, scarier than uranium. That was the biggest stench of Sodom, which the modern civilization raised to the pedestal of deity. You see, the violence of wrongheaded infidels caused more violence. Now they are wondering whose fault it was, and they are calling our children the hooligans.[51]

The CPE found that this was the case of hate speech, which was inconsistent with any religious doctrine.

In yet another case, the director of a public cultural institution (Sava Centar) and a member of the ruling party prohibited a press conference at which the Report on human rights of LGBT persons in 2008 was to be presented.[52] The director said that only decent people,

48 *See also* another recommendation where the CPE found a hate speech in an article published by the daily *ALO*. CPE, complaint no. 159/2010, opinion from 23 December 2010; CPE, complaint no. 162/2010, opinion from 27 December 2010.

49 *Blic*, Marković, 'Jedinstvena Srbija traži da Vlada zabrani Paradu ponosa' ['United Serbia Seeks that the Government Prohibits the Gay Pride'], 2 October 2012, available at <www.blic.rs/Vesti/Politika/345731/Markovic-JS-trazi-da-Vlada-zabrani-Paradu-ponosa> (last accessed 23 March 2013).

50 EBART, 'Parada ponosa ili prilagođavanje "političke volje"' ['Pride or Adjustment of "Political Will"'], available at <www.arhiv.rs/politika-i-homofobija-u-srbiji-izjave-politicara-u-srpskoj-stamp/> (last accessed 22 March 2013).

51 CPE, complaint no. 171/2011, opinion from 28 February 2011.

52 Human Rights Watch, 'Srbija: borba protiv homofobije' ['Serbia: Struggle against Homophobia'], 23 November 2009, available at <www.hrw.org/ru/news/2009/11/20/srbija-borba-protiv-homofobije> (last accessed 22 March 2013).

presenting decent contents, can organize meetings in this institution. After a very sharp public reaction, including the reaction of the Ombudsman, he apologized and explained that he cancelled the conference for security reasons.[53]

Unfortunately, it is also not uncommon for teachers or university professors to send very negative messages about the LGBT population. In one such case, during his lectures at the course *Theory of public opinion*, a university professor said that "homosexuality is a disease which should be deluded as stomach ulcers and that homosexuality can be cured only by the sex change".[54] According to the CPE, the professor's challenging of the decision to remove sexuality from the list of diseases contributed to the creation of a humiliating and offensive environment in relation to the LGBT people. It warned the professor that he must be careful not to be misunderstood when talking about homosexuality, insofar as certain false statements can contribute to the creation and maintenance of stereotypes, prejudice and intolerance towards LGBT people, establishing a humiliating or offensive environment.[55] In another case, the school was passive in protecting a high school student who was verbally and physically assaulted by his peers.[56] As he was regularly assaulted, he was forced to enrol part-time at school. He sent a letter to the principal, asking for police presence during his exam, but this request was denied. When he came to the exam, some ten peers shouted: "Kill, kill the fagot" and "Kill, slaughter, exterminate the fagot", and hit him. The CPE found that the school did not take adequate and prompt measures designed to overcome discriminatory attitudes of students towards the LGBT community and to prevent discrimination. The CPE ordered training of employees in order to secure their greater sensibility towards the LGBT population and training of students aimed at strengthening the spirit of tolerance, acceptance of diversity and non-discriminatory conduct.

9.3.2 Legal Status of Transsexuals

Another pertinent issue concerns the legal status of transsexuals. As for the LPD, it prohibits discrimination on the ground of sex change in Article 20. However, this article is not followed by a proper legislative framework that would assure equality of persons who

---

53 In his public statement on 25 February, the Ombudsman said that homophobia and discrimination are not permitted in Serbia. He said that this illegal and incomprehensible act needs to be corrected, as it caused a serious damage to this public institution and to society. It is simply incomprehensible that one important cultural institution banned the press conference of an NGO, which deals with human rights and whose key messages are equality, solidarity, non-violence and tolerance. *See*, *B92*, 'Smene ili ostavke u Centru "Sava"' ['Dismissal or Resignation at "Sava" Center'], 25 February 2009, available at<www.b92.net/info/vesti/index.php?yyyy=2009&mm=02&dd=25&nav_category=12&nav_id=346867> (last accessed 23 March 2013).

54 CPE, complaint no. 249/2011, opinion from 18 January 2012.

55 Poverenik za zaštitu ravnopravnosti, *Redovan godišnji izveštaj za 2012. godinu* [CPE, *Regular Report for 2012*], Belgrade, 2013, p. 69, available at <www.ravnopravnost.gov.rs/lat/izvestaji.php?idKat=16> (last accessed 25 March 2013).

56 CPE, complaint no. 299/2012, opinion from 8 February 2013.

changed their sex.[57] Significantly, amendments to the Law on Health Protection[58] and the Law on Health Insurance,[59] adopted in July 2011, provide the extension of mandatory health insurance and coverage of at least 65% of the cost of health services for gender reassignment for medical reasons. In 2012, the Ministry of Health established the Republic Commission for Transgender persons in order to set conditions under which they can exercise this right, but the Commission was suspended after the last political change. More importantly, despite the fact that gender reassignment in Serbia began some 20 years ago,[60] their legal status is still unresolved.[61] The Public Administration and Local Self-Government Ministry recommended that these persons initiate proceedings for the determination of the content of the document before the competent non-contentious courts, but the state authorities have not been applying a uniform practice with respect to entering the changes in the registers. This has resulted in legal uncertainty and further victimization of people who have undergone a sex change. Today, only in several Belgrade municipalities is it possible to enter new facts (new name and gender) in birth certificates and to receive new documents, while other local servants mainly refuse it.[62] Even if these new facts are entered in birth certificates, some institutions refuse to issue new documents (registration of cars, issuance of diploma, etc) because they seem not to understand the concept of privacy. Accordingly, the CPE issued an opinion in February 2012 recommending one faculty member not to correct data in the old diploma, but to issue a new diploma, based on the new identity.[63] In this case, the person left Serbia after graduation from a law faculty and went through a gender reassignment in Germany. The person continued to live in Germany, but wanted to receive new diplomas from all three levels of education. The primary and secondary school immediately issued new diplomas, but the law faculty invoked Article 102 of the Law on the Higher Education, which allows issuance of a new diploma only if it is invalid. The Faculty offered to make corrections to the existing diploma, not understanding that this solution violates the right to privacy and hinders social integration of this person. In the absence of domestic norms, the CPE directly invoked relevant international norms and standards and recommended the faculty to issue a new diploma, which

57 *See* Zaštitnik građana, *Poseban izveštaj o LGBT populaciji u Srbiji – stanje ljudskih prava i društveni položaj* [Ombudsman, *Special Report on LGBT Population in Serbia – Human Rights and Social Status*], Belgrade, September 2011, pp. 14-18.

58 *Official Gazette of the RS,* no. 107/2005, 72/2009, 88/2010, 99/2010 and 57/2011.

59 *Official Gazette of the RS,* no. 107/2005, correction 109/2005, 57/2011.

60 The gender reassignment is done in accordance with the jurisprudence of the ECtHR. *See*: *Van Kück v. Germany*, Application no. 35968/97, 12 September 2003; *Schlumpf v. Switzerland*, Application no. 29002/06, 8 January 2009.

61 *Supra* note 57, p. 14.

62 *Ibid.*, p. 18.

63 *See* CPE, complaint no. 297/201, opinion from 24 February 2012. This new trend is particularly emphasized in the jurisprudence of the ECtHR. *See Christine Goodwin v. UK*, Application no. 38957/95, 11 July 2002; *L v. Lithuania*, Application no. 27527/03, 11 September 2007.

was done within a short time. This recommendation was issued shortly before the decision of the Constitutional Court, which found that the municipal administration, declaring that it did not have the competence to enter new data in a birth certificate, violated the right of the complainant to dignity and free development of personality.[64]

9.4 Conclusion

Although the legal framework is mostly modern and in accordance with relevant international standards, and although some important decisions were brought in the last three years, discrimination against the LGBT population is still widespread. According to a recent survey, a quarter of the respondents do not know what the term discrimination means, while 60% believe that discrimination is very much present in our society.[65] Almost 14.5% believe that the LGBT population is discriminated against, and the social distance marker shows that there is a maximum distance against LGBT persons (even 79.5% respondents said that they would not accept an LGBT person as a family member).[66] There are many reasons for this situation, as documented in reports of independent bodies: frequent and widespread hate messages against the LGBT community and the lack of sufficient and genuine will to deal with this problem; existence of prejudices and stereotypes related to LGBT people that significantly impede the implementation of non-discrimination laws (even public officials enforce this prejudice in their statements); insufficient human rights programmes for education and sensitization of employees in public institutions; the lack of understanding of the human rights concept and international obligations that derive from the jurisprudence of relevant international institutions; the absence of measures designed to raise awareness and promote tolerance towards sexual minorities; the usage of school textbooks and other educational materials that contain texts filled with inadequate interpretation of homosexuality; the lack of genuine will of education authorities to deal with peer violence and discrimination based on sexual orientation in educational institutions; the role of media that very often spread hate speech and discriminatory attitudes towards the LGBT population. Illustrative are the words of the CPE in her public statement issued after the ban of Gay Pride in October 2012:

> It shows in the most direct way the high level of homophobia in Serbia. The atmosphere of fear, threats, violence and other severe forms of discrimination that are legally prohibited and punishable have reached the culmination and

64 Constitutional Court of Serbia, Už - 3238/2011, 8 March 2012.

65 *Supra* note 55, pp. 31-32.

66 *Ibid.*, p. 35. *See also* Razlika d.o.o., 'Izveštaj o položaju seksualnih manjina u Vojvodini' ['Report on the Position of Sexual Minorities in Vojvodina'], 2 December 2010, available at <www.autonomija.info/izvestaj-o-polozaju-seksualnih-manjina-u-vojvodini.html> (last accessed 31 March 2013).

> achieved its goal. Inability and unwillingness of the state to protect the constitutional right to peaceful gathering and freedom of speech show how little has been done in the previous years on promoting the rule of law and culture of peace and tolerance.[67]

All the aforementioned bluntly demonstrates that human rights culture, as a part of the larger liberal-democratic political culture, is not yet fully entrenched in Serbia. While the very members of the LGBT population are at times unaware of their rights and liberties, as well as unable to identify when these are violated, a far more intricate problem concerns the lack of readiness on the part of the majority, most importantly some institutional actors and parts of political elites, to recognize and respect the rights of persons belonging to vulnerable groups. Their indifference and, even worse, intolerance are a vivid reminder of how far Serbia is from the ultimate goal of democratic consolidation.

67 CPE, Public Statement Regarding the Ban of the Gay Pride, no. 1464, 3 October 2012, available at <www.ravnopravnost.gov.rs/lat/saopstenjaZaJavnost.php?idKat=6> (last accessed 31 March 2013).

10 Political Culture in Post-Conflict and Divided Societies: The Case of Bosnia and Herzegovina

Damir Banović

10.1 Introduction

Since political culture is a complex social phenomenon, and since there are different approaches to studying it, it is clear that there is no agreement among theoreticians and researchers regarding the dimensions of political culture.[1] Although numerous theoreticians have dealt with issues of political culture and its relevance for the existence and functioning of political institutions, *i.e.*, the possibility of introducing democratic political institutions, it was only in the 1960s that the works of Lucein Pye, Gabriel Almond and Sydney Verba[2] brought clear theoretical elaborations and operational methods of the concept of political culture. Pye claims that political culture is

> the set of attitudes, beliefs and sentiments which give order and meaning to a political process and which provide the underlying assumptions and rules that govern behavior in the political system. It encompasses both the political ideals and operating norms of a polity. Political culture is thus the manifestation in aggregate form of the psychological and subjective dimensions of politics. A political culture is the product of both the collective history of a political system and the life histories of the members of the system, and thus it is rooted equally in public events and private experience.[3]

Almond and Verba's definition of the concept of political culture essentially does not differ from Pye's. According to Almond and Verba, political culture refers to "the specifically political orientations – attitudes towards the political system and its various parts, and attitudes toward the role of the self in the system".[4]

---

1 Z. Popov-Momčinović, *Politička kultura u periodu tranzicije* (MA thesis on file at the University of East Sarajevo, East Sarajevo, 2008).

2 G. Almond & S. Verba, *The Civic Culture*, Princeton University Press, Princeton, 1963.

3 W.L. Pye & S. Verba, *Political Culture and Political Development*, Princeton University Press, Princeton, 1965.

4 Almond & Verba, 1963, p. 20.

What Almond and Verba's study demonstrated is that civic political culture complies with a democratic order and that this culture can sustain the stability of this order. The main feature of civic political culture is the ability of citizens to control contradictory political roles. The ability to achieve balance among different roles (subordinate, parochial and participatory) and contradictory orientations (cognitive, affective and evolutionary) is the main characteristic of civic political culture. This characteristic is obtained through political socialization and education. For a stable and functional democracy, it is not enough to have a high level of political competence, skills necessary for political cooperation and knowledge of political systems; instead, it is necessary to have an awareness of national identity and pride, developed social and political trust in other citizens, a balanced relation towards ruling elites, readiness to extend political cooperation when needed, and a deeper effective and not simply instrumental connection with the political order. According to Almond and Verba, this is the only way to ensure a democratic political system.[5]
Since the war of 1992–1995, there has been no theoretical and comprehensive empirical research on political culture in Bosnia and Herzegovina. There have been isolated cases of academic interest displayed by institutions for science and research,[6] *i.e.*, cases where focus is placed on research. In order to determine the type of political culture in Bosnia and Herzegovina, *i.e.*, of its combination, it is necessary to conduct comprehensive empirical research based on which we could be scientifically relevant when speaking about which type/s of political culture is/are dominating. However, as there is a lack of such research, the discussion could be based on particular and focused empirical research, as well as general attitudes that do not have to be particularly proven, including the fact that this is a transitional, post-conflict and divided society. Having this in mind, one can speak about what is possible, *i.e.*, a suggested situation and directions of development of political culture, as well as perspectives of development of democratic political culture from a scientific point of view. In that sense, this chapter will discuss the elements listed below, which determine the possibility of development and the nature of political culture in order to provide a picture of this possibility.

10.2 Determinants of Development of Democratic Political Culture in Bosnia and Herzegovina

Observing and determining the potentials of development of a democratic political culture is impossible to do outside the social context of Bosnia and Herzegovina's

5 V. Vujčić, 'Politička kultura i politička struktura: odnos političke kulture, strukture i demokracije', Part I, *Politička misao,* Vol. XXXVI, No. 1, 1999, pp. 120-121.

6 In that sense, MA theses dealing with political culture were Z. Popov-Momčinović, *Politička kultura u periodu tranzicije* (MA thesis on file at the University of East Sarajevo, East Sarajevo, 2008 and T. Lazić, *Teorije političke kulture i tokovi njenih transformacija u Bosni i Hercegovini* (MA thesis on file at the at the Faculty of Political Science of the University of Sarajevo, 2008).

society: its history, cultural patterns of the previous and current period, political structure, and the fact that this is a multicultural and divided society. What heavily burdens a political culture as well as the possibility of the development of a democratic political culture is its socialist legacy (and political culture encouraged in this period); its post-socialist transitional period, which cannot be separated from its conflict and post-conflict period (which were parallel to each other); the introduction of a democratic political system, and an entirely new complex state structure and consociational democracy.

10.2.1 The Socialist Legacy and the Post-Socialist Transitional Period

Political culture, as a culture in general, depends on experiences gained during historical development, *i.e.*, the development of a specific political community, which can be best seen in the example of transitional countries trying to establish a new political system because cultural sediments of the previous experience in one type of regime also exist in the new system.[7] It was precisely in their comparative research that Almond and Verba showed that one of the main determinants of existing political cultural patterns is political experience gained through history.[8] A study conducted by M. Kaase in 1994, covering Bulgaria, the Czech Republic, Hungary, Poland and the European part of Russia, showed that socialist experiences left important traces in the political awareness of citizens. The findings of this study speak about the fact that democratic consolidation in Central and Eastern Europe occurs and is occurring neither automatically nor in line with the realization of institutional changes. The political culture of these countries contains significant *sediments* of socialist ways of thinking that bring a great deal of ambivalence to their political sentiment.[9] The socialist period in Bosnia and Herzegovina,[10] in the shape of an economic, political and ideological monologue and social governance in a *top-down* manner, was suitable for the survival of traditional values, where the emphasis is placed on the individual being subordinate to the collective, on a strict social hierarchy, and a specific understanding of humans as subjects who work and produce while their civil rights are mainly neglected and violated. In the public sphere, people repeated official ideological

---

7 Popov-Momčinović, 2008, p. 15.

8 *Ibid.*, p. 31.

9 Vujčić, 1999, pp. 131-132.

10 Socialist Federal Republic of Yugoslavia was established at the second meeting of AVNOJ in Jajce on 29 November 1943, as a union of six peoples and six republics (Slovenia, Serbia, Croatia, Bosnia and Herzegovina, Montenegro and Macedonia) and at first it was called Federal Republic of Yugoslavia, which was changed at the third meeting of AVNOJ to Federal People's Republic of Yugoslavia. On 7 April 1963, the country was named Socialist Federal Republic of Yugoslavia (SFRJ). The dominant political role belonged to the Communist Party of Yugoslavia (KPJ), and later the League of Communists of Yugoslavia (SKJ). After Yugoslavia was thrown out of the Informbiro in 1948, the social and political system developed in the direction of self-governing socialism based on social ownership and socialist self-governance (*see* Lazić, 2008, p. 148 *et seq.*).

phrases, whereas in the private sphere they either shared their hostility towards the system or were indifferent towards it.[11] The starting point of establishing a political culture in socialist Bosnia and Herzegovina was the people's fight for their freedom based on which the following emerged: a common political and social worldview and system of values, a collectivist matrix of fraternity and equality and leaning towards the principles of social equality, and solidarity of all citizens and all peoples,[12] as well as resistance to fascism.[13] The analysis of the political culture of self-governance in the work of Franjo Kožul, in his *Political Culture of Self-Governance*, indicates specific occurrences in Bosnia and Herzegovina that are reflected in the following ways: 1) fear of using freedom offered by the system of self-governance; 2) political culture emphasizing the element of destruction: revolutionary principle of 'destroy in order to build'; 3) individuals continuously opposing the community, etc.[14] Therefore, types of parochial and subordinate political culture were created. Certain studies showed that perspectives, beliefs and values created during the communist period were *transferred* into the transitional period of post-communist countries. In this sense, Andrew Heywood, in his work *Politics*, states that communist countries were equal to liberal democracies in the process of transition.

> But there is a reason why now we are treating them as special systems. One: their communist legacy cannot be forgotten overnight [. . .]. Two: the transition itself has released powers and caused completely different problems than those of western polyarchies. This is why it is perhaps better to classify them as new democracies or half-democracies.[15]

For a post-socialist country such as Bosnia and Herzegovina, the transitional period has been a rather complicated process of overcoming the political past, solving the identity crisis, and adopting the elements of a democratic political system.[16] The transfer and revival of the characteristics of a political culture from the previous system in the new post-socialist period, after gaining independence in 1992, actually transferred the system of self-governance into nationalism, *i.e.,* into ethno-nationalism with dominance of the particular over the general, and a noticeable rise of religious fundamentalism in the public space.[17] The citizens are aware of their political rights and express the need to participate

---

11 Popov-Momčinović, 2008, p. 43.

12 *See* Decisions of ZAVNOBiH as of 1943 and 1944.

13 Lazić, 2008, p. 206.

14 *Ibid.*, p. 151.

15 A. Heywood, *Politika,* Clio, Beograd, 2004, p. 70.

16 Andrew Heywood identifies three problems of post-socialist countries: 1) Overcoming political and cultural consequences of communist regimes. One-party system and censorship prevented the development of civil culture, which emphasizes participation, negotiations and consensus; 2) Problems arising from the process of economic transition; 3) Weakness of state government when facing ethnic and national tensions (*Ibid.*, pp. 70-72).

17 Lazić, 2008, p. 151.

in the public sphere, but in practical terms, the political behaviour of citizens is characterized by apathy and indolence in relation to politics.[18] The transition from a socialist to a democratic political system includes not only normative changes that enable democratic pluralism, decentralization of the government and the establishment of the civil sector, but also changes that occur within subjective dimensions of political culture. Considering the fact that there are certain categories that are difficult to change (perspectives, beliefs and values), we should not be surprised to see that changes in political cultures, in the sense of development of a democratic political culture, do not occur at the same pace as changes associated with establishing new institutions and changes at the normative level.[19] The reason for such tendencies in post-communist countries is an important historical, *i.e.*, communist, legacy that includes "firm social structures, a low level of social political mobility, the lack of establishment of civil structures and setting religious and cultural specificities of different social groups aside".[20] As some theoreticians have emphasized,[21] the key role for the development and stability of young democracies certainly belongs to the orientation of citizens towards new systems and values. However, the problem of studying post-communism and post-socialism is quite complex because this is a mixture of old and new regimes, old and new societies and because this is a unique hybrid resistant to change that often varies from country to country. In the territory of the former Yugoslavia, the problem is much more complex because this is a territory where, during the 1990s, the transition emerged as a form of resistance in a pre-modern age.[22]

10.3 The Influence of the War in Bosnia and Herzegovina (1992-1995) on the Development of Political Culture

Compared to the conflicts in other Yugoslav republics, the war in Bosnia and Herzegovina lasted the longest – three and a half years – and the number of victims was the largest, at approximately 100,000.[23] This was a tri-polar conflict where, simply put, Serbs, Bosniaks and Croats fought against one another.[24] The reason for the conflict before the war was the issue of whether Bosnia and Herzegovina should remain a part of Yugoslavia: most

18 *Ibid.*, p. 10.

19 *Ibid.*, p. 142. The processes of transitional countries in which changes occur at the normative level in the sense of changes in constitutionally legal systems, passing new laws and amending the old ones without changing the social basis was the topic of the work of N. Wichmann, *Democratization Without Societal Participation*, LIT Verlag, Berlin, 2007.

20 B. Galić, *Politička kultura novih demokracija*, Available at <www.hsd.hr/revija>.

21 S.P. Huntington, *Treći talas: demokratizacija na izmaku dvadesetog veka*, CID, Podgorica, 2004.

22 Popov-Momčinović, 2008, p. 40.

23 <www.idc.org.ba/presentation/index.htm>.

24 According to the last census held in 1991, 44% were Muslims, 31% were Serbs and 17% were Croats. The rest of the population declared themselves as Yugoslavians, national minorities, or they refused to declare themselves. Available at <www.fzs.ba/popis.htm#_POPIS STANOVNIŠTVA 1991 I STARIJI>.

Bosniaks and Croats advocated the idea of secession, while a vast majority of Serbs in Bosnia and Herzegovina wanted the republic to remain part of Yugoslavia. This issue was the subject of a referendum held between 29 February and 1 March 1992, when most Bosniaks and Croats voted for secession, while the Serbs mainly boycotted the referendum. After the secession of Bosnia and Herzegovina, the cause of the conflict changed, at which point the conflict turned into a war. The question arose of whether the state should stay within internationally recognized borders.[25] During the war, there were several governing zones. The institutions of the Republic of Bosnia and Herzegovina were able to ensure their governance only in one part of the country, and the others were controlled by the internationally unrecognized para-state formations of Republika Srpska and the Croatian Community of Herzeg-Bosnia.[26]

There is no single position regarding the nature of the war, either within the academic community[27] or among Bosnia and Herzegovina's different ethnic communities. A survey was conducted 10 years after the war, with 95% of the Bosniaks and 73% of the Croats arguing that the war in Bosnia and Herzegovina was a war of aggression, while 84% of Serbs polled said that it was a civil war.[28] Opinions regarding the unified state, the formation of parallel structures during the war, and the nature of the conflict in Bosnia and Herzegovinaare only several indicators of different perspectives of ethnic groups related to many political issues. There have been and continue to be many attempts to find a solution for these issues within the consociational governance model established after the war. Along with these issues, facing the consequences of the war and the accommodation of groups in a newly established state structure are burdensome topics that continue to significantly influence the development of a democratic political culture in Bosnia and Herzegovina.

The fact that there is almost no political consensus proves that there is no developed democratic political culture among political elites. This implies the acceptance of an established model of decision-making and representation of the collective. At the same time, this is a precondition for the transition into the phase of balancing between collective and individual representation in the political system of Bosnia and Herzegovina. The consequences of the war were deeper divisions among the ethnic groups in Bosnia and Herzegovina, which affected public trust in institutions, as well as the issues of the existence of a state, which significantly influences the performance and the efficiency of a political system. The transitional period cannot be separated from the post-conflict period, which had an influence on the development of political culture in Bosnia and

25 T. Gromes, 'Dejtonski mirovni sporazum', *in* D. Banović & S. Gavrić (Eds.), *Država, politika i društvo u Bosni i Hercegovini – analiza postdejtonskog političkog sistema,* University Press – Magistrat, Sarajevo, 2011, p. 39.

26 *Ibid.*, p. 39.

27 G. Marković, *Bosanskohercegovački federalizam*, Službeni glasnik – Unversity Press – Magistrat, Belgrade/Sarajevo, 2012, pp. 37-50.

28 Gromes, 2011, p. 40.

Herzegovina, and which is also characterized by traditional and subordinate elements in this period, of which the most notable are: 1) mythically influenced awareness; 2) the dominance of the collective over the individual and 3) a considerable lack of trust in state institutions.[29] In the post-conflict period, there has been significant progress regarding the return of refugees, as well as in reconciliation and mutual tolerance among the people at large.[30] Trust and ethnic tolerance are preconditions for functioning public institutions. A study conducted in 2010, entitled *What Croats, Bosniaks, and Serbs think of one another and what they think of Bosnia and Herzegovina*, showed that although these ethnic groups have been living together for centuries, they in fact know quite little about one another and that their mutual perception is burdened with stereotypes from the past and the war. Relations among people are not good, and they are burdened with a considerable lack of trust in one another, mutual cooperation is very low, and there is no common vision about either the past or the future of the country.[31] A likely reason for such poor relations should be sought in the last war, as most qualifications listed above were created during the conflict or as a result of of the conflict. War and war traumas are ever present in all aspects of living in this state, and they place a heavy burden on mutual relations. According to the study, there is almost no consensus among different ethnic groups about the cause of the war, and each ethnic group has its own view and believes its own "truth".[32] The study also showed the relations of the three ethnic communities towards the state. When describing Bosnia and Herzegovina, they mostly agree that it is "a divided country without a future, and a country of three constituent peoples".[33] Furthermore, the study demonstrated that when it comes to building a joint state, there is no common goal: each constituent people has its own specific national goals and its own perspective of the state.[34] The study also illustrated potential regarding the development of mutual relations. This is supported by the fact that people included in the survey increasingly recognized positive values of the other constituent peoples, and the level of negative stereotypes has significantly decreased in the past ten years.[35] This study showed the influence and importance

29 According to a study by the United Nations Development Program (Quarterly report January-March) as of 2001, the decrease of trust in public officials in Bosnia and Herzegovina was affected by the belief of people involved in the survey, namely that there is a lot of corruption, crime, white collar crime and other misuse of positions. It is rather worrisome to observe that all surveys up to now have shown an increase of such beliefs. More in D. Vejnović, 'Politička kultura u Bosni i Hercegovini', *infra* note 30.

30 D. Vejnović, 'Politička kultura u Bosni i Hercegovini',*Lokalna samouprava*, Vol. II, June 2004, p. 57.

31 B. Skoko, *Što Hrvati, Bošnjaci i Srbi misle jedni o drugima, a što o Bosni i Hercegovini*, Friedrich Ebert Stiftung, Sarajevo, 2011, p. 15.

32 *Ibid.*, p. 16.

33 29% of the people chose both descriptions. For Bosniaks, B-H is a divided, multiethnic European state of three constituent peoples; for Croats, B-H is a divided country of three constituent peoples under the control of the international community; for Serbs, B-H is a state of three constituent peoples under the control of the international community. More in *ibid.*, p. 18.

34 *Ibid.*, p. 19.

35 *Ibid.*, p. 20.

of the war regarding mutual relations among ethnic groups, and that relations of trust and mutual tolerance are significant conditions for a functioning democratic political system. The situation in which group members believe that others are using state institutions for their own particular interests does not contribute to establishing the basis for a functional state. A consensus among ethnic group members can be found when discussing the fact that Bosnia and Herzegovina is a divided country (even though it is unclear how they understand the concept of this division), which is one of the preconditions of a social revival of the consociational model. There is still no agreement regarding the internal structure of the country. In other words, no common ground has been reached regarding the decision to either abolish entities or create new ones. This demonstrates that national issues that cause tensions among the ethnic groups have not yet been resolved.

10.4 Applying the Multicultural Concept in the Divided Society and Perspectives on the Development of a Democratic Political Culture

The society of Bosnia and Herzegovina is multicultural, multi-confessional and deeply politically divided. These facts serve as the basis for a consociational or concordational model of governance with collective rights, collective representation, a wide coalitional government, veto mechanisms, a complex state structure,a high level of decentralization, and a permanent conflict among political elites. Formally, this system can be characterized as democratic,with numerous political parites, periodic parliamentary and local elections, equal active and limited passive electoral rights,[36] freedom of assembly and association (as preconditions for a functioning civil sector), and freedom of media. Constitutional limits are set on the passive electoral rights of constituent peoples regarding the entity in which they live, *i.e.*, of the "Others" regarding their candidacy for central state bodies: the Presidency of Bosnia and Herzegovina and the House of Peoples of the Parliamentary Assembly of Bosnia and Herzegovina, both formally and thus practically set limits on the development of democratic practices and democratic political culture in the form of political participation and elections. Introducing democracy formally does not necessarily

36 Restrictions put on passive rights lower the democratic potential of citizens in the entire territory of the state. In particular, passive electoral right is limited to constituent peoples considering parts of the state in which they live: Croats and Bosniaks in Republika Srpska cannot be candidates for membership of the Presidency of B-H which comes from the territory of Republika Srpska, and Serbs living in the Federation of B-H cannot be elected members of the Presidency coming from the territory of the Federation. Passive electoral right is also limited for those who belong to the group of *the Others* when it comes to membership of the Presidency of Bosnia and Herzegovina and the choice of delegates of the House of Peoples of the Parliamentary Assembly of Bosnia and Herzegovina. Even the European Court of Human Rights has stated that this is a discrimination of *the Others*, particularly in the case of *Sejdic and Finci v. Bosnia and Herzegovina* as of 2009.

mean the existence of democratic practices; instead it is only one of the preconditions for its establishment, as well as for the establishment and development of democratic political culture. Lijphart analyzed the phenomenon of consociational democracy and the relation between political culture and political structure in the criticism of a one-sided approach to research.[37] Lijphart discovered that some countries do not have a developed set of values and perspectives with the label of democratic political culture of Almond and Verba, and that democracy still functions successfully. In particular, in many countries that are divided on the basis of religion, language, ethnicity or ideology, agreement is achieved through constitutionally-set mechanisms and the agreement of elites that overcome cultural differences among groups. However, even in such democracies, there has to be at least a modicum of consensus regarding the state. In order for such a system to function, citizens need to have a positive opinion of the established system and support for agreement among elites. In that sense, Lijphart was writing of different political subcultures within segments, and thus differentiated between centrifugal and centripetal political cultures. In centrifugal political cultures, there is a consensus of subcultures that recognize the legitimacy of one another regarding participation in governing and social resources. The Netherlands and Austria are examples of such a system. On the other hand, in some societies there are centripetal powers that dominate over the centrifugal and do not enable consensus, which is the case in Northern Ireland.[38] Bosnia and Herzegovina is an example of centripetal political culture because it still does not have a consensus regarding the existence of the state and the application of the consociational model that was introduced by the Constitution.

Bosnia and Herzegovina is a classic example of the application of the concept of multicultural politics[39] (which gradually evolve) and of a predominantly collectivist representation – constituent peoples and national minorities with a different range of rights. The Preamble of the Constitution of Bosnia and Herzegovina[40] states that "the carriers of sovereignty are "constituent peoples" (Bosniaks, Croats and Serbs), along with "Others" and "citizens of

37 A. Lijphart, *Demokracija u pluralnim društvima,* Globus – Školska knjiga, Zagreb, 1992.

38 Z. Popov-Momčinović, *Politička kultura* (Reader for students on file at the Faculty of Philosophy of the University in East Sarajevo).

39 Bosnia and Herzegovina is not an exception when it comes to the conflict of specific consociational mechanisms. One of such examples is the one of South Tirol (Italy). Mechanisms of representation of ethnocultural identities in other countries have mainly been developed in the context of minorities, *i.e.,* the exceptions of the liberal-civil concept of neutrality of a state in relation to culture, language and tradition. "Where there are elements of ethnic federalism, political representation at the level of a state is mainly ensured on a territorial principle (*i.e.,* at the principle of representation of territorial units) – such as the case of Canada. Also, in contexts where identity as such plays a vital role in political life (*e.g.,* in Belgium), politically relevant identity is determined on the basis of a linguistic group." E. Hodžić & N. Stojanović, *Novi – stari ustavni inženjering?,* Analitika, Sarajevo, 2011.

40 According to the decision of the Constitutional Court of B-H on constituency of the peoples, No. U-5/98, the Preamble is considered a normative part of the Constitution of B-H.

Bosnia and Herzegovina". When this provision is applied and interpreted, we can conclude that there the following population categories or groups exist:

1. Constituent peoples (*i.e.* Serbs, Bosniaks and Croats);
2. National minorities, totalling 17, according to the Law on National Minorities;[41]
3. Nationally undecided or those individuals who for certain ideological reasons do not wish to declare themselves regarding their ethnic identity.These individuals either are not the same ethnicity as one of the constituent peoples or of one of the many ethnic minorities. They tend to view identity as a fluid or changeable category. They may also include individuals from so-called "mixed marriages".

Therefore, the principle of exclusively collective representation and the dominance of collective rights in the political system of Bosnia and Herzegovina has been the cause of the exclusion of the civil principle observed as an abstract category. This concept of a citizen is not recognized in the constitutional system of Bosnia and Herzegovina because being a political subject in Bosnia and Herzegovina involves filling gaps with national or ethnic content, or refusing to express one's opinion of it. However, recognizing the category of ethnically undecided citizens (within the category of the Others) at the middle level of territorially-political organization of government,[42] does not mean that this partially introduced the civic principle. Instead there is a logical consequence of exclusively collective representation, and this consequence is the following: in case you do not belong to any of the groups listed, then there is nothing else but to belong to a group of ethnically undecided people through which you should articulate a certain common group interest that in reality does not exist. Further application of the consociational model also includes introducing collective rights: political representation of ethnic groups through a system of quotas or proportional representation in legislative, executive, judicial and governing institutions (based either on explicit constitutional norms or on constitutional custom); complex decision-making process: a two-thirds process, consensus or special, so-called, entity voting, mechanisms for the protection of vital national interest (right to veto) and similar.[43] Bosnia and Herzegovina has

41 Art. 3 of the Law on Rights of National Minorities, *Official Gazette of B-H,* Nos. 24/03 and 76/05 states: "A national minority, in terms of this Law, shall be a part of the population-citizens of B-H that does not belong to any of three constituent peoples and it shall include people of the same or similar ethnic origin, same or similar tradition, customs, religion, language, culture, and spirituality and close or related history and other characteristics. B-H shall protect the status and equality of members of national minorities as follows: Albanians, Montenegrins, Czechs, Italians, Jews, Hungarians, Macedonians, Germans, Poles, Romas, Romanians, Russians, Rusins, Slovaks, Slovenians, Turks, Ukrainians and other who meet requirements referred to in Paragraph 1 of this Article."

42 After the Decision of the Constitutional Court of B-H on the constituency of peoples U – 5/98 as of 2000 (the decision contains four partial decisions as of 29 January 2000, 18 February 2000, 1 July 2000 and 18 August 2000), relevant provisions of entity constitutions were proclaimed unconstitutional regarding the Constitution of B-H.

43 More on the consociational model and social preconditions for consociational democracy in: G. Marković, *Bosanskohercegovački federalizam*, Službeni glasnik – Unversity Press – Magistrat, Belgrade/Sarajevo, 2012, pp. 215-246, and M. Kasapović, *Bosna i Hercegovina: podjeljeno društvo i nestabilna država*, Politička kultura, Zagreb, 2005.

fulfilled most conditions for the development of the consociational model of democracy. Its society is plural because it covers three segments based on the lines of division of the population into three nations, which then formed an entire set of organizations and institutions, and which function as separate sub-systems. Each social segment has its own political, economic, religious, cultural, athletic, charity and other organizations, its own educational systems, systems of values, tradition, media, manifestations and other forms of organizing and expressing its specificities. Although this is a divided society, ethnic groups do not necessarily avoid cooperation in different fields of social life by advancing social processes that are going on within them, including the transportation of services, capital and goods, organizing joint cultural manifestations, establishing sports competitions, and establishing a confederation of different unions, etc.[44] Cooperation between elites and segments is easily facilitated via communication because, from a linguistic perspective, all segments speak the same language.[45] However, democratic stabilization and consolidation are not enabled because a minimum of consensus on the part of political elites regarding the existence of the state, interpretation of constitutional norms on representation of groups and levels that apply either proportional or quota systems, the scope of jurisdiction of the state and federal units, and the range of constitutional reforms does not exist.

Democratic instability does not necessarily have to be caused by the lack of democratic political culture. The fact is that there is no true opposition. This is due to the need to represent all social segments in the government, violating the freedom of individuals in favour of the freedom of a collective, a large coalition and the right to veto that make decision making harder, as well as the subordination of the competence of public administration to a proportional system of equal representation of segments. This contributes to strong clientelism, and increases criticism of the consociational model as such.[46]

Freedom of association and political participation are the first formal preconditions for democracy. This influences political culture by making participation more possible. With these preconditions, citizens have the opportunity to form associations ideologically in order to fight for political governance through the right to elect and choose certain political parties compatible with their ideological view. Of course, this does not exhaust individuals acting as political subjects, but it is a very important part of democratic political practice, which at the same time shows tendencies in a transitional and divided society. Since 1990, and since mass national movements and the first multi-party elections, political parties in Bosnia and Herzegovina have lost this characteristic. In the first multi-party elections, national parties such as the Party of Democratic Action (Stranka demokratske akcije,or SDA, which represents Bosniaks), the Croatian Democratic Union (Hrvatska

44 Marković, 2012, pp. 215-217.

45 Linguists agree that people in Croatia, Serbia, Bosnia and Herzegovina and Montenegro speak one polycentric standard language, which linguistics treats as Serbo-Croatian. More on this in: S. Kordić, *Jezik i nacionalizam,* Durieux, Zagreb 2010.

46 Kasapović, 2005, pp. 69-72.

demokratska zajednica, or HDZ,which represents Croats) and the Serbian Democratic Party (Srpska demokratska stranaka, orSDS, which represents Serbs) won 84% of the votes.[47] From 1996 until 2002, parliamentary elections were held every two years on the basis of the OSCE's temporary electoral rules. These short election cycles were implemented in an attempt to change voter orientation, shifting allegiance away from national, or ethnically oriented, parties and towards civil parties. However, election results make clear that this goal was not achieved. In the first post-war parliamentary elections in 1996, national parties won 96% of the mandates in total, and they were also successful in 1998. In 2000, non-ethnic parties won 47% of the votes and thus formed a government that, for the first time, did not contain exclusively ethnic parties or a coalition based on ethnic quotas.[48] In 2002,the Central Election Commission of Bosnia and Herzegovina organized elections based on the Law on Elections of Bosnia and Herzegovina. These elections once again brought ethnically-oriented parties to power, with the lowest voter turnout observed since 1990, at a mere 53.95%. The next elections were held in 2006. This time there were 36 parties, eight coalitions, and 12 independent candidates. A study conducted by the Friedrich Ebert Foundation at that time emphasized that:

> The last elections are characterized by several interesting elements: a bigger turnout, a very active and organized civil society, a clear fight between nationalist rhetoric and rhetoric of people's everyday problems, overlapping and progress regarding the support between different ideologies and political parties, and finally, peaceful and well-controlled elections.[49]

Although new political parties emerged, according to analysis and research, the citizens basically chose the *status quo*. In 2010, the Social-Democratic Party won the most votes of any single party in the elections. However, the sum of the votes obtained by national parties, in particular the SDA, HDZ and SNSD (Alliance of Independent Social Democrats – Stranka nezavisnih socijal demokrata), was even greater. However, the post-election period was characterized by long negotiations, lasting 14 months, related to forming the government at the state-level due to different opinions regarding group representation. According to the results found in a study on socio-psychological characteristics of voters and abstainers in Bosnia and Herzegovina,citizens' political activities are mainly voting from election to election. Their low interest in parties exposes the gap between parties and voters. This enables parties and their presidents to act independently and irresponsibly

47 T. Topić, 'Hibridni režim i političke partije u Bosni i Hercegovini',*in* S. Puhalo (Ed.), *Socio-psihološki profil glasača i apstinenata u Bosni i Hercegovini,* Art print, Banja Luka, 2007, p. 35.

48 *Ibid.*, p. 35.

49 F.E. Stiftung, *Analysis of Results of Parliamentary Elections in Bosnia and Herzegovina,* Sarajevo 2006, p. 1.

towards voters. There is an impression that parties have power but no real relations with civil society. Another indicator of this gap are the pre-electoral coalitions that break after the elections (for example, the post-electoral break between the Croatian Party of Rights – Hrvatska stranka prava/HSP and the HDZ 1990), and the creation of post-electoral coalitions over which citizens exercise absolutely no influence.[50] Since the beginning of the multi-party system, the decrease in the number of voters has been evident.[51] This is often explained by apathy, scepticism of citizens regarding possible progress, a lack of trust in political parties, and the factual protectorate of Bosnia and Herzegovina, where voters do not see the purpose of their political activism. The country may be rightly termed a protectorate given that the High Representative in Bosnia and Herzegovina has the possibility to change the Constitution, pass laws, change the authorities, etc.[52]

According to the above-mentioned study, since the elections in 2006, voters in Bosnia and Herzegovina, regardless of the party that they vote for, consider themselves and their ideas ethically superior, and express the need for a leader and intolerance to new ideas. Charismatic leaders of political parties and their nationalist rhetoric were acceptable for most disappointed voters. All voters expressed nationalism (except those of the Social-Democratic Party). Conformism can be seen among all voters, and all of them equally accept both conservative and liberal ideas (which show that voters still do not differentiate between these two ideas). Also, the research showed that voters trust the influence of an outside force more (luck, destiny or God) than they trust their own influence on their lives.[53] Therefore, we still have the elements of a subordinate-parochial political culture of trusting leaders (now political parties), a lack of tolerance, which is an important condition for a functioning political system of a divided society, and the influence of outside factors on life as dominantly pre-political, in which political subjects are seen as objects of the flow of history. Other focused and non-systematic studies showed that the main features of political culture are still provincialism, a patriarchal mentality, and mistrust towards the 'other'.[54]

Experience so far has shown that the activities of political parties in Bosnia and Herzegovina, to a significant or considerable extent, are determined by national affiliation. Regardless of their profile, most parties advocate ethnic interests.[55] Bosnia and Herzegovina is characterized by a hyperinflation of political parties (nominally, there are 97 registered parties) in

50 I. Šijaković, 'Izbori i demokratija', *in* S. Puhalo (Ed.), *Socio-psihološki profil glasača i apstinenata u Bosni i Hercegovini*, Art print, Banja Luka 2007, p. 66.

51 In 1990, the turnout was 74.1%; in 1996, the turnout was 79.3%; in 1997, the turnout was 61.3%; in 1998, the turnout was 62.7%; in 2000, it was 64.4%; in 2002, it was 53.9%; in 2004, it was 46.8%; in 2006, the turnout was 55.3%. *See* Puhalo, 2007, p. 79.

52 *Ibid.*, p. 79.

53 *Ibid.*, p. 132.

54 D. Vejnović *et al.*, *Politička kultura i govor mržnje u Bosni i Hercegovini*, Evropski defendologija centar za naučna, politička, ekonomska, socijalna, bezbjednosna, sociološka i kriminološka istraživanja, Banja Luka, 2011, p. 86.

55 Topić, 2007, p. 35.

a political space where there is one political party for every 33,000 citizens.[56] Such a large number of political parties confuse voters, and political parties themselves are not clearly ideologically positioned as leftist or rightist.[57] A great number of political parties claim that we still cannot talk about transitional stabilization. According to the index of democracy of the British magazine *The Economist* (which takes into consideration both the process of elections and pluralism, civil freedom, functionality of governments, political participation and political culture), Bosnia and Herzegovina belongs to the group of countries with a hybrid regime.[58] The term *hybrid* refers to countries that have not completed the process of transition yet; hence, they can be found somewhere in between totalitarian regimes and democracies, which is also related to the type of political culture that follows this transitional period and that is still not participatory.

Civil society is an important part of the development of a political culture. According to Ivan Šijaković,

> if we observe the civil society of Bosnia and Herzegovina nowadays, we can see that it is at the very beginning of its establishment and forming and that we can see only vague lines of possibly establishing an independent, autonomous (from the state and pathological occurrences), strong and influential civil society.[59]

The study on *Social aspects of the political system of Bosnia and Herzegvina* by Amila Ždralović shows that the constitutional and legal conditions for the formation of a civil society are fulfilled, but that there is still a difference between what is *de jure* proclaimed and *de facto* applied. A normative framework surely enables organizations to be established in the civil sector, and a certain number of organizations can certainly be considered those of the civil sector. However, many organizations have the following features: 1) associations are inactive; 2) activities of these associations do not influence the development of civil society; 3) they do not follow the work of state bodies and the application of public policies; 4) there is a dominance of associations based on common interests of their members; and 5) most associations are oriented towards their donors. Although there are many registered associations (12,189), very few can actually be called organizations of civil society.[60] The reasons for the lack of motivation of citizens can be found in

56 A. Arapović, *Izborni sistem Bosne i Hercegovine: Kritička analiza i kompilacija izbornog zakonodavstva,* Centri civilnih inicijativa, Tuzla, 2012, p. 107.

57 Popov-Momčinović, 2008.

58 Topić, 2007, p. 13.

59 Šijaković, 2007, p. 60

60 A. Ždralović, 'Društveni aspekti političkog sistem BiH',*in* D. Banović & S. Gavrić (Eds.), *Država, politika i društvo u Bosni i Hercegovini – analiza postdejtonskog političkog sistema,* University Press – Magistrat, Sarajevo 2011, p. 200.

the sociocultural patterns of Bosnia and Herzegovina's society of that prefer the ethnic to the civil. Ethno-political communities are constitutional and legal categories, and through their actions they reproduce the collective and not the individual. However, it is questionable whether Bosnia and Herzegovina can be observed from a civic perspective in which individual identity dominates over particular collective identities. This question arises due to the fact that three dominant ethnic groups exist in this divided state, as well as the fact that this system reinforces particular collective identities. In this case, there is no space for the individual as such.

10.5 CONCLUSION

The question of identity and values remains a part of the debates in Bosnia and Herzegovina. Values of a socialist society have disappeared in the transitional period, and new and much stronger identifications have emerged: ethno-religious collectives that made groups closed and left them unprepared for re-examining their established identities and the possible creation of multiple identities. Feeling comfortable and secure in one's collective identity closes a phase in political consolidation, and in a divided society it closes the opportunity to recognize the other and different, to give their existence legitimacy, participation in governance and allocation of resources, all of which open up the potential for the further development of a democratic system. The problems of predominance of the collective occur in situations when individuals do not identify themselves through ethnic dimensions and yet have a formal right to democratic and political participation. Topics involving mutually recognizing collectives and unidentified individuals still burden the political system, and resolving these issues remains a condition for the development of elements of a participatory and centrifugal political culture. Perhaps it is wrong to analyze political culture in Bosnia and Herzegovina by comparing it with thepolitical cultures of national states, as it is evident that these represent different social conditions and different institutional systems. Instead, perhaps it would be better to conduct a comparative analysis of systems and political cultures in divided societies: what conditions do we need to make one consociational model functional? It could be a democratic political culture in which the condition of minimum consensus regarding certain questions mexist. An additional burden for the transitional period is also found in the post-conflict situation: facing the past and creating a sense of trust among ethnic groups. Assessing the type of political culture in Bosnia and Herzegovina on the basis of a few empirical studies is not sufficient. The development of a democratic political culture is burdened by a socialist legacy, the country's recent past, and the search for identity and the status of individuals. Finally, the complete lack of consensus among ethnic groups and the issues that arise as a result of different interpretations of the nature of the political system further destabilize the consociational model.

11 Political Identities and Citizenship in Montenegro

Bojan Spaić

11.1 Introduction

Until only a few years ago, there was very little research assessing and analysing Montenegrin politics, most of it from the late nineties.[1] Now, the situation has improved a lot. Political and social scientists in the region are making an effort to supplement their observations on political structure and political culture with contemporary research on values by conducting detailed surveys like the *European Value Survey* and the *World Value Survey*.[2] Nevertheless, their data, thoughts, attitudes and observations have still not been consolidated, and a paradigmatic interpretation of the evolution of political culture after the downfall of the socialist system and subsequent regional conflicts has not yet been developed.

One of the major issues of contemporary Montenegrin political theory and science that has not been resolved, or even tackled, is certainly the discrepancy between the official (constitutional) concept of citizenship and particular ethnic and national identities.[3] The aforementioned issue represents a key problem owing to the fact that the political developments in Montenegro in the last two decades (and especially after 1997) could be characterized as a politics of identity, a political competition predominantly determined by, on the one hand, political parties' attitude towards identity and, on the other hand, voters' choice of identity.

As it turns out, this issue poses not only a theoretical but also a political problem that, considering the fact that national identity issues have persisted, if not escalated, remains a constant trait of Montenegrin politics. In this chapter, I shall try to present and analyse 1) some basic characteristics of the Montenegrin political system and its development in the last two decades, 2) general characteristics of Montenegrin political society and

1 The extensive research by P. Jovanović and M. Marjanović focused on the political culture in Montenegro and had quite a few problems, by the authors' own admission: P. Jovanović & M. Marjanović, *Politička kultura u Crnoj Gori*, CID, SoCen, Podgorica, 2002. The other research that had some different aims and a stricter scope was done in M. Bešić & B. Đukanović, *Svetovi vrednosti*, CID, Podgorica, 2000.

2 The first European Value Survey in Montenegro was conducted in 2008.

3 A similar subject emerges in a Berkeley article by Andrei Milivojević and Miloš Bešić, but is focused on the changing identities in Montenegro in relation to the referendum for independence: A. Milivojević & M. Bešić, 'Wither the Union? Interim Findings on the "Changing" Ethnic Makeup of Montenegro and the Independence Referendum', *Newsletter of the Institute of Slavic, East European, and Eurasian Studies*, Vol. 23, No. 1, 2006, pp. 18-26.

political culture, 3) the official concept of citizenship in order to 4) come up with some meaningful conclusions on the relationship between citizenship and politically construed national identities as well as to provide a partial explanation of identity construction.

11.2 State and Party System

The Montenegrin party system, built on state paternalism and clientelism as an inheritance from the socialist era, could be defined (according to classification by Giovani Sartori)[4] as a party system with a single predominant party. The Democratic Party of Socialists, as a pragmatic-hegemonic party that had inherited from the League of Communists all of the public resources management and patron-client connections with voters, won elections until 1997 in a political environment divided along the lines of being for or against Slobodan Milosevic's regime. Until that moment this party was absolutely dominant in Montenegrin politics "among all strata".[5] The growing distress with life in The Federal Republic of Yugoslavia under the rule and influence of Serbian politics caused the dominant Montenegrin party to split into two factions: the reform-oriented Democratic Party of Socialists (DPS) and the conservative-oriented Socialist People's Party (SNP). DPS kept the bond and continuity with the unitary Democratic Party of Socialists and the Communist Party, presenting itself as a civically oriented party clearly politically aligned against the regime of Slobodan Milošević. SNP, owing to strong ties with Serbia, transformed itself into a party for persons of Serb nationality in Montenegro. This internal split in the ruling party formalized the division among Montenegrin citizens into those who supported a union with Serbia and those oriented towards the independence of Montenegro. This, in turn, led, due to the electoral victories of DPS, to the faction of the once unitary party that grew sceptical towards the common state and to the gradual dissolving of bonds with Belgrade.[6] After the decline of the Serbian regime, and especially after its complete demise in 2000, Montenegrin party divisions and discrepancies shifted towards issues of identity: DPS, with an anti-Milošević orientation, became the bearer of the idea of Montenegrin national identity and independence, whilst the SNP, as the pro-Milošević party, defined itself as a party of national Serbs, supporting the idea of the maintenance

4 A detailed explanation of this classification and its application on Montenegrin political system is given in O. Komar, *Birači u Crnoj Gori: Faktori izborne i partijske preferencije* (Ph.D. thesis on file at the Faculty of Political Science, Podgorica), pp. 50-51. *See* G. Sartori, *Parties and Party Systems: A Framework for Analysis*, European Consortium for Political Research Press, 2005.

5 M. Bešić, Nacionalizam versus građanska opcija u Crnoj Gori, *in* D. Vujadinović *et al.* (Eds.), *Između autoritarizma i demokratije: Civilno društvo i politička kultura*, Vol. 2, CEDET/CEDEM/CTCSR, Podgorica/Beograd/Zagreb, 2004, p. 20.

6 Milivojević & Bešić, 2006, p. 18.

and survival of the union.[7] This was the crucial turning point from the perspective of national identity of the citizens of Montenegro, which will be addressed further on.
The described party system division is closely related to the divide that followed the constitution of the Montenegrin political community after the five-decade-long 'communist experiment'. During the period stretching from the fall of the socialist federation until the introduction of the Constitution of Montenegro as an independent state in 2007, in trying to find the modes of joint existence with Serbia, Montenegro has changed its constitutional order three times. The last and still valid Constitution established Montenegro as an independent state with a republican model of government for the first time since 1918. In the pre-referendum period, the divides that caused the split of the main political party were followed by a further society-wide division into:

- *Unionists* – those supporting union with Serbia (predominantly consisting of the orthodox population of Montenegro who declared themselves members of the Serbian nationality), and
- *Independentists* – those supporting Montenegro as an independent state (predominantly consisting of the orthodox population who considered themselves Montenegrins, but also members of Albanian, Muslim, Bosnian and Croatian minorities).

Furthermore, this divide was nationally determined, as the Montenegrins, Bosnians and Albanians openly and strongly supported independence, while the Serbs voted for the common state.[8] This political conflict has been, at the level of state regulation, definitively resolved by a referendum vote in May 2006 on independence from the Union of Serbia and Montenegro (formed in 2003).This vote notoriously (and as insisted upon by the international community) required a majority vote of 55% for the proclamation of independence.
Despite the unconditional acceptance of the results of the referendum by all of the significant Montenegrin political subjects, the solution of the long-standing issue of independence has not brought the long-expected catharsis in public space and political discourse. Political development has, due to established socio-identity issues, remained focused on the politics of identity. This has led to the establishment of nationality (seen as a socio-demographic characteristic) as a determinant of voter behaviour.[9] Changes within the party system (as determined by fracturing of the main political party) as well as

7 Despite the fact that Yugoslavia (SFRJ) broke up with the escalation of nationalism and the demise of the common socialist ideology (Bešić, 2004, p. 200), the national divide in conflict-free Montenegro gained prominence only after the weakening of bonds with Serbia. Only then "the national issue becomes a national problem" *Ibid.*, p. 202. A detailed account of the election system in Montenegro can be found in V. Pavićević, 'Izborni sistem Crne Gore', *in* Vujadinović *et al.* (Eds.), 2004, pp. 211-229.

8 Milivojević & Bešić, 2006, p. 18.

9 As the detailed study on voter behaviour in Montenegro by Olivera Komar clearly shows: Komar, *supra* note 4.

the uncertainty of the institutional framework led to polarization of the once homogeneous national structure in favour of strictly defined national lines. This fact directly caused the decrease of more than 20% of those declaring themselves as Montenegrins, when compared with the results of the population census in 1991, in which 61.68% of the population declared themselves Montenegrins. At the same time, the number of those declaring themselves Serbs has grown from 9.43% to 31.99%.[10]

Before proceeding to possible explanations of such fluctuations in national identity, let us address and summarize some basic characteristics of the political culture in Montenegro, and the concept of citizenship as proclaimed by the Constitution of 2007.

11.3 Political Culture

Studies on political culture from the end of 1990s identified some general characteristics of Montenegrin political society that have to be taken into consideration in order to understand its political culture. The methodology of every single empirical study of political culture must tackle the fact that ties between citizens in Montenegro are still influenced by the tribal society that Montenegro once was. That does not mean that it still displays all of the characteristics of tribal societies; it just means that human interactions are still often viewed through tribal optics. The individual is never only an individual – he is always a member of a family (symbolized by a family name) and a member of a tribe. The other traits are the following:

- *Identity.* For more than two centuries, Montenegro has had a clear, defined and unchanged geographical, cultural and historical identity.
- *Political community autonomy.* The aforementioned identity has been expressed during this period through an autonomous political community. It is important to point out that identity and political community were never monolithic and homogeneous. During almost its entire history, Montenegro has been spanning a huge internal division between the need for state autonomy and the need for integration. Later on, we shall discuss the manner in which these facts determined contemporary politics in Montenegro.
- *Cohabitation of ethnic communities.* Until 1878, when the first larger territorial expansion occurred, Montenegro was a traditional, mono-cultural and mono-confessional community. Despite the introduction of new peoples and religions in its territory, the concept of multi-ethnicity in Montenegro has resulted in neither a melting pot process nor assimilation; on the contrary, it has been developing towards a model of cohabitation of ethnic entities. Therefore, Montenegro shows a higher degree of ethnic tolerance in comparison with neighbouring countries.

10 *See* Milivojević & Bešić, 2006, p. 18.

- *Small numbers law.* The size of a country and of its population influence political development and relations, which could result in a lack of real public opinion: "Public opinion is not anonymous enough, that way it wouldn't be public either, nor are there huge groups and 'masses' whose movements could create dynamics elsewhere".[11]
- *The need for belonging.* The size of the political system conditions the constant need for adherence to larger alliances. Throughout history this need has resulted in special ties to Russia, and the professed belonging to the Serb and the Yugoslavian national and religious corpus.
- *Changes in state order.* Montenegro enters a process of accelerated modernization and development out of a specific form of tribal organization, under political governance, but without Church governance. None of the modes of government in the last 200 years have managed to establish new traditions and ways of life, and for this very reason the community has mostly remained traditionalist and devoted to old values and customs.
- *Relation towards government.* The government is understood as "indigenous, domestic, ours": "The absence of ethnic and cultural distance, small or surmountable (to overcome) status and economic distance, when compared to other and different historical arrangements, resulting in a simple, informal and often very rational communication between the citizen (population member) and the government".[12]
- *Clientelism.* High expectations from the authorities favour exchanges based on a "personal clientelism model".[13]
- *Egalitarianism.* Montenegrin society is predominantly egalitarian: "Ruling roles, the position in the state apparatus, are the main prerequisite for economic preference gain".[14]
- *Current divisions.* Transitional processes taking place since 1990 have resulted in three society-wide lines of division: socio-economic, ethnic and one related to relations with Serbia.[15] The major issue addressed will be the relationship and influence of the aforementioned division lines.

Recent studies intended to classify political culture in Montenegro that are mostly based on the facts above used Almond's classification into *parochial*, *participative* and *subject* forms, including their *sub-forms*. According to one author of the new generation, who has analyzed these issues, a political culture within this reference system can be defined as subject-participative, where the subject elements consist of:

1. Low level of awareness of systems input functions. System input functions are those related to a society input into government by means of political socialization,

11 Jovanović & Marjanović, 2002, p. 16.
12 *Ibid.*, p. 17.
13 Komar, *supra* note 4, p. 102.
14 Jovanović & Marjanović, 2002, p. 18.
15 *Ibid.*, pp. 14-18.

recruitment, interest articulation, interest aggregation or political communication. In a system in which these functions are weak, irresponsibility and unresponsiveness of government occurs, annihilating a participative political structure of the liberal-democratic political system.

2. Poorly developed awareness of the role of an individual pertaining to system functioning. This can primarily be seen in some general citizen duties that are routinely avoided, such as the evaluation of the work of government and state apparatus, calling to accountability, demanding rights' protection, organizing towards various interests and ideas, etc. An individual is unaware of the fact that he or she is an important part of the system, or that the system might depend on his or her behaviour. In that way, an individual is setting himself or herself free of individual responsibility, which is one of the prerequisites of a liberally democratic system.
3. Paternalistic expectations from the state to provide conditions for the life of an individual. This does not imply that the state should provide equal conditions for all, or the conditions for a successful and operating economic system that would stimulate new jobs and economic development (for everyone, again). These expectations are related to demands on the state to take care of individual interests of society members. They can easily get transformed into a very specific clientelism (hierarchic) relationship, often seen in societies that undergo transitional processes.[16]

Participative elements that are strengthening due to the formal liberal-democratic constitution of the Montenegrin political system are still being normatively analyzed. The reason for such an analysis and interpretation lies in those factors that, besides influencing the political process, influence the development of participative political culture and the weakening of subject ties. These factors are the following:

1. Political socialization in Montenegro at all levels, from family and friends to institutional modes of socialization, diverges towards the development and maintenance of authoritarian characteristics. Authoritarianism is a feature of subject, and not participative political culture. Therefore, a turnover of this process is needed, emphasizing the importance of political learning – not just as knowledge acquiring, but with a focus on how that knowledge has been acquired.
2. Interest articulation mechanisms enhancement. One of the major differences between participative and subject political culture is a weak input in the second one. Government does not act on the basis of input obtained from citizens. This is partly due to the fact that citizens are not being conscious or choose not to be conscious of their capabilities, or their obligations and responsibilities towards government. Therefore, any local or interest-based organizational activity should be supported, as well as

16 Komar, *supra* note 4, p. 118.

rapprochement of the citizens and authorities in general, and not on particular levels. The leaders in this process should be various citizen societies, the non-governmental sector, media and political parties.

3. Political communication. A very low level of dialogue culture, which lies not only in the government's responsibility, but in media responsibility as well, characterizes public communications in Montenegro. Participative political culture assumes the presence or existence of a well-informed citizen, who knows where to get the desired information, even though he or she does not have enough time to inform himself or herself. The problem is that information in Montenegro is often emotionally oriented, highly intonated pro or against the government, and rarely contains genuine analysis and argumentation. This kind of media space does not stimulate an apprised citizen's participation in public debates, resulting in the presence of several (always the same) individuals discussing specific topics within the public media space.
4. Quality control in all the spheres of public authorities. Quality control indirectly increases contractive, and decreases status-based society relations. Particularly if an individual cannot hide himself behind the wall of society ties or power relations, thus being obliged to take responsibility for the quality of his work, the sustainability of client-patron relations becomes impossible.
5. Decision-making transparency. This is another mechanism for weakening client-oriented social ties. If there are existing mechanisms that make a decision-making process transparent and verifiable, client-based ties lose their significance, and the focus naturally shifts towards quality.[17]

Despite the fact that political culture in Montenegro can be defined as subject-participative, it is clear that a predominant factor in Montenegrin political culture is still the subject one. It is the consequence of a fast political order change, the perpetuation of identity issues on the political scene, as well as client-oriented relations between voters and political parties and a traditional paternalistic understanding of the state. Following the aforementioned Montenegrin political culture characterization, I proceed to the analysis of the concept of citizenship as embodied in the Constitution.

11.4 MULTICULTURALISM, NATIONALISM AND CITIZENSHIP

In political theory, citizenship has been understood by taking into account rights, political status and identity forms,[18] as "membership in a self-governing political community".[19]

17 *Ibid.*, pp. 19-20.
18 Based on the classical definition of citizenship provided by the British social scientist Thomas Humphrey Marshall (1893-1981) in the article 'Citizenship and Social Class' from 1949.
19 R. Belamy, *Citizenship – A Very Short Introduction*, Oxford University Press, New York, 2008, p. 3.

A citizen is a member of a political community who enjoys the rights and assumes the duties of membership.[20] Generally, the term *citizenship* is used to name a set of political activities that assume public rights and obligations towards one's political community. Voting has often been considered one of those key activities, and in that sense, citizenship often implies a democratic political order; in other words, citizens' activities in democratic states. In this way, a democratic citizen is determined by: 1) membership in a democratic political community, 2) possession of the rights and benefits that this membership implies and 3) participation in political, economic and social processes.[21] Nowadays, the concept of citizenship is anchored in the republican and liberal traditions:

1. The republican model of citizenship potentiates the primacy of citizens' interest to use his political rights in participating in a common decision-making process on important social issues (it accents obligations to the detriment of rights). In other words, in the traditional republican frame, political status (active participation in public activities and institutional performance) has a key position in the definition of citizenship.
2. The liberal citizen profile shifts the focus to interest in social and economic activities, as well as freedoms. It defines an attitude towards politics based on interest in rights preservation and focuses on the prevention of rights limitation by the state. The liberal profile emphasizes rights and freedoms as key points in the determination of citizenship.[22]
3. The third profile of citizenship actually presents a multicultural opposition to both the liberal and the republican model, by which the term *citizen* designates a member of a political community irrespective of his specific identity or identities (cultural, ethnic, religious, gender, racial, etc.). This 'third model' is better understood as a position in political theory and practice, which focuses on the dichotomy between individual and collective rights. The main argument of the multicultural criticism of the liberal model of citizenship is that the proclaimed neutrality of value is in fact illusory and that, accordingly, citizenship founded on equal rights and freedoms represents a charade

20 W. Norman & W. Kymlicka, 'Citizenship', *in* R. G. Frey & C.H. Wellman (Eds.), *A Companion to Applied Ethics*, Blackwell Publishing, Oxford, 2003, p. 210.

21 Belamy, 2008, p. 7. After the weakening of the welfare state, political theorists, in searching for the active citizen, have turned to market economy, civil society or the state. The arguments against the welfare state in the 1980s have mostly been concentrated on the politics of dependence that this form of state creates for entire categories of population (single mothers, unemployed etc.). In the 1990s, after the fall of real socialist regimes and the struggle of Eastern European societies to (re)constitute democratic societies, the interest in theory and practice was shifted to the civil society. The insistence on the central role of state institutions in the education of the citizen came as a critique of the standpoint that connects citizenship with the civil society or the market economy.

22 *Ibid.*, p. 43. A certain degree of complementarity between these two models, owing to the fact that there is no consensus within either one, is often taken as an argument that the differences between them can even be annulled (M.P. Gaige, 'Citizen: Past Practices, Prospective Patterns', *in* J.V. Ciprut (Ed.), *The Future of Citizenship*, The MIT Press, Cambridge, 2008, p. 121.)

in favour of the social group that is factually dominant. A multiculturalist answer to this issue lies in the claim that acceptance of a set of minority rights does not dilute the citizenship as a form of identity; on the contrary, it fortifies it.

These issues have opened a whole range of debates between universalist and differentialist conceptions of citizenship; the first group holding that the basis of civic identity is mainly the transcendence of particular identities, and the latter who holds that this very transcendence and its insistence on institutions that are blind to social differences is not only illusory, but also gives advantage to dominant social groups, maintaining that the liberal concept of citizenship is modifiable without danger to the functioning of institutions in liberal democracies. However, even at first glance these two positions are not completely contrary. The contemporary political reality encompasses the possibility that the instability of the political community can occur due to the insistence on equality in rights based on the conception of universal citizenship.

Will Kymlicka and Wayne Norman have introduced a classification of requests put forward by minority social groups to liberal democracies from a multiculturalist perspective: 1) the request for exemption from laws that discourage or make harder some practices that are specific to particular cultural communities, 2) the rights for aid in acting in a political society which the majority group does not require (affirmative action that enhances the possibilities for members of minority groups; the rights to use one's own language in communication with official institutions) and 3) a rare set of requests to limit the freedom of people who are not members of the cultural community in order to protect that cultural community (limitation of the usage of the English language in Quebec), and requests to incorporate traditional and religious rules in the official legal system. And while this set of requests is handled to a certain degree by liberal democracies, there is also another set that can jeopardize the entire liberal conception of citizenship and with it the liberal state itself: 1) representation within governmental institutions (special electoral units, reserved spots in the parliament for ethnic, religious and other groups) and 2) the request for self-governance within cultural communities (especially those that are territorially concentrated). Kymlicka and Norman also speak about a set of requests that involve the symbolic recognition of importance and status of a group in a wider state community, such as mentions in the state anthem, flag, public celebrations and so forth.[23]

From this perspective, the main problem that is often connected with fears of multiculturalism is encapsulated in the question of whether the recognition of minority group requests in liberal democracies has disintegrative potential, and whether their recognition endangers the classical concept of citizenship. The problem of citizenship is mainly a problem of identity and recognition, which is essentially a problem of political philosophy,

23 Norman & Kymlicka, 2003, pp. 218-220.

but also a problem of institutional arrangements that can be derived from multicultural demands. Ideologically, the aforementioned problem is presented as the questioning of the value neutrality of liberalism that is put in an absurd position to defend its openness to different modes of a good life as only one mode of a good life.[24]

In another paper, devoted exclusively to multicultural citizenship, Kymlicka emphasizes the relation between the liberal conception of citizenship and multicultural demands for particular rights. He is particularly keen on elaborating the incompatibility between civic identity and particular identities in the domain of a liberal democratic political community in order to establish which of the multicultural demands represents a danger to the liberal state. His final conclusion is that it is possible to integrate multiculturalism into the liberal concept of citizenship with the recognition of polyethnic rights to participation, but he also puts forward many reservations when it comes to the set of rights of self-governance that can be recognized by diverse cultural communities.[25] If we add the dangers of imposing a collective identity to this problem, we come to a knot that is not easily untied either in theory or in practice. It then seems reasonable to operate with the Habermasian concept of constitutional patriotism, a liberal idea of just institutions as conditions to the development of the sense of universal belonging to the liberal democratic community, enriched by the idea of differentiated citizenship in the amount, which according to Kymlicka, does not lead to the disintegration of this community.

It is clear from the previous discussion that the liberal and republican concepts of citizenship encompass civic identity as a sense of belonging to a political community in which citizens have equal rights and equal status. The multicultural profile poses this problem quite differently, by including problems of the neutrality of human rights, the political value of collective identities in a political community, modes of good life, positive liberty etc. In regard to the civic identity in Montenegro, it will be shown that the liberal concept of universal citizenship enriched by the republican ideal of participation by means of political dialogue and the involvement in political procedures quite reasonably and in a way naturally includes some concessions to the multicultural model. Different modes of recognition can thus be justified in a liberal state up to the moment in which the particular tendencies in a society do not become fundamentally opposed to the universalist model of citizenship (radical multiculturalism).

---

24 "Liberal democracies can accommodate and embrace many forms of cultural diversity, but not all. [. . .] Liberal principles impose two fundamental limitations on minority rights. First, a liberal conception of minority rights will not justify [. . .] the demand by a minority culture to restrict the basic civil or political liberties of its own members [. . .] Liberal justice cannot accept any such rights which enable one group to oppress or exploit other groups." (W. Kymlicka, *Multicultural Citizenship*, Clarendon Press, Oxford, 1995, p. 152.) Further theoretical and philosophical assessments of the relation between constitutional democracies and politics of recognition of cultural differences can be found in A. Gutmann (Ed.), *Multiculturalism*, Princeton University Press, Princeton, 1994.

25 Kymlicka, 1995, pp. 264-271.

Theoretically and historically, nationalism is not only a "strategy to form identity of one's political society members, but rather a strategy in competition for participation in the sharing of 'political goods'". From this point of view, János Kis considers the

> establishment of a national state in ethnically divided society [. . .] as the overtaking of control of these goods by one national group [. . .]that are divided through authorities, limiting the others in the acquisition of goods from a generally limited source".[26]

As opposed to a national strategy, Montenegrin legal order acquires a post-national strategy (in which citizenship is the main principle of integration of political order), thus making it one of the most important Constitutional determinations. Article 1 of the Montenegrin Constitution from 2007 defines Montenegro as an independent and sovereign state with a republican governance model, a civic, democratic, ecological and a state view of social justice, based on the rule of law. One of the basic determinants of the state of Montenegro is that it is a civic state, and this is, according to Mijat Šukovic, "one of the most important determinations of the Montenegrin constitutional profile".[27] Within his detailed analysis of the constitutional concept of a civic state, Šukovic unambiguously determines some of its key components as strictly defined by the constitution. Therefore, these key components should serve as a guideline and boundary for all the public policies after the promulgation of the Constitution of 2007.

Šukovic states that the key moments in the constitutional elaboration of a civic state concept are the following: 1) The equality of rights and freedoms for all Montenegrin citizens, irrespective of their group differences, identities, belongings; 2) The citizen is the holder of sovereignty and 3) Specific individual rights guaranties for the members of ethnic minorities (that can, nevertheless, be used within a community, but strictly for the purpose of assuring equal status in accomplishing these rights). Considering the fact that the concept of universal citizenship is in this case obviously merged with multicultural rights, this third component requires special attention. The drafters of the constitutional post-national concept of citizenship disregarded liberal fetishism in terms of rights equality by arranging the rights of 'minorities' in the following way:

Members of non-dominant and ethnic groups (national minorities) are guaranteed the following rights and freedoms to be used individually or within a community with the others: 1) to express, preserve, develop and publicly show their national, ethnic, cultural and religious belongings; 2) to choose, use and publicly express their national symbols and national holidays; 3) to use their own language and writing in private, public and professional

26 J. Kiš, *Na putu prevazilaženja nacionalne države* (paper presented at the conference *Kolektivna prava – za i protiv*, Novi Sad, 1996).

27 M. Šuković, *Ustavno pravo*, CID, Podgorica, 2009, p. 181.

environment; 4) education in their own language and writing in public institutions, where educational curriculum involves the history and culture of the minorities; 5) in regions with a significant percentage of minority population, all the public authorities have to act within the public services and processes also in the language of the minority; 6) to found educational, cultural and religious societies, materially supported by the State; 7) to write their own anagraphical data in their own original language in official identity documents; 8) in regions with a significant percentage of members of non-dominant and ethnic groups, traditional local names, names of the streets and blocks, as well as topographic signs, are to be written also in a language of a minority; 9) authentic representation in the parliament of Montenegro and in local parliaments, in which they participate as a significant part of the population (principle of affirmative action); 10) proportional representation in public services, bodies of state, and local self-governing bodies; 11) media and information in their own language; 12) to establish and maintain contacts with citizens and societies outside Montenegro, with whom they share common national and ethnic origin, cultural-historic heritage and religious beliefs and 13) to found a council for special rights' establishment and protection.

It is to be noted that the Constitution guarantees representative and polyethnic rights according to the principle of affirmative action (as explained in the *Lund recommendations*), without guaranteeing self-governance rights. Representation rights that belong to polyethnic rights (propositions 9 and 10, Article 1 of the Montenegrin Constitution from 2007) are in theory interpreted as a demand to participate.[28] According to the above-mentioned determinations, the supranational character of the state, its value and authority, are not something derived from particular nations and cultures, but something that actually precedes them.[29] The same principle has to be taken into account in the case of identity, based on the fact that a supranational identity does not have to be taken as a primary one, although its existence is necessary in order to provide for the functioning of liberal democratic institutions. At any rate, the set of civil rights guaranteed by the Constitution of Montenegro is in accordance with the concept of differentiated citizenship (which assumes disparity in legal status of some of society's groups, but with the objective of inclusion of these groups),[30] as developed by the multicultural theory.[31]

In great part, this fact recognizes the Montenegrin social reality, which is essentially and declaratively a highly multicultural one, and provides the best imaginable legal framework to harmonize Montenegrin citizenship's universalistic pretensions with the demands of collective identities. This is also in accordance with the constitutional determinations of the EU that are directed towards a Europe of citizens based on common political culture

28 "[B]asic impulse beside the demand on representative rights is integration, and not separation." V. Kimlika, *Multikulturalno građanstvo*, CID, Podgorica, 2004, p. 258.

29 *Ibid.*, pp. 264-265.

30 J.V. Ciprut, 'Citizenship: Mere Contract, or Construct for Conduct', *in* Ciprut 2008, p. 12.

31 A great number of liberal theorists, especially those concerned with issues of justice and the importance of institutional arrangements for the functioning of liberal democracies, question the concept of differentiated citizenship: Kimlika, 2004, pp. 253-257.

and respect for fundamental political principles, which shifts all the cultural differences into the private domain.

So the Constitution takes a post-national conception of citizenship as a nucleus of social integration that should in fact constantly direct state policies towards special care about issues of which conditions need to be accomplished to provide every citizen with equal liberty of choice (equality for all citizens) to lead his or her own individual way of life within a supranational identity. Nevertheless, this should not imply in any sense that other identities within society are less important; they are just bounded by some restriction in the case that they act as demands or requests. Particular communities in which we can act (*e.g.*, cultural and ethnic communities) are not a foundation for society's political constitution. In a society's political constitution, rational and institutional ties among people should play a determinant role, not ties related to group identities (emotional and irrational).

This certainly does not provide an identity pattern as consistent and stable as the one supplied by a society integration based on an ethno-national principle. The nation, as a strategy of state arrangement, provides a common ethos that represents a connective tissue and a substantial, ethical basis for procedural and rational organization of society. Nevertheless, citizenship as a strategy has its own rationales. Habermas' fundamental insight into his theoretical interpretation of a post-national (civil) identity as a basic form of identity is based on the idea that a political culture for a citizen within a civil state is the same as a nation presents for its member in a national state. Therefore, a political culture (in the case of Montenegro, a subject political culture) is one that, in the absence of emotional and irrational substantial fundamentals to society's political organization, plays a role of ethical space out of which institutional and procedural arrangements gain value.

11.5 DIFFERENTIATION OF POLITICAL IDENTITIES

The post-national conception of citizenship adopted in the Montenegrin Constitution of 2007 is meant to serve as a basis for Montenegrin democratic consolidation according to a universal citizenship model, after the announcement of the independence of Montenegro as the state.[32] In a universalist citizenship model, national identities are ideally supposed to be unrelated to ethnic identities, with the first cutting across the second and

32 W. Merkel mentions four criteria on the basis of which the level of consolidation of the political system should be accessed (W. Merkel, *Transformacija političkih sustava: Uvod u teoriju i empirijsko istraživanje transformacije*, Fakultet političkih znanosti Sveučilišta u Zagrebu, Zagreb, 2011, p. 98): 1) Constitutional consolidation – the level of structure that encompasses the answer to the question of whether the constitutional framework is consolidated, 2) Representative consolidation – the level of participants that encompasses the answer to the question of whether they accepted the rules of the democratic game as the only possible. 3) Consolidation of behaviour of informal political participants that encompasses the question of whether they have accepted democratic procedures as the only possible. 4) The consolidation of the civic society that encompasses the answer to the question of whether the citizens have become active participants in democratic decision making. *Ibid.*

transcending it. But, eight years after the referendum on independence and despite the constitutional declarations, issues of identity are strongly present in the Montenegrin public sphere. Studies have shown that this is primarily due to the fact that voters' mobilization is still taking place along the lines of their nationality. With DPS still ruling as a moderate Montenegrin party, with allies that are either nationalist Montenegrin parties or parties of national minorities (Bosniak, Muslim, Croat, Albanian), and the opposition, often labelled as the opposition to the state of Montenegro and not to the ruling parties owing to its tendency to appeal to members of Serb nationality that strongly supported the union with Serbia, the party politics are still very much concentrated on national issues, especially during the heat of the elections. Only recently, several new parties formed in the post-referendum period that have tried to minimize the national burden of the Montenegrin political scene (*Movement for Changes* and *Positive Montenegro*). In spite of their efforts, they are still tacitly required to declare themselves as Montenegrin or Serb parties in order to raise their chances in the political battle.

And while the above-mentioned could fit well into the common practice of a relatively new democratic polity, the data from regular population censuses in the last couple of decades clearly shows how the numbers of 'declared identities' are even now in a state of fluctuation:[33]

Table 1

	1948	1953	1961	1971	1981	1991	2003[3]	2011
Montenegrin	90.7	86.6	81.4	67.2	68.5	61.9	43.2	44.98
Serb	1.8	3.3	3	7.5	3.3	8.3	32	28.73
Albanian	5.2	2.3	5.5	6.7	6.5	6.6	5	4.91
Bosniak							7.77	8.65
Muslim[1]			6.5	13.3	13.4	14.6	3.97	3.31
Croat	1.8	1.5	2.3	1.7	1.8	1	1.1	0.97
Yugoslav		5.6	0.3	2.1	5.7	4.3	0.3	0.19
Others[2]	0.6	0.6	1.1	1.6	0.8	2.4	6.7	8.26
Total Pop.	377,189	419,873	471,894	529,604	584,310	615,035	620,145	620,029
	9	3	4	4	0	5	5	9

Sources: Petrović, 'National Composition of Yugoslavia's Population,' Yugoslav Survey (1992) and Zavod za statistiku Crne Gore. As for the data from 2003 and 2011, the official documents that were used can be found on <http://monstat.org/eng/index.php>

Notes: Grey means the category did not exist; 1) Muslims were counted as a religious group in 1961 and as a nation in 1971; the data for 2003 merges for simplicity the categories of Muslim and Bosniak; 2) Includes all remaining groups and, in 2003, foreign citizens, those that declined to state and unknown; and 3) New methodology, excluding citizens living abroad for over a year and including foreigners.

33 The data can be found in the article of Milivojević and Bešić up to the year 2003: Milivojević & Bešić, 2006, p. 19. I adapted the table to suit the needs of this article. The data from the last census was compiled and added by me.

One has to bear in mind that these dramatic shifts in the number of Serbs and Montenegrins are only to a small degree (if any) due to immigration. Newcomers to Montenegro almost never change their ethnic identity.[34] The reasons for such shifts must lie elsewhere. Common theoretical assumptions on the relation between national and ethnic identity provide us with two possibilities for explaining these seemingly dramatic declines in the number of members of a nation in Montenegro. The key to these assumptions is the way that national identity is defined.

The first considers national identity as continuous with ethnic identity. This essentialist hypothesis would entail that ethnic characteristics determine the membership to a nationality. An ethnic community is, in theory, determined through six attributes: 1) a collective common name; 2) myths about common ancestors, with the ethnic group being understood as a superfamily, based on a wider conception of kinship, composed of mutually connected families; 3) common historical memories that can also take the form of a myth; 4) one or more differentiated elements of a common culture and 5) connection to a determinate homeland that also has a mythical and subjective character. This involves a commitment to the territory understood as the holy land of the ancestors, as a homeland in which they rest and that is consecrated by their blood. The most important element of ethnic identification is the connection and the devotion to a territory and not the actual ownership or inhabitation. It exists even when the members of an ethnic group are separated from the homeland. f) The feeling of solidarity in major parts of the population.[35]

The second assumption that could explain the shifts in identity tells us that national identity is built upon rational and interest-based grounds. In the second case, the constitution of a national identity has been associated with the civil understanding of a nation, in which the unique national identity is being created within a state, irrespective of particular identities. When trying to apply the aforementioned assumptions to the Montenegrin political community, we arrive at the conclusion that both explanations are mixed and unclear. To prove this, let us take as an example two currently dominant divides in Montenegro in terms of identity:

- The first divide cuts across the orthodox population and is the one that marked Montenegrin public development and political struggle after 1997 – the division between those who declare themselves as Serbs and those who declare themselves as Montenegrin. The ethnic traits of those two lines of the orthodox population are basically the same. They share the same tradition, history and language.
- The second divide has most of the common characteristics of the first one, but it applies to the population of Muslims. This population in Montenegro has traditionally expressed its national identity either as Muslim (with a capital M that was used to differentiate between national belonging as opposed to religious) or as Yugoslav.

34 Bešić, 2004, p. 20.

35 A. Smit, *Nacionalni identitet*, Čigoja štampa, Beograd, 1998, p. 40; D. Vuković, *Nacionalni identitet i globalizacija*, Čigoja štampa, Beograd, 2011, p. 18.

> After the second term lost its meaning, the Muslim population started dividing itself towards two lines: the line that continues following Muslim identity as a tradition, and the second one that accepts Bosniak identity as their national identity.

As previously mentioned, a recent study in Montenegro showed that national identity continues to be a key predictor of voter behaviour. According to the data presented and the view of national identity as a rational and interest-based preference, it seems that this aspect of voter socio-demographic behaviour not only appears on the input side, but is also strongly present on the output side. In other words, the results of political competition directly influence voters' expression of national identity. If this assumption is on the right track, fluctuations in the number of Serbs and Montenegrins on one side and of Muslims and Bosniaks on the other could only be explained if national identities are understood as (mainly, or even completely) political identities. These identities, for the purpose of this chapter, have been determined as politically construed cultural-historical identity, as fluid constructs based on the changing preference of the citizen and the voter.[36] Therefore, Montenegrin divides seemingly confirm that: "[P]olitical identities are less primordial than they are contingent and changing [...] [and] amenable to being constructed or ordered by political institutions and political choices".[37]

This remarkable trait of Montenegrin transitional and post-transitional experience, namely that some ethnic identities present themselves as partially or totally constructed based upon the individual preferences conditioned by different identity determinations, remains a subject for the empirical and theoretical study of society and politics. A true politics of identity, in which cultural-historical identity is created based on the projection of their value in Montenegrin political space, is currently active exactly in this sense. National identities in Montenegro are politically influenced in a manner that allows us to talk about them as fluid identities – self-determinations of a social group that are not based on any kind of substantial ethnic characteristics, such as language, tradition or origin.

11.6 Conclusion

Some of the conclusions based on the discussion so far could be as follows: 1) Montenegrin society is pronouncedly multicultural, not only on the basis of the trivial criterion that several cultures live within the boundaries of one political community, but also in the sense that cultural differences are taken as politically important. The political valence of different cultural identities is reflected in the existence of identity-conditioned demands

36 This deviates significantly from the definition of political identity as constituted by "interests and programs" D. Rodin, 'Kulturno-povijesni i politički identitet', *Politička misao*, Vol. XXXV, No. 2, 1998, pp. 52-53.

37 J.J. Linz & A. Stepan, *Problems of Democratic Transition and Consolidation: Southern Europe, South America, and Post-Communist Europe*, Johns Hopkins University Press, Baltimore, 2011, p. 366.

for integration, representation and self-governance (*i.e.*, demand for polyethnic, representational and self-governing rights). The liberal and democratic bases of the modern state of the West have broadened the space for respect for cultural differences in a traditionally rational and egalitarian political sphere, with the term multicultural democracy that designates a political system in which cultural differences are respected on the state level. 2) Montenegro is constitutionally committed to the concept of a civic state that primarily entails that the civic identity is the primary identity with political value. Considering the multicultural rights that are recognized in the supreme legal document, this identity is not opposed to particular identities, nor is it envisaged as a collective identity that 'swallows' all the others. The explicitly proclaimed intent of the makers of the constitution is a transnational civic identity that leaves space for the recognition of particular identities by respecting certain polyethnic rights and cultural differences. 3) The cultural and political spheres in Montenegro show strong signs of perpetuating certain identity divides in the society. These mainly relate to issues of political identity in the long period before state independence. The institutional arrangements formed under the influence of Western liberal democracies and under the imperative of European integration provide a good basis for the minimization of the existing divides (especially when keeping in mind that those divides run mainly along the lines of political identities and not along the lines of cultural identities), but public policies are not recognized as inclusive and open, which makes it difficult to put aside those issues. 4) The analysis of political culture in Montenegro shows that it is necessary to strengthen its participative element, with subject elements remaining strong.

By connecting the dots of political structure, party system, political culture, the constitutional concept of citizenship and the differentiation of national or political identities, the prospects of a weak constitutionally proclaimed supranational civic identity come into conflict with the politics of identity that are persisting despite the resolution of issues related to Montenegrin statehood. Based on the facts exposed, it seems evident that we could, in of the absence of specialized empirical data, speculate on (at least partial) party-client construction of national identities in Montenegro. As we were able to see, it is not the case that political parties are gaining voters' confidence during the electoral competition only through appeal to determined and pre-existing national identities. On the contrary, by taking into consideration that the mentioned national groups belong to the same ethnicity, it is clear that what is going on is that the national identity is 'chosen' on a pragmatic-client basis. Furthermore, this is not a classic case of what Claus Offe calls *the ethnification of politics*, precisely because the identities are not existent prior to the political struggle that makes them emerge and shapes them.[38] In the cases described,

38 Vuković, 2011, p. 30.

these identities can therefore be termed as fluid identities or political identities in the sense of politically formed national identities. The question posed in a cited paper that analyzed flip-flops in identity identification remains reasonable: "If a sizable proportion of erstwhile Montenegrins became Serbs, could they 'go back' and under what conditions?"[39] The census data that was presented does not let us draw definite conclusions, but allows us to speculate on a possible answer.

It seems that variations and fluidity in national identities present a baseline for politics of identity perpetuation, which still appears as a determining factor for Montenegrin election results. The predominant party mostly manifests her relative failures as punishment for unsatisfactory governance only at the local level, remaining stable on the state level (also due to the high coalition potential with smaller national parties). It cannot be expected that this domination of national divisions and their political value are going to decrease in years to come. The dominant party's insistence on preserving gained independence, as well as Serb national parties' insistence on symbolic national issues (such as flag, parts of the state anthem etc.) fortify this national course in Montenegrin politics. In the pre-referendum period one of today's prominent Montenegrin social scientists wrote this about the national divides that we analyzed:

> What are the prospects of further maintenance of the national matrix in Montenegro as a socio-political platform? Very bad! [. . .] These predictions rest on the assumption that the nationalist option will have less and less adherents in the future development, while the civic option, aided by external factors will be gaining strength, organization and numbers.[40]

It is quite obvious that this prediction is wishful thinking. If our assumption on the fluidity of national identities is true, the consistence in this course of identity politics appears to be pragmatically significant as well. Giving up the established rhetoric based on issues of national identity, considering the fact that the citizens' national determination is fluid, could seriously affect parties' success at elections, leading to irreparable voter loss.

39 Bešić, 2004, p. 24.

40 *Ibid.*, p. 210.